STARTING OUT!™

The Complete Re-Entry Handbook

Building Essential Life Skills

2010 Edition

---

www.startingout.com

User Access Code: RE4949

Consulting Editors

William H. Foster, Ph.D.

Dean and Professor
Muskie School of Public Service
University of Southern Maine
Former Deputy Commissioner
New Jersey Department of Labor

Carl E. Van Horn, Ph.D.

Professor of Public Policy
Bloustein School of Public Policy
Rutgers University
Director, John J. Heldrich Center
for Workforce Development

About the Editors

William H. Foster, Ph.D.

Dr. Foster is Dean of the Muskie School of Public Service at the University of Southern Maine. Before joining the Muskie School, he was the senior vice president and chief operating officer of The National Center on Addiction and Substance Abuse (CASA) at Columbia University. Prior to that, Dean Foster served as executive director of a Congressional commission on social security, chief of staff and deputy commissioner of the New Jersey Department of Labor, and a policy advisor to Senator Bill Bradley. He also spent 17 years on the faculty at the University of Illinois and Rutgers University. Dr. Foster holds a Ph.D. in Counseling Psychology from the University of Wisconsin at Madison.

Carl E. Van Horn, Ph.D.

Dr. Van Horn serves as both professor of public policy at the Edward J. Bloustein School of Planning & Public Policy at Rutgers University and Director of the John J. Heldrich Center for Workforce Development. He has been director of policy for the State of New Jersey, senior economist at the Joint Economic Committee of the U.S. Congress, and chair of the Public Policy Department at the Bloustein School of Planning and Public Policy. Dr. Van Horn has advised the National Science Foundation and was appointed by President Clinton to a Presidential Emergency Board to mediate disputes between labor and management in the railroad industry. He holds a Ph.D. from Ohio State University.

Starting Out, Inc.
P.O. Box 68
Damariscotta, ME 04543

Tel	1–207–563–3800
Fax	1–207–563–3823
Email	amy@startingout.com
Web	http://www.startingout.com

STARTING OUT!™

The Complete Re-Entry Handbook

http://www.startingout.com
User Access Code: RE4949

Consulting Editors:

William H. Foster, Ph.D.
Dean and Professor,
Muskie School of Public Service,
University of Southern Maine
Former Deputy Commissioner,
New Jersey Department of Labor

Carl E. Van Horn, Ph.D.
Professor of Public Policy,
Bloustein School of Public Policy,
Rutgers University
Director, John J. Heldrich Center for Workforce Development

Disclaimer

Copyright Protection

2009–2010 Edition

Senior Publishing Staff:

Daniel R. Goldenson
Chairman & Publisher

Seth Goodall
Executive Vice President

Daniel L. Braverman
Senior VP, Research & Marketing

Amy R. Winkle
VP, Editorial Development

Graham Walsh
Re-Entry Sales Manager

Sara A. Rosario
Production Editor

Contributing Editor:
Kate Kastelein

Book Design:
Firefly, LLC

Printing and Distribution:
DS Graphics, Inc.

Customer Service:
amy@startingout.com
1–207–563–3800

Corporate Address:
Starting Out, Inc.
Day-Nash Building
277 Main Street
P.O.Box 68
Damariscotta, ME 04543

Sign Up | About Us | Contact | Change Edition

EMAIL PASSWORD LOGIN

New User? Sign Up Here »

STARTING OUT!™

in maine

Prisoner Reentry Edition

Today's Feed: Vehicle Make/Model Search fo

Career Resources by State
87 Life Management Articles
230+ In-Depth Career Profiles

The Book | Career Finder | Benefits Locator | National Resources

Practical How-To Articles with Links to the Best Websites on Each Subject

80 Detailed Chapters Covering These Important Topics:

ORDER NOW

Chapters | Our Advisors | Endorsements

Starting Out!™ in Maine

- Living and Working in Maine
- Breaking the Barriers to Employment
- How to Address Your Background in Your Resume, Application, and Interview
- Inmate-Friendly Employers
- Where to Find it in Maine
- Maine Career Resources
- Welcome to the University of Maine System
- Welcome to the Office of the Governor
- Opportunity Maine College Incentive Program

Special Information for Guidance Counselors and College Deans

- Choose Your State - Go!

230+ In-Depth Occupational Profiles

- Airline & Transportation Industry (5)
- Architecture, Design, & Planning (3)
- Arts & Entertainment (15)
- Banking, Finance & Investment (8)
- Biological & Chemical Sciences (8)
- Business (18)
- Clergy & Faith-Based (5)
- Conservation & the Environment (8)
- Engineering (20)
- Farming, Ranching, & Forestry (4)
- Fashion/Cosmetics/Interior Design (4)
- Funeral Industry (3)
- Government & Military Service (10)
- Healthcare (45)
- Hospitality & Tourism (6)
- Insurance (4)
- Law & Public Safety (14)
- Media & Communications (13)
- Real Estate & Construction (9)
- Sports, Athletics, & Fitness (7)
- Teaching & Library Science (11)
- Trade & Industry (9)

Benefits Locator

Federal Benefits
Examine 1000+ benefit and assistance programs for every need

Student Aid
Search student financial aid programs, scholarships, and grants

Military Benefits
Explore military programs for education, health, and financial assistance

GO!

Register for Online Access

Register to Access Additional Online-Only Features!

Email:

Password:

Access Code:

GO!

National Resources

Federal Information Index
Handy Federal Resources, A to Z

Site Glossaries
Business, Health & Technical Terms

GO!

Students| College Navigator | Careers | Military | Federal Jobs | Student Jobs | Health Guide | Money | Volunteers

Web Design & Development by Firefly of Maine

Visit the State Selector and Career Finder on the web at:
www.StartingOut.com | User Access Code: RE4949

Table of Contents

Introduction

The Challenge of Re-Entry

Looking at the Numbers

Each year, nearly 700,000 men and women are released from prison into communities across the United States. Many do not make a successful transition: two-thirds are arrested within three years and one-half are returned to prison, either for parole violations or new crimes. These trends need to change.

This revolving door phenomenon is costly in terms of human and social impacts on crime victims, returning prisoners, their families, and the communities in which they reside. And, the criminal justice system is extremely costly to society, diverting huge sums of money that could be better spent on education, healthcare, and housing.

Studies Look at Re-Entry Experiences

Since 2001, the Urban Institute has been conducting research to understand the process of prisoner reentry and identify factors associated with reentry success and failure, with the goal of informing policy and practice.

Studies show that offenders experience high rates of physical health conditions, mental illness, and substance abuse in correctional populations. In re-entry surveys, respondents typically had one or more chronic health conditions at the time of their release. About 7 in 10 also report levels of pre-prison substance use consistent with abuse and dependence.

Most ex-offenders often lack sufficient education and need further training and guidance.

The Daunting Task of Re-Entry

Returning prisoners face distinct challenges with regard to finding housing and employment, reconnecting with family members, abstaining from substance use and crime, and avoiding a return to prison. Anecdotal evidence suggests several reasons why prisoners with health problems often have a more difficult reentry process than others.

Returning prisoners face multiple, often simultaneous tasks as they embark on the process of reestablishing their lives outside prison—finding housing, getting a job, having enough money to live on, reconnecting with children and family—and these intermediary steps influence the ability to live a drug-free and crime-free life.

Re-Entering Society is an Opportunity for Positive Change

The Starting Out! Re-Entry Handbook, with its *Companion Workbook*, are designed to be useful tools for ex-offenders to deal with these difficult challenges in the following ways:

1. They map out the path to re-entry, step by step.
2. They explain what you need to do before your release.
3. They offer solid assistance on job searching.
4. They outline every public assistance program that can help you.
5. They re-focus your attention into constructive areas: family, job, and church.
6. They challenge you to join support groups to help with re-entry.
7. They explain drug and mental problems and where to find help.
8. They encourage responsible social and sexual behavior.
9. They point the way to good training programs.
10. They get you thinking about being a good citizen.

The Help is Out There for Ex-Offenders

It stands to reason that successful guidance, job assistance, and treatment of your health conditions will all increase your chances of reentry success. For example, when you utilize the nearest CareerOneStop office in your community, you will find helpful, caring people who will point you to job training opportunities and friendly employers who accept ex-offenders.

When you get assistance with pressing physical and mental problems, including drug addiction, you will feel better and be in a position to hold a job and support yourself. Getting help with a substance abuse problem should be your Number 1 task.

You Need to Succeed

When you leave incarceration, everyone wants you to succeed: your counselors, your family, your community, your church, and your friends. But you, and you alone, are the only person who can move on beyond your criminal past to a new life. Take the challenge of re-entry very seriously. Change your life. You will be a far happier human being, and will become a productive member of society.

Part I

Preparing for Re-Entry

Chapter 1

Personal Identification Documents

Minnesota Department of Corrections

Proper identification is required to cash a check, take a driver's test, or get a job. Forms of acceptable identification include the following:

Birth Certificate

A birth certificate provides proof of when and where you were born. A certified copy of your birth certificate can be useful when providing identity in certain situations, such as applying for a driver's license, retirement benefits, passport, or assistance programs.

You may request an application form and requirements for a certified copy of your birth certificate from your caseworker. Information needed for application includes:

- **Payment for a certified copy.** Ask your caseworker for assistance and information.
- **Notarized signature.** Most states require your signature be notarized if you are requesting a copy of your birth certificate by mail. Notaries are available at all correctional facilities. Once you are released, you may locate notaries in your community by searching the local Yellow Pages.

Part I

Social Security Card

Social security is a part of almost everyone's life, no matter what your age. If you have never applied for a social security card and are over 18, you must apply in person. If you would like a free duplicate card, you must request an application from your caseworker or transition staff. Your caseworker can send a form letter to accompany the application, verifying your name.

State Driver's License and ID Card Requirements

To apply for a current driver's license in your state, an identification card, or an instruction permit, you may present a copy of an expired driver's license, instruction permit, or state identification card. Each state has its own rules which you can learn at any state motor vehicle bureau.

If you *do not* have one of the items listed above, you must usually present one **primary** and one **secondary** document. The primary document must contain your full legal name (first, middle, last) and the month, day, and year of your birth.

If your full legal name is different from the name on your primary document or state driver's license, instruction permit, or state identification card, you must also present a certified copy of a marriage certificate or a certified copy of a divorce decree or other court order. The divorce decree or other court order must specify the name change. The name that will appear on your new driver's license, instruction permit, or state identification card is the name that is on your primary document or legal name change document.

Documents are subject to verification and may not be accepted if altered. Any document that is not in English must be accompanied by an approved English translation.

Any documents listed previously or a primary document listed in this chapter that does not contain your full legal name or only contains a middle initial means that you must also present **another primary or secondary document** that indicates your **full legal name.**

If your license is stolen or lost but still valid, check with your motor vehicle bureau about the procedure to get a duplicate by mail. You can find motor vehicle bureau telephone numbers in a local telephone book.

Primary Documents

✓ *Certified copy of a birth certificate issued by a government bureau of vital statistics or board of health in the United States (U.S.), District of Columbia, Guam, Puerto Rico, or the U.S. Virgin Islands.*

✓ *Certificate of Birth Abroad (FS-545 or DS-1350) issued by the U.S. Department of State.*

✓ *Report of Birth Abroad of a United States Citizen (FS-240) issued by a U.S. embassy.*

✓ *Certified copy of an adoption certificate from a U.S. court.*

✓ *Unexpired identification card (Form DD-2), issued by the U.S. Department of Defense.*

✓ *Unexpired U.S. passport.*

✓ *Unexpired passport from a country other than the U.S. with an unexpired I-551 stamp or an unexpired I-94 arrival and departure form.*

✓ *One of the following unexpired documents issued by the U.S. Department of Justice:*

- *Certificate of Naturalization (N-550, N-570, or N-578)*
- *Certificate of Citizenship (N-560, N-561, or N-645)*
- *US Citizen Identification card (I-179 or I-197)*
- *Permanent Resident or Resident Alien card (I-551 or I-151)*
- *Northern Mariana card (I-873)*
- *American Indian card (I-872)Employment Authorization card with photo (I-688, I-688A, I-688B, or I-766)*
- *Re-entry Permit / Refugee Travel Document (I-571)*

✓ *A Canadian birth certificate or naturalization certificate with a valid I-94 form attached. Must be presented with a photo Secondary Document issued by a Canadian government agency.*

Secondary Documents

- ✓ *Another primary document.*
- ✓ *Photo driver's license, state identification card, or permit issued by a U.S. state, the District of Columbia, Guam, Puerto Rico, the U.S.Virgin Islands, or a Canadian province or territory, that is current or expired for five years or less.*
- ✓ *Certified copy of a U.S. or Canadian court order with full legal name and date of birth.*
- ✓ *Employee photo identification card from a government jurisdiction in the U.S. or Canada.*
- ✓ *Certified copy of a birth certificate from a government jurisdiction other than the U.S., the District of Columbia, Guam, Puerto Rico, or the U.S.Virgin Islands.*
- ✓ *Current identification card (DD-1173 or DD-214) issued by the U.S. Department of Defense.*
- ✓ *Certified copy of a government-issued marriage certificate.*
- ✓ *Unexpired color-photo permit to carry a firearm or concealed weapon, issued by a U.S. police department or sheriff.*
- ✓ *Current pilot's license issued by the Federal Aviation Administration.*
- ✓ *Certified secondary or post-secondary school transcript containing full legal name and date of birth.*
- ✓ *U.S. nonmetal, non-laminated social security card or Canadian social insurance card.*
- ✓ *Current secondary school student identification cards with student's name, photograph, and date of birth or unique identification number.*

Chapter 2

How to Address Your Background in Your Job Search

Our Place D.C.
Chrysalis: Changing Lives Through Jobs

According to the US Department of Justice, more than 59 million criminal-history records are on file at state repositories nationwide. The Bureau of Justice Statistics reports that the number of prison releases is growing, with more than 700,000 ex-offenders rejoining the community each year.

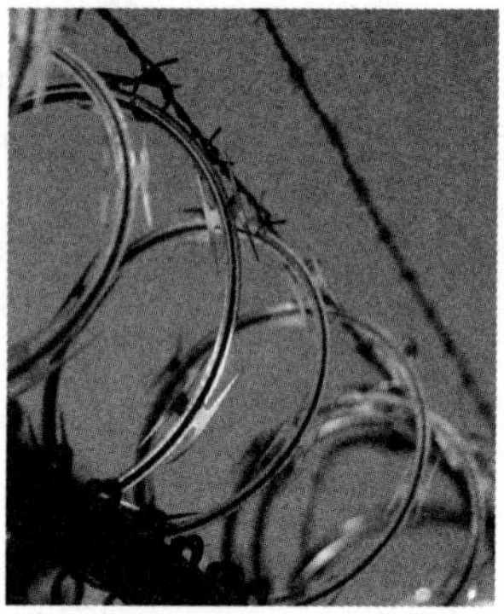

Individuals with criminal histories face numerous obstacles when seeking employment, so it's important they make the one document that can open doors—the resume—as effective as possible.

Resume Tips

- **Don't Reference Your Criminal Background**
  The purpose of a resume is to help you secure a job interview. For your resume to work, it must highlight your top qualifications for the position and demonstrate that you would be an excellent employee. While it's important to be honest on your resume, revealing information about a criminal background is best handled in a face-to-face interview.

  Many states prohibit employers from asking about an arrest record but allow them to inquire about past convictions. Check with your state's attorney general's office (find this by visiting *www.naag.org* and clicking on the interactive map) to determine what employers can and cannot ask you. If the employer asks a legal question regarding your criminal history, briefly explain what happened, but keep it positive and don't dwell on the past. Explain that you have learned from your mistakes and are currently interested in making a positive contribution to the employer's operation.

When completing job applications that ask about your conviction record, you must be honest. Select "yes" when asked if you have been arrested, and in the section that asks you to provide the details, write something like "will explain in interview."

☛ Highlight Related Training/Work Experience

If your criminal background includes prison time and you took advantage of training or work opportunities during that time, you may include these experiences on your resume.

Write the name of the facility and your title (e.g., "Arthur Kill Correctional Facility, Commissary Clerk") in your resume's Work Experience section. Treat this position as any other position and write about key skills you developed and any positive contributions you made. If you completed further education while in prison, write the name of the sponsoring institution along with the details of your training in your Education section. Keep in mind that employers are less interested in your early career; prison-related activities from more than 10 years ago can be omitted.

☛ Don't Emphasize Unrelated Experience

If your work or educational experiences from prison are unrelated to your career goal, they should not be featured prominently on your resume. The most effective resumes are targeted to an objective; your related experience and training should be the focus of your resume. You may, however, add an Additional Experience section to your resume and briefly list your prison-related work or training if you need to cover a big time gap.

- **Use Available Job Search Resources**
  If you were recently released from prison and are in a work-release program, take advantage of job search services offered by your facility. A placement specialist may be able to help you find employment or offer guidance that will facilitate your search. Many states offer tax credits to employers as incentives to hire ex-offenders.

Application Tips

Do not give up all hope of getting a job when you see questions about your criminal record on a job application! The job application is the place to make yourself stand out from the other applicants. Filling out an application does not guarantee that you will be hired, but filling it out completely and honestly may increase the possibility of getting hired and keeping your job. The following is a list of helpful hints for answering questions about your criminal record on a job application:

- ✓ The key to answering questions like these is to know your record. Take a copy of your record with you when you fill out the application, but do not show it to the employer.
- ✓ Read the question carefully. Often employers are only interested in felony convictions. For example, an employer will often ask, *"Have you ever been convicted of a felony?"* If you have only been convicted of a misdemeanor, then you should answer "No."
- ✓ Answer truthfully. Remember: If you lie on your application, you can be fired or denied a job. It is pretty easy for an employer to check your record and there is nothing you can argue to get your job back. Also, it is a crime to lie on an application for some federal and other government jobs.
- ✓ Sometimes questions give time limits. For example, a common question is, *"Have you been convicted of a crime in the past seven years?"* You can answer "No" if your last conviction was more than seven years ago.
- ✓ *"Have you ever been convicted of a crime, offense or violation of the law?"* Remember the difference between conviction and arrest: A conviction is a guilty plea or court's

finding of guilt. An arrest that does not lead to conviction is any arrest that is dismissed, no papered, nolle prosequi, not guilty by reason of insanity, or a finding of not guilty. Also remember that you do not have to spend time in prison to have a conviction on your record. Probation, time served, community service, and other alternatives to prison can be the results of convictions.

✓ *"Have you ever been charged with a crime?"* You only have to respond "Yes" about a "charge" if you were arraigned. If the arrest was "no papered," you were never charged with a crime. If you were arrested and let go without ever appearing before a judge, you were probably no papered. Look on your criminal record to make sure. Also, remember that a crime includes both misdemeanors and felonies (but not most traffic offenses).

✓ There is a difference between adult and juvenile convictions. In some states or circumstances you do not have to reveal your juvenile records. In D.C., for example, juvenile records are not considered convictions. Ask about the laws in your state to be sure.

✓ What if you don't answer the question? There are risks to not answering. To the employer, it may appear that you do not understand the question. The employer may also jump to the conclusion that you have a record and are not willing to talk about it. Instead of not answering the question, you can avoid saying "Yes" or "No" by writing, "I will discuss this in an interview."

✓ Do not just say "Yes." Most questions ask you to explain why you answered "Yes" to a question about your criminal record. There are several ways you can do this:

- » Make your answer a "Yes, but..." answer. Type a statement that explains your conviction and highlights the positive about your circumstances. An example might be explaining your charge, but noting that you learned how to use computers in a prison program. Bring copies of this statement when you fill out your application, and attach it to the form.
- » Another explanation is to write *"I will explain in an interview."* You can answer "Yes" to the question or leave it blank if you use this method.
- » Another option is to simply list your conviction and disposition when you are asked to explain.

✓ "Fighting back" convictions for domestic abuse victims: If you were the victim of domestic abuse and you were convicted on assault, battery or another offense as a result of defending yourself, you should explain this to the potential employer even though you may not want to discuss the abuse.

In the end, only you can decide what is the best way to handle the tough questions. Do not let an application scare you away from applying for a job you want! You never know when someone might want to give you a chance.

The Interview

☛ **Can an Employer Choose Not to Hire Me or Fire Me Because I Have a Criminal Record?**
Some jobs require criminal background checks or a "police clearance" to apply for them. Your boss or the company you work for might also do a background check—including a criminal records search—on you after you start working there.

When a company hired by your employer does a background check, the employer gets a copy of your criminal record. This is why it is important for you to get a copy of your criminal record from these places and make sure they are accurate.

☛ **What Are Employers Allowed to Ask on a Job Application or in an Interview?**
There are a number of types of questions that you are not legally required to answer, like your marital status, religion, living situation, plans for the future, and so on. You should be aware of what these are and decide how to handle them. You don't have to answer them, and you don't have to volunteer this sort of information even if you are asked open ended questions. If you are asked inappropriate questions when interviewing, be polite and try not to be defensive. It may just be someone trying to be helpful and tell you about their good benefits, or the interviewer may not really understand how they sound or even realize they shouldn't be asking. Give people the benefit of the doubt, and try to give a diplomatic response.

- If you are African-American or Hispanic living in D.C., for example, employers cannot ask you questions about arrests that did not lead to convictions. However, if you are applying to a high security job, such as working for the police department, they can ask you such questions.

- Employers cannot make you pay for a copy of your own criminal record.

- Examples of Unlawful Inquiries: All inquiries relating to arrests, such as "*Have you ever been arrested?*" (Note: Arrests are NOT the same as convictions. An innocent person can be arrested, remember.)

- Examples of Lawful Inquiries: There are none, relating to arrests. Legal inquiries about convictions are: *"Have you ever been convicted of any crime? If so, when and where?""Have you ever been convicted under criminal law within the past five years (excluding minor traffic violations)?"* It is permissible to inquire about convictions for acts of dishonesty or breach of trust. These relate to fitness to perform the particular job being applied for, as stipulated by FDIC requirements.

How to Explain your Criminal Record on a Job Interview

The following points are some suggestions for answering questions about your criminal record in an interview:

- **Come prepared with an explanation.**
  When you have a criminal record, acknowledging and explaining it can be the best way to avoid being discriminated against because of your past.

- **Steer the conversation to the positive.**
  Sometimes employers will start questioning you about the details of your conviction. You should politely and respectfully tell the interviewer that you prefer not to talk about the details of your conviction, and remind him or her of the positive things you accomplished while incarcerated or since your release.

- **Focus on your life NOW.**
  One point you want to get across in the interview is that you are moving away from your criminal past. You can talk about your experiences since being incarcerated, or the anticipation and challenge of holding a job you can be proud of. Again, if you get stuck talking about your conviction, steer the conversation back to the present.

- **Stay relaxed to show confidence.**
  It is important that you do not "freeze" when asked questions about your criminal record. Body language is part of the interviewer's impression of you, so if your attitude changes abruptly, the interviewer will sense your nervousness. If you look like you do not know how to answer questions about your conviction, the interviewer might think you are not being honest.

- **Practice interviewing with a friend, family member, or some other trusted person.**
  Get comfortable with admitting that your conviction happened and then practice moving on to other topics. Practicing will help you stay calm when you have to answer the tough questions in a real interview.

  Applying for jobs and interviewing can be hard work but even if you do not get the first job you interview for, you will get better at it each time you try.

Keep in Mind, A Criminal Record Can Bar You from Jobs in Certain Fields.

Be prepared, some placed may not legally be allowed to employ you. The following information relates to the Washington, D.C. area, but may also be relevant where you live.

- **Hospitals, Jails, Charities**
  A background check is required to work as a non-licensed employee at a place that provides direct care for people (like a hospital, a juvenile home, a jail or prison, an institution for the mentally ill, or a charity organization). Convictions for some crimes will bar you from employment in this area. If you have been convicted of any of the following crimes anywhere in the U.S., you can-

not get a job working in a facility in health care, community residence facilities, or hospice and home care (remember that pleading guilty is the same as being convicted):

» *Murder, attempted murder, or manslaughter;*

» *Arson*

» *Assault, battery, assault and battery, assault with a dangerous weapon, mayhem or threats to do bodily harm;*

» *Burglary*

» *Robbery*

» *Kidnapping*

» *Theft, fraud, forgery, extortion or blackmail*

» *Illegal use or possession of a firearm*

» *Trespass or injury to property*

» *Rape, sexual assault, sexual battery, or sexual abuse*

» *Child abuse or cruelty to children or*

» *Unlawful distribution, possession or possession with intent to distribute a controlled substance. Remember: If you have only a first-time offense for simple possession, you can get this expunged from your record.*

☛ Department of Recreation and Parks

Volunteer work for the D.C. Department of Recreation and Parks also requires a background check, and volunteers will be barred for the same convictions previously mentioned.

☛ Banks

You cannot work in a bank or financial institution if you have been convicted of an offense involving dishonesty, breach of trust, or money laundering. For most convictions, the bank can ask for an exception, but for some crimes—such a fraud, burglary, theft, and money laundering—you cannot work in a bank for 10 years after the conviction. In addition, an employer can fire someone who has a conviction for dishonesty, breach of trust, or money laundering.

- **Any Job That Requires Carrying a Gun**

  An example of this type of job would be a security guard. If you have been convicted of a misdemeanor crime of domestic violence, you cannot buy, own, or carry a firearm. Any felony conviction (not only for domestic violence), or any Civil Protection Order (CPO) against you also bans possession or use of a firearm. Thus, if you have been convicted of misdemeanor domestic violence, have a current CPO against you, or have any felony conviction, you are not permitted to hold a job that requires that you carry a gun.

Licensing Requirements and Criminal Records

You may be required to get a license to join a profession or advance in a career. However, you will not be allowed to get certain licenses if you have been convicted of particular crimes. The general rule for most occupational licenses is that you must not have been convicted of an offense which bears directly on your fitness to be licensed.

Digging Deeper

Video: Employment Tips – Resume Advice for Ex-Convicts

http://albuquerque.jobing.com/video

Type "Resume Advice for Ex-Convicts" into the Search Videos box and click on this video. This short video offers advice on addressing your criminal record on your resume, and how to show the positive side of your experience, such as education or work experience gained in prison. Other videos offer advice on intervewing, searching for jobs, and keeping your job.

The Wizard of Jobs: Ex-Felon Resources

http://www.thewizardofjobs.net/exfelons.html

Here you will find an alphabetical list of links to a variety of ex-offender resources. There are links to federal and state resources, as well as programs and non-profits. Also included are helpful articles on related topics. Browse the list, and see which resources can help you.

Chrysalis: Changing Lives Through Jobs: Career Center

http://www.changelives.org/career.html

Chrysalis offers a number of online resources on its Career Center page. There are links to job search engines, as well as articles on resumes, cover letters, interviewing, and thank you letters. Under "Learning computer skills" and "All about the internet," you will find online lessons and tips to help you improve your skills in these areas.

Ex-Offender Employment Information Handbook

http://www.bop.gov/inmate_programs/emp_info_handbk.pdf

Don't be intimidated by the size of this document! It is full of helpful information on a variety of employment-related topics. From information about employment programs to job search tips and a sample resume, you will find a lot of resources to help you fin a job. In addition, there is information about non-job-related subjects, such housing, voting rights, education, and how to get a driver's license.

Our Place D.C.

http://www.ourplacedc.org/pages/documents/FOPIssue202006.pdf

The mission of this Washington, D.C.-based non-profit is "to support women who are or have been in the criminal justice system by providing the resources they need to maintain connections with the community, resettle after incarceration, and reconcile with their families." While many resources are only for women in the D.C. area, their newsletter offers advice and inspiration to people anywhere. You can find articles on employment, health, legal issues, family, and abuse as well as interviews with real people who have made it through tough situations.

Chapter 3

Dress for Success: Personal Hygiene, Grooming, and Attire

Adapted from an article prepared by Columbus, Georgia Technical College

Employers hire people they believe will "fit" into their organization.

Skills, experience, and qualifications are important, but so are dress and grooming. Your appearance expresses motivation and professionalism. When in doubt, err on the conservative side and make a statement of who you are. Your clothing and grooming should create the image that will help you get the job offer.

First Impressions

Most of us have heard the expression, *"A picture is worth a thousand words."* Remember this when preparing to meet with a prospective employer. The picture you create will greatly influence your chances of being hired. Most employers form a first impression during the first seven seconds of a meeting. Not much is said in this short time; early judgment is based strictly on appearance. Furthermore, studies reveal that employers consistently ask the question, "Does the individual look right for the job?"

Here are some basic guidelines:

- ✓ *Be clean and neat, including your fingernails, teeth, shoes, hair and face*
- ✓ *Wear clean clothes suitable for the type of work you seek*
- ✓ *Don't smoke during an interview*
- ✓ *Try to avoid visible body piercing and excessive cologne or perfume*
- ✓ *Arrive ten minutes early and arrive alone*
- ✓ *Smile; be friendly*
- ✓ *Demonstrate a positive attitude*
- ✓ *Use good eye contact*
- ✓ *Shake hands firmly*
- ✓ *Use good manners*
- ✓ *Don't interrupt and don't argue!*
- ✓ *Don't chew gum*
- ✓ *Take resumes and/or other pertinent information*

Clothing

The clothes you wear affect your attitude and confidence levels. When people take the time to dress for success, they tend to feel good about themselves. Image alone will not win the job offer, but it will go along way in building respect.

There are no absolute rules regarding dress. Your selection will vary based on your occupation, location, and preference. A business suit for a construction job or overalls for an office job would not be appropriate dress! The goal is to look the part, and your appearance should be consistent with your occupation. Neat, clean work clothes would be suitable for assembly, production, or warehouse positions. Sales and office positions require business clothes. A conservative suit would be the recommended style for professional and managerial positions.

Common sense and good taste are the best guides in selecting clothing for the interview. Avoid faddish styles and loud colors. Jewelry should be conservative and kept to a minimum. Clothing should fit comfortably. You want the employer to focus on your skills, not on your clothes.

Grooming

Personal grooming is just as important as what you wear. You may select the right clothes, but neglecting personal hygiene can ruin the image you wish to present. Review the following grooming checklist before meeting with the employer.

ITEM	GROOMING
Hair	Clean, trimmed, and neatly combed or arranged.
Facial Hair (Men)	Freshly shaved; mustache or beard neatly groomed.
Fingernails	Neat, clean, and trimmed.
Teeth	Brushed teeth and fresh breath.
Breath	Beware of foods which may leave breath odor. Beware of tobacco, alcohol, and coffee odor. Use a breath mint if needed.
Body	Freshly bathed/showered; use deodorant. Remove body piercings, tongue rings, and cover tattoos if possible.
Make-Up (Women)	Use sparingly and be natural looking.
Perfumes/ Colognes/ After Shave	Use sparingly or none at all. Your "scent" should not linger after you leave.

Goals of Appropriate Dress and Grooming

The primary goal is to "feel good" about the way you look and project a positive image. When you feel good about yourself, you naturally convey confidence and a positive attitude. These nonverbal messages are as important in the interview as the verbal skills you use in selling your qualifications. Persistence and follow-up are the keys to a successful job search. If you are serious about employment, plan your follow-up. There is no such thing as a wasted effort, and the only dead lead is the one you chose to kill. Situations change and the employer who is not hiring today may be looking for someone with your qualifications in the future.

An interview isn't a beauty contest, but how you dress and your overall appearance almost always get noticed by the interviewer. Don't give the interviewer a chance to rule you out because you didn't feel like ironing your shirt or polishing your shoes. Dress in a business-like, professional manner, and you will be sure to fit in wherever you interview.

Chapter 4

Public Assistance for Ex-Offenders

Starting Out! Research Group

Introduction: Planning Ahead for a Successful Re-Entry

The key to a successful transition into your new community is early preparation. Approximately 120 days prior to your release date, it is important that you begin to make contact with as many federal and state supportive service agencies as possible. In order to qualify for specific benefits or services, a counselor or caseworker will need specific information regarding your particular situation.

Keep in mind that in order for you to obtain supportive services from state and federally funded organizations, you must apply, and you must meet certain eligibility requirements. Service organizations must evaluate each applicant individually, because the level of assistance and the length of eligibility can vary greatly depending upon various circumstances such as age, disability, income potential, specific skills or trade certifications, level of education, number and age of dependents, etc.

Part I: Necessary Documents for Program Eligibility

Before applying for assistance, you will be asked to provide documentation. Read Chapter 1 of this book for a complete explanation of the types of documents you need to assemble. These items may be applied for by inmates prior to release through their

Case Management Counselor. Here are some of the most common documents you will need:

1. **Social Security Card.** If you've lost your card, contact a local Social Security Office and apply for a replacement card.
2. **Birth or Marriage Certificate.** If you need a copy of your birth or marriage certificate, you must contact the Division of Vital Records in the states where you were born and were married.
3. **Orders of Release.** These documents will be issued to you upon your release.
4. **High School Diploma or GED Information.** The purpose of providing General Educational Development (GED) information is to enable those who do not have a copy of the high school equivalency to obtain one. Many employers will not hire if an individual does not have a high school diploma or equivalent (GED).

Part II: What to Expect from Government Assistance Programs

☛ Federal Programs

Federal programs are generally designed to help people who need work, housing, public assistance, and other services. While each program has different standards for participation with low income being the most common requirement, there are no federal programs exclusively for ex-offenders. However, there are a number of beneficial programs that can offer general types of assistance, and these are listed further on in this chapter and in Parts IV and V dealing with employment and training.

To learn about all federal benefits programs, not just for ex-offenders, the government operates a special website for consumers, *www.govbenefits.gov.*

☛ State and Local Programs and Where to Find Out About Them

Most assistance programs are administered locally by community agencies. You can find the addresses for them in the local telephone book's blue pages and on the internet. One of the first stops you should make is to the state employment service offices to help you with job leads. Their local addresses are located in the blue pages of the telephone book.

Read Chapter 21 of this book, "Searching for a New Job," to learn about federal, state, and local assistance for employment and training.

☛ Non-Federal Offender Assistance

If you are a non-federal offender in a state or local correctional institution, you should ask education services staff at your correctional institution for information about community, state, and private programs to help ex-offenders.

☛ Local Sources of Help and CareerOneStop Offices

Assistance may also be available from local faith-based organizations. Your local library may offer public access to the internet and provide employment information specific to your community. If there is a One-Stop Career Center in your area, be sure to visit it for job leads, training, and other services that can help you and your family. Always explain your situation when you visit any assistance services agencies and, if they cannot be of assistance, do not forget to ask for a referral to another agency or private organization that may be able to help you. **For a full explanation of employment assistance, refer to Chapter 21.**

Part III: Are There Loans or Grants Available for Ex-Offenders?

☛ Beware of Bogus Offers of Loans and Grants

The internet is filled with websites that promise that they can help you get loans and grants from the federal government for almost any purpose. These offers are not reliable, as the federal government does not freely give out money, except under formal programs with special qualification as noted below. Do not spend your own money on any of these services, as you will not only lose your payment, but you will lose valuable time and only be disappointed.

There are a number of agencies in the federal government that do provide loans, grants and assistance, such as for farmers, small businesses, and certain qualified projects, although it is often difficult to qualify for this type of assistance. The best source for these programs is the Catalog of Federal Domestic Assistance. It is available at some libraries and from the Government Printing Office (GPO). Information is also available from the Federal Citizen Information Center at 1-800-FED-INFO, or on the internet: *www.pueblo.gsa.gov.*

☛ Small Business Administration

There are no small business loans or grants specifically for ex-offenders. However, if you have plans to start a new business and are teaming up with others who have had business experience, you can learn about the Small Business Administration (SBA) which works with local banks. The SBA does not provide direct loans. They do provide loan guarantees for certain businesses that borrow from lending institutions. They do not provide specific grants or low interest rate loans to ex-offenders for business start-up or expansion. For further information, you may want to contact the Small Business Administration, 409 Third Street, S.W., Washington, DC 20416 or view its website at: *www.sba.gov.*

Part IV: Social Security Assistance: Understanding Eligibility

The Social Security Administration oversees a number of different benefit programs, including retirement benefits, disability benefits, dependents benefits, and survivors benefits. You must visit or speak with your local Social Security Office about eligibility for different programs.

✗ **Social Security and Supplemental Security Income (SSI) Benefits** are not payable for the months that you are confined to a jail, prison, or certain other public institutions for the commission of a crime. In addition, you are not automatically eligible for Social Security or SSI benefits when you are released. In all cases, you must apply for benefits with a Social Security Office if you think you qualify. Although you cannot receive benefits while you are confined to jail or prison, your spouse or children, if they are eligible, can be paid benefits on your record. Inmates should consult their counselor for assistance with this process.

- ✗ **Social Security Disability Benefits** can be paid only to people who have recently worked and paid Social Security taxes, and who are unable to work because of a serious medical condition that is expected to last for at least a year or result in death. The fact that an individual is a recent parolee or is unemployed does not qualify as a disability.

  Who decides if I am disabled? The Social Security Administration will review your application to determine if you meet basic requirements for disability benefits. They will look at your age and whether you have worked long enough and recently enough. The office will send your application to the Disability Determination Services (DDS) office in your state. The DDS will decide whether you are disabled under the Social Security law. They will use the medical evidence from your doctors and from hospitals, clinics, or institutions where you have been treated and any other information they have available. Once a decision is reached, you will be sent a letter. If your claim is approved, the letter will show the amount of your benefit and when payments will start.

- ✗ **Social Security Retirement Benefits** can be paid only to people who are 62 or older. Generally, you must have worked and paid taxes into Social Security for 10 years to be eligible.

- ✗ **Supplemental Security Income (SSI) Benefits** can be paid to people who are 65 or older or blind or disabled and who have low income and few resources. No SSI benefits are payable for any months that you reside in prison.

- ✗ **Ticket to Work Program** is administered under the Ticket to Work and Work Incentive Improvement Act of 1999 provides an opportunity for people who receive social security disability benefits to work. It provides training and employment opportunities for disabled individuals while allowing them to continue to receive social security benefits. To learn about programs and eligibility in your area, go to: *www.yourtickettowork.com*.

- ✗ **Future Social Security Benefit Estimates** are available from the Social Security Administration based upon the amounts you have paid in during your working years. You can get a free Personal Earnings and Benefit Estimate Statement by calling 1-800-772-1213 and asking for Form SSA-7004. (All calls are confidential.) The website is *http://www.ssa.gov*.

Part V: Department of Labor Programs

The following programs are offered by the U.S. Department of Labor. **Refer to Chapter 21, which deals with employment, for a full explanation of each one:**

- ✓ *CareerOneStop*
- ✓ *Veterans Employment and Training Service*
- ✓ *Veterans Workforce Investment Program*
- ✓ *Homeless Veterans' Reintegration Program (HVRP)*
- ✓ *Job Corps*
- ✓ *Disability Employment and Training Services*
- ✓ *Native American Employment and Training Services*
- ✓ *Older Workers Employment Program*
- ✓ *Registered Apprenticeships*
- ✓ *Employer Tax Credit Programs for New Hires*
- ✓ *Federal Bonding Program*

Part VI: Education and Training Assistance

Once you are released from incarceration, you will have many opportunities to pursue additional education and training. Here are some of those opportunities:

☛ **CareerOneStop** Your local CareerOneStop Office offers different types of training programs, apprenticeships, and educational guidance.

☛ **Federal Student Financial Aid**

☛ **Adult Education** Almost every community offers adult education classes in numerous fields. Try to make time to take one or two courses that will advance your career.

Part I

Part VII: Department of Veterans Affairs: Programs for Ex-Offender Veterans

Check with your nearest Veterans Administration Office to learn about possible assistance for substance abuse, mental health, disability compensation, vocational rehabilitation and employment. Inquire about the following programs:

1. *Veterans Vocational Rehabilitation and Employment Service (800-827-1000)*
2. *Veteran Affairs' Montgomery GI Bill (888-GI-BILL-1 or 888-442-4552 or http://www.gibill.va.gov/)*
3. *Health Care for Homeless Veterans (803-776-4000, extension 7697)*
4. *National Coalition for Homeless Veterans (NCHV)*

NCHV provides a comprehensive source of information for America's homeless veterans (including current and ex-offenders), and the programs available to them in each state. Visit *http://www.nchv.org*, call 800-VET-HELP, or write to 333 ½ Pennsylvania Avenue, SE, Washington, DC 20003-1148.

Part VIII: Individual and Family Assistance Programs

☛ Credit Reporting

You can request a free credit file disclosure, commonly called a credit report, once every 12 months from each of the nationwide consumer credit reporting companies: Equifax, Experian, and TransUnion. The easiest way to get your report is to go to: *www.annualcreditreport.com*. You can also call Equifax (877-576-5734), Experian (888-397-3742), or TransUnion (800-680-7289) directly.

A credit file disclosure provides you with all of the information in your credit file maintained by a consumer reporting company.

☛ Food Stamps

The Food Stamp Program enables low-income people to buy nutritious food to improve their diets. Food stamp recipients spend their benefits on eligible food in authorized retail food stores with paper coupons or electronic benefits on Electronic Benefits Transfer (EBT) cards. EBT is an electronic system that allows a recipient to authorize transfer of their government benefits from a federal account to a retailer account to pay for products received.

Visit the U.S. Department of Agriculture's pre-screening tool at www.foodstamps-step1.usda.gov to determine your eligibility. For information by phone, call the toll-free information number: 1-800-221-5689.

☛ Housing

Check with community housing assistance organizations in your area for information on low-income housing options. You can also check listings in the blue pages of the telephone book under "Housing" to locate contact numbers.

For those who do not have access to local information, contact the U.S. Department of Housing and Urban Development (HUD), 451 7th Street, S.W., Washington, DC 20410. The telephone number is 202-708-1112, TTY: 202-708-1455.

Ex-offenders with drug and sex offender convictions are ineligible for public housing in most localities. However, if you are not excluded, you can also inquire about eligibility for "Section 8 Rent Subsidies."

For information about both availability and eligibility restrictions, go to *www.hud.gov* and click on "Renting" listed in the left-hand column.

☛ Homelessness Programs

There are homeless shelters in most cities in the U.S. In addition, the U.S. Department of Health and Human Services offers many programs, grants, and services for the homeless. For more information, contact the U.S. Department of Housing and Urban Development, 4517th Street S.W., Washington, DC 20410. Telephone: 202-708-1112, TTY: 202-708-1455, or contact the local department of health and/or human services in the blue pages of your telephone book.

Additional information can be obtained from your local office of United Way about the Emergency Food and Shelter Program (EFSP).

☛ Medical Assistance

For information on medical assistance, contact the health department at the location where you are released. You can find its number in the blue pages of the local telephone book. You may also write to the Department of Health and Human Services 200 Independence Ave, SW., Washington, DC 20201. You can also call its office at 1-877-696-6775 or 202-619-0257 or find information on the web: *www.hhs.gov*.

The Centers for Medicare and Medicaid Services *(http://www.cms.hhs.gov)* offers health coverage for certain populations based upon eligibility.

Medicare is a health insurance program for people age 65 or older, people under age 65 with certain disabilities, and people of all ages with End-Stage Renal Disease (permanent kidney failure requiring dialysis or a kidney transplant).

Medicaid is available only to certain low-income individuals and families who fit into an eligibility group that is recognized by federal and state law. Medicaid does not pay money to you; instead, it sends payments directly to your health care providers. Depending on your state's rules, you may also be asked to pay a small part of the cost (co-payment) for some medical services Medicaid is a state administered program and each state sets its own guidelines regarding eligibility and services.

☛ Children and Families of Adult Offenders

The National Institute of Corrections (NIC) offers a number of programs on re-entry. For information, click on "Projects" at its website, *www.nicic.org*, or call the Family and Corrections Network at 434-589-3036 to get information over the telephone.

Local Social Service Programs may be available in your community that can benefit the families of adult offenders. These programs are often offered by non-profit organizations or as part of the Department of Social Services in a city or state. Check with your corrections counselor about locating such assistance, or call the Health Department, Human Services Department, or Social Services Department of your city.

☛ Child Support Enforcement

The Child Support Enforcement (CSE) Program is a federal, state, and local effort to locate parents, their employers, and/or their assets; to establish paternity if necessary; and to establish and enforce child support orders. State and local CSE offices provide day-to-day operation of the program. The federal role is to provide funding, issue policies, ensure that federal requirements are met, and interact with other federal agencies that help support the CSE program.

In most states, CSE offices are listed under the human services agency in the local government section of the telephone directory. If there is not a separate listing, the human services agency information operator should be able to give you the number. Call your CSE office to learn how to apply for enforcement services and what documents (birth certificates, financial statements, etc.) you need to provide. They will answer your questions, or refer you to the state office that can. Be sure to indicate your release destination.

☛ AIDS Treatment and the AIDS Access Project (http://www.atdn.org/)

The AIDS Treatment Data Network is an independent, community-based, not-for-profit organization that provides treatment access information and advocacy, case management, supportive counseling, and English and Spanish language information services to men, women, and children with AIDS, HIV and those co-infected with hepatitis. Click on The Access Project to find links to resources and assistance in every state. You can also request assistance by calling 800-734-7104, extension 22.

☛ Sexually Transmitted Disease (STD) and HIV Hotline

The Federal Centers of Disease Control and Prevention (CDC) operates an STD/HIV Hotline providing anonymous, confidential information, prevention information, and referrals to clinical services in every state. Only New York State provides public treatment services.

The nationwide toll-free number in English is 800-227-8922, in Spanish it is 800-344-7432, and TTY is 800-243-7889. Find more information on the web at *www.cdc.gov/std* and *www.cdc.gov/hiv/*.

Part I

☛ Domestic Violence Emergency Help

The National Domestic Violence Hotline (NDVH) serves as the only center in the nation that is available for victims, friends and family who often call for life-saving help. The hotline operates 24 hours a day in more than 140 languages: For assistance call 1-800-799-7223 or 1-800-787-3224 (TTY) or visit the website: *www.ndvh.org*.

☛ Mental Health and Chemical Dependency Resources

Staff at the national/regional agencies listed below should be able to direct callers to mental health and chemical dependency resources in specified communities.

Substance Abuse and Mental Health Services Administration
1 Choke Cherry Road
Rockville, MD 20857
1-800-662-HELP
www.samhsa.gov

Mental Health America
2001 N. Beauregard St. 12th Floor
Alexandria, VA 22311
1-800-969-6642
www.nmha.org

National Alliance for the Mentally Ill
Colonial Place Three
Post Office Box 2345
Arlington, VA 22201-3043
1-800-950-6264
www.nami.org

The National Clearinghouse for Alcohol and Drug Information
2107 Wilson Blvd., Suite 300
Rockville, MD 20847-2345
1-800-729-6686
Hablamos Español: 1-877-767-8432

Part IX: State and Local Re-Entry Benefits and Services

☛ State, Municipal, and Non-Profit Re-Entry Services

Some states, municipalities, and non-profit organizations operate Re-Entry Centers which function as service locations for offenders released from a correctional facility. For example, the Commonwealth of Massachusetts operates regional re-entry offices. The re-entry centers help ex-offenders by providing them with necessary services, on-going treatment, and support in the community where these ex-offenders are returning. Ask your corrections counselor if there is a re-entry service center or office in or near your community.

☛ General Emergency Relief and Temporary Assistance to Needy Families

Benefits that could be available to former prisoners vary by state, and one must research these benefits on a state-by-state basis. Check to see whether you are eligible for Temporary Assistance to Needy Families (TANF). Some states have General Emergency Relief which consists of limited financial assistance to individuals and families. If you are eligible for assistance from SSI, you may or may not be eligible for General Relief. Because General Relief is a local program, the kind of assistance available varies from agency to agency. Ask your local State Social Services representative what kinds of General Relief assistance are available, including possible benefits for needy families, including food stamps, benefits for the unemployed, for the disabled, for those undergoing medical treatment.

☛ State Rehabilitation Benefits

Check with your state's Department of Rehabilitation Services for available vocational rehabilitation for individuals with physical or mental disabilities.

Part X: Non-Profit and Service Organizations

There are many non-profit, service, and prisoner advocacy organizations in every state that assist recently released prisoners to transition into society. Among the more well-known such agencies are the Salvation Army, Volunteers of America, YMCA and YWCA, churches and faith-based organizations. Every corrections facility has lists of local non-profits that assist ex-offenders.

Chapter 5

Immediate & Temporary Housing for Ex-Offenders

Minnesota Department of Corrections

Finding a place to live will be difficult for some. For others, there will be no choice because of Department of Corrections requirements. Some may be mandated to live at a Residential Re-Entry Center (RRC), sometimes referred to as a "half-way house," or to a Comprehensive Sanction Center (CSC) which has more structured transition programs. Below we explain each of these alternatives.

If you have no restrictions on where you live, think hard before deciding to move back into your old neighborhood. There may be people and activities there to pull you back into committing crimes.

Some will have a supportive friend, relative, or family member to live with and housing may not be a major concern, while others will need to explore different options.

When looking for housing, keep in mind where it is located relative to your workplace, what transportation is available, and what stores are in the area.

Community Correction Centers/Residential Re-entry Centers

Re-entering offenders from federal and state prisons may face different options.

Most non-violent federal prison inmates will complete their period of federal prison incarceration in some type of Community Corrections Center (CCC) or halfway house (RRC). The Bureau of Prisons normally requires inmates to remain in federal prison until at least 90% or more of their sentence has been completed. Only then will they become eligible for a transfer to a Community Corrections Center.

What is a Comprehensive Sanction Center (CSC)?

The CSC concept was created to facilitate the development and implementation of individualized community program plans tailored to offenders' specific needs. Approximately 45% of federal inmates in community-based programs are housed in CSCs. While similar to RRCs, CSCs offer a more structured system for granting inmates gradual access to the community. CSCs also require that inmates participate in more programs, including intensive treatment programs for substance abuse education, life skills training, mental health counseling, education, employment assistance, and monitoring.

The **Second Chance Act** provides that, "*the Director of the Bureau of Prisons shall, to the extent practicable, ensure that a prisoner serving a term of imprisonment spends a portion of the final months of that term under conditions that will afford that prisoner a reasonable opportunity to adjust to and prepare for re-entry of that prisoner into the community. Such conditions may include a community correctional facility.*"

Temporary Shelter Providers and Referral Agencies

Some offenders may need temporary shelters after completing community-based transition programs. Below is a list of types of temporary shelter programs in many communities across the U.S.:

1. **United Way 2-1-1, formerly First Call for Help,** is a service that can assist you in finding temporary shelter like the ones listed below. Resources are accessible to you through the library transition resource center, the internet (after your release), and by dialing 211.

2. **Community Action Agencies** provide services to reduce the effects of poverty in the community. Many provide energy assistance, winterization, housing, and emergency

shelter services. These agencies are also a good source of information and referral for related services. To find an agency near you, go to *www.communityactionpartnership.com* and click on the "Find a Community Action Agency" button under the Community Action Network tab. You can also call 202-265-7546 or write the Community Action Partnership at 1140 Connecticut Avenue, NW, Suite 1210, Washington, DC 20036.

3. **County Social Services Agencies** sometimes administer low-income financial assistance programs, as well as other assistance programs such as Medical Assistance, Emergency Assistance, and Food Stamps. They may provide referrals for overnight shelter. There are strict state and federal guidelines for the above programs so immediate monetary assistance may not be possible.

4. **Drop-In Centers** provide a variety of services, which may include food, clothing, and support. The centers serve as sources of information, and daytime shelter. Availability is limited to larger metro areas.

5. **Emergency and Overnight Shelters** offer lodging for a short period of time (usually one or two nights) until other arrangements can be made through the county or other programs. You may use 2-1-1 (First Call for Help) to help locate these shelters. There is no charge for staying at most emergency shelters. Some charity-sponsored shelters may require that you participate in their programs to use their shelter.

6. **Salvation Army Units** provide shelter vouchers to individuals in need. They may also help out with meals and other essential needs. These units may also offer medical checkups, AA programs, job skill training, and counseling. For more information, write to: The Salvation Army National Headquarters, 615 Slaters Lane, PO Box 269, Alexandria, VA 22313. You can also find a local program by visiting *www.salvationarmy.org*, and searching for centers near your location.

7. **Transitional (halfway housing)**—Some offenders are mandated to this type of housing as a condition of their release and to provide some structure as the offender adjusts to life on the outside. If space is available, others may also live there, provided they meet the shelter's guidelines. You may use 2-1-1 (First Call for Help) to help you locate transitional housing in your area or you may want to ask your caseworker for assistance:

- *May provide shelter for up to one year.* • *Expects you to be accountable at all times and cooperate with any programming identified by the referring agency.*
- *Provides opportunity to ease back into the community by gaining employment, accumulating savings, developing a plan of working toward independent living, and establishing community support services.* • *Includes support services (such as counseling and job search help) in addition to food and shelter.*
- *Provides you time to save money for your own place. Costs will depend on services provided.*

8. **Sober Housing**—Sober housing is NOT a treatment program and often will not accept sex offenders.
   - *Provides long-term support, allowing residents to stabilize and develop healthy relationships with other people pursuing similar goals.*
   - *Generally, the only requirements are sobriety and lawful means of paying bills. Often, there is no second chance—a resident who "uses" one time will be "out."*
   - *Is much less expensive than an apartment and makes saving money for more independent living easier.*

   These units may also offer medical checkups, AA programs, job skill training, and counseling. For more information, write to: The Salvation Army National Headquarters, 615 Slaters Lane, PO Box 269, Alexandria, VA 22313. You can also find a local program by visiting *www.salvationarmy.org*, and searching for centers near your location.

9. **Homeless Shelters:** Most cities offer homeless shelters for temporary use. Check your community's Yellow Pages or visit the national homeless shelter directory at: *http://www.homelessshelterdirectory.org/*.

10. **Single Room Only (SRO) Housing** is usually furnished housing with shared bath or kitchen facilities that is made available to income eligible individuals at reduced rates.

11. **YMCA and YWCA Rooms** are available in many cities at very low nightly rates to tide you over while you find more permanent housing.

12. **Church and Faith-Based Housing Assistance:** Seek advice from your local church or from local faith-based organizations about temporary housing available in your community.

Chapter 6

Managing Your Money: A Quick Primer

Minnesota Department of Corrections
Starting Out! Research Group

When you are released from federal prison you will usually receive $100 gate money, plus any money you have saved. The amount of money you will be given may be different in your state prison system. Nevertheless, you should begin your budgeting with this money and with any money you may receive from friends and relatives.

Think about needs you will have immediately upon release. Avoid the temptation to spend this money impulsively, as fun money. Include it in your overall budget plan.

Where Will My Money Come From?

As you leave incarceration, you may not have a job waiting for you or relatives who can help support you until you can get a job. For this reason, you must manage the little money you may have saved as carefully as possible while you are trying to get a job. Until you get your first job, you may have to depend upon emergency shelters, community, and faith-based services to get by.

Once you have money coming in from a job, you need to establish good habits right away, so you do not spend more than you have.

Understanding Your Income and Taxes

You will not receive your full hourly pay or salary in your paycheck, so be prepared! Your employer will be taking out state and federal taxes and possibly other items such as insurance or union dues, leaving you with a lower amount to spend than you may have expected. Be sure you understand your pay stub which should list all items that may have been deducted from your gross pay. If you have questions, you should always ask your employer or personnel manager to explain your pay stub.

Managing Your Savings

If you have built up some savings or are given some money by friends or relatives, try not to spend it all at once. You will need it as an emergency cushion. Only use your savings if you have no other source of money.

Keeping Track of Your Spending

The first step in making a spending and saving plan is to start keeping track of where you money is coming from and where it is going. You have to know how much you are spending and what you are spending it on before you can make a spending and savings plan.

You need to keep track of your spending for at least one month before you can get a good picture of where your money goes. At the end of the month, total the amount you have spent for each spending category.

For example, for January your list might look like this:

	Date	Item	Amount
1	January 1, 2008	Rent (1 bedroom)	$550.00
2	January 1, 2008	Video rental	$4.50
3	January 2, 2008	Bus pass	$30.00
4	January 5, 2008	Groceries	$45.00
5	January 7, 2008	Shoe polish	$5.00

6	January 10, 2008	Shampoo	$4.50
7	January 12, 2008	Gas	$21.50
8	January 15, 2008	Electric Bill	$45.50
9	January 18, 2008	Groceries	$75.00

At the end of January and each new month, you should know where your money came from and how you spent it. Using a separate sheet of paper, copy the following chart and place the above amounts in the right categories:

Snapshot of My Personal Budget

Sources of My Money	Month 1	Month 2	Month 3	Month 4
Gate Money				
Earnings				
Savings Used				
Personal Loans				
Total Money Available				

How I Spent My Money

Housing	
Utilities	
Food	

Laundry	
Family Necessities	
Medical	
Automobile and Transportation	
Clothing	
Recreation and Entertainment	
Personal Improvement	
Gifts, Church, and Charity	
Taxes	
Child Care	
Union/Professional	
SAVINGS	
TOTAL AMOUNTS SPENT	
SUBTRACT EXPENSES FROM INCOME TO SEE HOW YOU DID	

Managing Your Money

Once you understand where your spending money is coming from and how it is being spent, you can begin to make decisions to avoid spending more than you have. On the earning side, you may need to increase your income by working more hours or getting a second job. And on the expense side, you may have to cut out items that you just can't afford.

Always plan to have enough money for the most vital necessities, such as food and shelter. As your income increases, you can afford to take on more expenses and begin to enjoy the fruits of your labor.

Stay Away From Loans and Credit Cards

Above all, DO NOT BORROW and DO NOT GET A CREDIT CARD. Borrowing means you don't have enough money on hand to meet your daily expenses. If you borrow and lack income, you will not be able to pay the loans or credit cards back, and you will suddenly find yourself with large debts and debt collectors coming after you. This can only lead to more serious problems.

Chapter 7

Putting It All Together: Making a Personal Re-Entry Plan

Starting Out! Research Group

Question: Why should I make a re-entry plan?

Answer: A well-thought-out re-entry plan will lead to a more successful transition back into society, and may also increase your chances of being released on time and to your preferred area. Counselors and Community Corrections Officers (CCO) like to see re-entry plans. It shows them that you are serious about your release and serious about your life.

Part I: The Benefits of a Personal Re-Entry Plan

✓ *A good plan will help you to know where you are going and how you intend to get back into society.*

✓ *Planning ahead and writing a re-entry plan will get you thinking about all the things you need to do and know before you are released, so you can take advantage of programs and assistance in your current facility.*

✓ *Many items require long-term planning, such as building marketable skills while incarcerated.*

✓ *Preparation involves getting your identification documents together. This work can and should be accomplished before your release.*

- ✓ *While incarcerated, you can learn about managing your money, improving your interpersonal skills, and getting help with substance abuse and mental health issues.*
- ✓ *A Re-Entry Plan can help you identify weaknesses and strengths in your education, and identify ways of getting help with basic academic skills. You may be able to earn a GED while incarcerated.*

Part II: My Goals and Objectives Upon Release

Every plan should have a series of objectives and goals that explain your life plans, how you will approach life on the outside, and what you intend to accomplish so you will be able to turn your back on criminal activity. You may already have accomplished some of your life objectives while incarcerated. Why not make a list of what these accomplishments and personal improvements are?

Part III: My Personal Support System on the Outside

A support system includes the people in your life who you can talk to about problems and successes. These people may also be able to offer you assistance, whether it be advice, a ride to work, or a job lead. A good support system is important to your success on the outside. Consider the following questions about your potential support system.

- » *What family members will help you? Do you have a spouse waiting for you? If you have children, what is your current relationship with them and how do you plan to improve it when you are released?*
- » *What friends can you count on when you are released? Will they help you stay out of trouble? Will you avoid those who are a bad influence?*
- » *Can your family and/or friends help with housing, transportation, finding a job, and other necessary steps?*
- » *Will you get financial and emotional support from your family and/or close friends?*
- » *Do you have access to a vehicle?*

» *Do you have childcare obligations upon your release?*

Part IV: My Future Address Upon Release

You must know where you will stay, including the address, telephone number which you can give to others, the residential manager or landlord, the cost of your housing, and how you intend to pay for it.

Part V: My Employment Plans

Have you found a job before your release? If so, write down the details, such as name of your employer, address, phone number, supervisor's name, work schedule, transportation requirement, and expected pay.

If you do not have a job prior to release, you need to work actively on your employment plans, including your resume, job search efforts, networking with prior employers or contacts, or your skill development to take on a special type of job.

Part VI: My Education and Training: Past, Present, and Future

Write down details of your education. Did you finish high school? If so, list the name and location of your high school. Do you have a GED? If not, do you plan to take a GED course? Did you take any other courses, such as at a community college, job training or career school, or college or university? If so, write down all the details for your resume.

If you plan to get more training, have you located a program? Do you know the eligibility and costs? How will you pay for it?

Part VII: My Finances

☛ My Finances and Support

If you do not have employment or if you are awaiting a paycheck, how do you plan to support yourself? Have you become eligible for any financial benefits?

☛ My Budget

You should prepare a budget, as shown in Chapter 62. How much money you will generally be making compared to the money that you will be spending on things like: food, housing, clothing, utilities, etc.?

Part VIII: My Transportation

Getting to and from your job is an important consideration. How do you plan to get to the job you have waiting or a future job? Have you checked out public transportation options? Do you have or are you getting a driver's license?

Part IX: Stipulations of Judgment and Sentence

☛ Requirements for Release

Upon your release, you will most likely have certain conditions to live by. What are the court's and the Department of Corrections' requirements for your Earned Release Date (ERD) under your community supervision? Be sure to include this information in your plan, so you can easily keep track of it.

☛ Required Programs and Counseling

If you are required to do Moral Recognition Therapy (MRT), Anger Stress Management, Support Groups, Domestic Violence (DV) Counseling, Outpatient treatment or any other mental health/addiction treatments, the date, times and locations of these should be part of your re-entry plan.

☛ Legal Financial Obligations

If you are required to pay Legal Financial Obligations (LFO), such as fines, fees, or restitution, how do you plan to pay monthly? Be sure to include these amounts in your monthly budget.

- ✓ *How much do you owe?*
- ✓ *How much are you required to pay each month?*
- ✓ *Where do you have to submit payments to?*

☛ Restrictions and Restraining Orders

You need to make sure that your counselor and CCO know what is required of you in your Judgment and Sentence (J&S) this would include:

- ✓ *Any restraining orders*
- ✓ *Any restrictions (i.e. living arrangements)*
- ✓ *Area restrictions*

Part X: My Spare Time Plans

Part of the reward for re-entering society is to enjoy some of your hobbies and interests in your spare time. Why not make a list of things you would like to do upon your release?

Part II

Problem-Solving and Goal-Setting Skills

Chapter 8

Building Decision-Making and Goal-Setting Skills

Daniel R. Goldenson, Publisher, Starting Out, Inc.
William H. Foster, Ph.D., Dean and Professor, Muskie School of Public Service, University of Southern Maine

Introduction

This book is called Starting Out! for a good reason. It is about building life management skills along side academic and occupational skills, and then applying those skills to many practical issues, from educational choices to occupational possibilities, from health and nutrition to housing and volunteering.

We have catalogued more than 80 different life decision areas into 20 topics, beginning with education and training, followed by such areas as employment, insurance, investing, taxes, housing, and emergency preparedness. Each area provides a number of brief, fact-filled chapters developed by federal government departments and agencies that serve the interests of citizens across the United States.

To begin, it is important to focus on two of the most valuable life skills: (a) the ability to evaluate and weigh options and then make solid decisions, and (b) the ability to select and reach longer term life goals.

Decision Making at a Basic Level

One of the most common forms of decision making involves examining the "pros" and "cons" of a particular course of action before moving ahead. Let's say the question is: *Should*

I purchase a used car with high mileage? Here is a useful way to analyze the decision.

PRO	CON
The car is very cheap—only $500.00.	High mileage cars may require costly and often unexpected repairs.
I will have my own means of transportation which will save me time.	Operating costs, such as gasoline and insurance are expensive.
I can consider jobs in more locations, and use the car for recreation.	If the car is used a great deal, I may have to elimnate other items in my budget.

If you still really want a car and think the "pros" mostly outweigh the "cons," you can try to address some of the negative aspects as part of your decision to purchase the car. *Here is what you might do:*

- ✓ I will have a mechanic check out the car carefully before I buy it, and will only buy a car that seems currently to be in good condition and that anticipates no large long-term costs.
- ✓ Gasoline is expensive, so I will limit my car use carefully to keep my costs down. I will also shop for car insurance and get advice about which type of policy will be the most economical to purchase.

Part II

Decisions with Many Variables: Follow a Step-by Step Process

1. **Analyze the problem or situation.** Define what you wish to achieve or resolve. Collect appropriate information and input from useful sources and from others. Be objective rather than emotional. *For example, a common problem is spending too much money everyday. Begin by making a list of every item, service, or activity that you spent money on during the past month. Try not to leave anything out.*
2. **Narrow down your focus or divide the problem into pieces.** Making decisions is always easier if you can simplify the choices or options. *Now, divide your list between items that were absolutely necessary (food, medicine, and housing are examples), fairly necessary (cell phone, gasoline, and internet services) and not necessary (costly entertainment and junk food).*
3. **Consider options / Develop solution alternatives.** As you consider options and alternatives, also think "outside the box." *One way of keeping items in your*

budget that are expensive is to earn some extra money to pay for them. A budget has two sides: the income side and the expense side, and you can make changes to either.

Now it's time to make a budget, so you don't spend more than you have. Force yourself to examine each of your expenses, trimming those that you can do without so you live within your means. This step may be painful, as you may have to give up some of the things you enjoy. If you add to your income, however, you may be able to keep some of the items that are important to you. This will lead to a more satisfactory overall conclusion.

4. **Evaluate the solution alternatives.** Look at both the positive and the negative consequences of each alternative. Some alternatives will be more desirable than others, but life always involves choices that are hard to make. *For example, if you have to eliminate certain expenses, try to think of less costly ways of including some of those activities or items, such as borrowing books from the library instead of purchasing them. Or, as noted above, try to earn some extra money to help balance your personal budget.*
5. **Make choices and arrive at a decision.** Make choices that have the least negative consequences and which still solve the problem and help meet your goal *In this example, arrive at a practical budget that takes into account your necessary and optional expenses, and your ability to earn extra money if that is part of your solution.*
6. **Implement the plan and evaluate the decision.** Put your decisions into effect. Make further changes in the plan if needed, again using the steps of the decision-making process. *Test out your new budget for a few weeks. Make adjustments along the way until your budget truly works. For a decision to be sound, you need to accept the consequences of your actions and be comfortable with the result.*

Decision Trees

Decision Trees are useful tools for helping you to choose between several alternative choices or courses of action, often involving multiple decisions and steps. Decision trees can have many branches which you add as you keep asking yourself: Is this the end of the choice or must I make a further choice?

For example, a decision tree can help you decide how you want to handle regular snow removal on a long driveway. It will help clarify all the options so you can assign a cost to each, and then arrive at a final decision. In this case, if you use the do-it-yourself approach, you still must decide how much to spend on equipment. A key consideration would be whether you could clear other driveways to make extra money, thereby making the purchase of a snowblower feasible.

Here's how this decision tree might look:

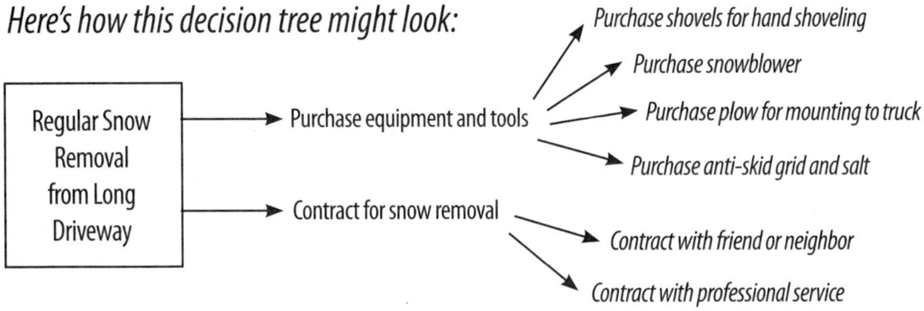

☛ **How to Create a Decision Tree:** Start a Decision Tree with a decision that you need to make. Here's what to do:

» *Draw a small square to represent the decision on the left hand side of a large piece of paper, half way down the page.*

» *From this box draw out lines towards the right for each possible solution, and write a short description of the options. Keep the lines apart as far as possible so that you can expand your thoughts.*

» *At the end of each line, consider the results. If the result of taking that decision leads to other decisions, continue the process of listing each possibility. At a certain point you will have listed all the options so that you can begin to make final choices and arrive at your ultimate decision.*

Goal Setting

The goal-setting process is somewhat similar to decision-making, but often involves long-term plans or objectives that evolve over time. For example, your goal might be to learn a new software language, take a knitting course, master a new language, or become a certified life guard. These goals will take time to achieve, and you will have to make many decisions along the way to realize your goal successfully.

Normally, goal setting includes making a clear goal statement that defines a final objective or goal, creating a plan for reaching the goal, and a way to measure or assess your achievement of the goal. **There are a variety of processes that can be used to set goals. Important goal-setting steps include:**

» *Set a goal.*

- *Look at options to meet the goal.*
- *Establish a plan.*
- *Think about rewards for reaching the goal.*
- *Monitor your progress toward the goal.*
- *Evaluate progress. If needed, adjust the goal and redo the plan.*

Problem-Solving and Conflict Resolution Methods

Conflict resolution is a special type of decision making and involves a separate set of skills. You may think you know what steps to take to resolve a problem or conflict, but others may see things very differently. Disputes of this kind are very common, since there are often many different ways of viewing and then approaching a problem.

Here are the three major conflict resolution skills that become useful:
1. Negotiation **2.** Mediation **3.** Consensus Decision Making

Each of these processes has similar characteristics, including: **1.** Parties identify their own needs and interests. **2.** Parties communicate their particular needs and interests openly and exhaustively. **3.** Parties work cooperatively to find solutions to meet those needs and interests. **4.** Parties stay focused on the problem and persist in their deliberations. **5.** Parties work cooperatively to find a mutually acceptable solution.

Each problem-solving process has similar steps: **1.** Agree that you disagree (agree to negotiate; set the stage). **2.** Take turns talking (gather perspectives/identify interests). **3.** Restate what you think you heard (explain the other's viewpoint). **4.** Come up with a solution that works for both parties (create and evaluate options/generate agreement).

Negotiation

Negotiation is a problem-solving process in which there are face to face efforts by those involved to resolve the dispute or problem. Representatives of those involved may also meet face to face to negotiate on behalf of the disputing parties.

☛ Steps in Negotiation:

- *Agree that you disagree and you will try to negotiate.*

» *Take turns talking; look at things from the viewpoint of the other party.*

» *Describe what you want, how you feel, and the reasons for your wants and feelings.*

» *Take the other person's point of view and then summarize your understanding of what he or she wants and feels and the reasons for his or her wants and feelings.*

» *Think of several ways to solve the conflict in a way that works for both parties (create win-win options).*

» *Choose the best way and make an agreement to do it.*

» *Get outside help if unable to resolve the conflict.*

Mediation

Mediation is a problem-solving process in which the two parties in the dispute are assisted by a neutral third party known as the "mediator". Face to face meetings of the parties involved, or their representatives, occur during the mediation process. Mediation is commonly used in place of court trials, since it is much less expensive and far easier to pursue.

Consensus Decision Making

Consensus decision making is a group problem-solving process in which all of the parties in the dispute, or representatives of each party, work together to resolve the dispute. A plan of action is created that all parties can and will support. Consensus decision making may or may not be facilitated by a neutral party.

Conclusions

Decision-making and goal setting skills are valuable to develop, since they can be used very effectively throughout life. We face small decisions every day, but periodically we face much larger and sometimes more complicated decisions. And, most people have certain career or family goals in mind that may take years to realize, but these goals directly impact the decisions we make along the way. At times decision-making involves others who have other goals and other views than your own. In such circumstances understanding various approaches to such shared decision-making is essential. So knowing the basics of negotiating, mediating and consensus is a useful skill to acquire.

Chapter 9

What is Critical Thinking?

Daniel J. Kurland, Author, *I Know What It Says. . . What Does it Mean?* and *The Fundamentals of Critical Reading and Critical Writing*
Available online at www.criticalreading.com

No one always acts purely objectively and rationally. We connive for selfish interests. We gossip, boast, exaggerate, and equivocate.

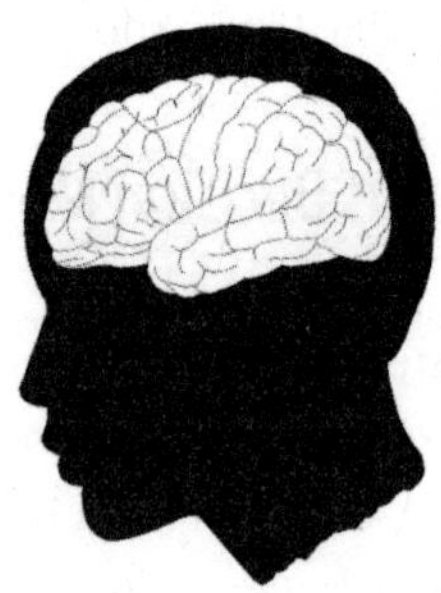

It is "only human" to wish to validate our prior knowledge, to vindicate our prior decisions, or to sustain our earlier beliefs. In the process of satisfying our ego, however, we can often deny ourselves intellectual growth and opportunity. We may not always want to apply critical thinking skills, but we should have those skills available to be employed when needed.

Critical thinking includes a complex combination of skills. Among the main characteristics are the following:

Rationality

We are thinking critically when we:

» *rely on reason rather than emotion,*

» *require evidence, ignore no known evidence, and follow evidence where it leads, and*

» *are concerned more with finding the best explanation than being right analyzing apparent confusion and asking questions.*

Self-awareness

We are thinking critically when we:

» *weigh the influences of motives and bias, and*

» *recognize our own assumptions, prejudices, biases, or point of view.*

Honesty

We are thinking critically when we recognize:

» *emotional impulses,*

» *selfish motives,*

» *nefarious purposes, or*

» *other modes of self-deception.*

Open-mindedness

We are thinking critically when we:

» *evaluate all reasonable inferences*

» *consider a variety of possible viewpoints or perspectives,*

» *remain open to alternative interpretations*

» *accept a new explanation, model, or paradigm because it explains the evidence better, is simpler, has fewer inconsistencies, or covers more data*

» *accept new priorities in response to a reevaluation of the evidence or reassessment of our real interests, and*

» *do not reject unpopular views out of hand.*

Discipline

We are thinking critically when we:

» *are precise, meticulous, comprehensive, and exhaustive*

» *resist manipulation and irrational appeals, and*

» *avoid snap judgments.*

Judgment

We are thinking critically when we:

» *recognize the relevance and/or merit of alternative assumptions and perspectives and*

» *recognize the extent and weight of evidence*

In sum,

» *Critical thinkers are by nature skeptical. They approach texts with the same skepticism and suspicion as they approach spoken remarks.*

» *Critical thinkers are active, not passive. They ask questions and analyze. They consciously apply tactics and strategies to uncover meaning or assure their understanding.*

» *Critical thinkers do not take an egotistical view of the world. They are open to new ideas and perspectives. They are willing to challenge their beliefs and investigate competing evidence.*

Critical thinking enables us to recognize a wide range of subjective analyses of otherwise objective data, and to evaluate how well each analysis might meet our needs. Facts may be facts, but how we interpret them may vary.

By contrast, passive, non-critical thinkers take a simplistic view of the world.

» *They see things in black and white, as either-or, rather than recognizing a variety of possible understanding.*

» *They see questions as yes or no with no subtleties.*

» *They fail to see linkages and complexities.*

» *They fail to recognize related elements.*

» *Non-critical thinkers take an egotistical view of the world*

» *They take their facts as the only relevant ones.*

» *They take their own perspective as the only sensible one.*

» *They take their goal as the only valid one.*

Effective Problem Solving

Adapted from guidance resources prepared by The University of South Australia

As a student you are likely to be involved with a wide range of school courses and programs, possibly some part time work, home activities, and social activities with family and friends. At some time during these activities, challenges, issues or problems will arise. Most students deal with challenges daily and solve problems almost automatically. Sometimes, however, there will be a significant issue which is difficult to solve quickly or automatically. You will then want to know, 'How do I solve this problem?' The first aim of this article is to explain the problem solving process.

In addition to assisting you with an immediate issue, problem solving is also a life skill. Educators believe that problem solving is a critically important skill that applies to every aspect of our lives. We become successful problem solvers when we apply logical, critical, and creative thinking to the issues we face. And so the second aim of this article is to help you become an effective problem solver.

☛ What is problem solving?

Problem solving is a tool, a skill and a process. It is a tool because it can help you solve an immediate problem or to achieve a goal. It is a skill because once you have learned it you can use it repeatedly, like the ability to ride a bicycle, add numbers, or speak a language. It is also a process because it involves taking a number of steps.

You can engage in problem solving if you want to reach a goal and are prepared to face obstacles along the way. As a student, your goals are likely to be many and varied. You might want to write more effectively, increase the number of your friends, get a job, become computer literate, buy a car, or improve your fitness. So it is likely that in working towards your goals you will encounter some barriers.

At the point at which you come up against a barrier you can engage in a problem solving process to help you achieve your goal. Every time you use a problem solving process you are increasing your problem solving skills.

☛ A seven-step problem solving cycle

There are a variety of problem solving processes, but each process consists of a series of steps, including identifying an issue, searching for options, and putting a possible solution into action. It is useful to view problem solving as a cycle because sometimes a problem needs several attempts to solve it, or the problem changes. Figure 1 shows a seven-step problem solving cycle.

Figure 1: The Seven-Step Problem Solving Cycle

To solve a problem, take the steps, one at a time.

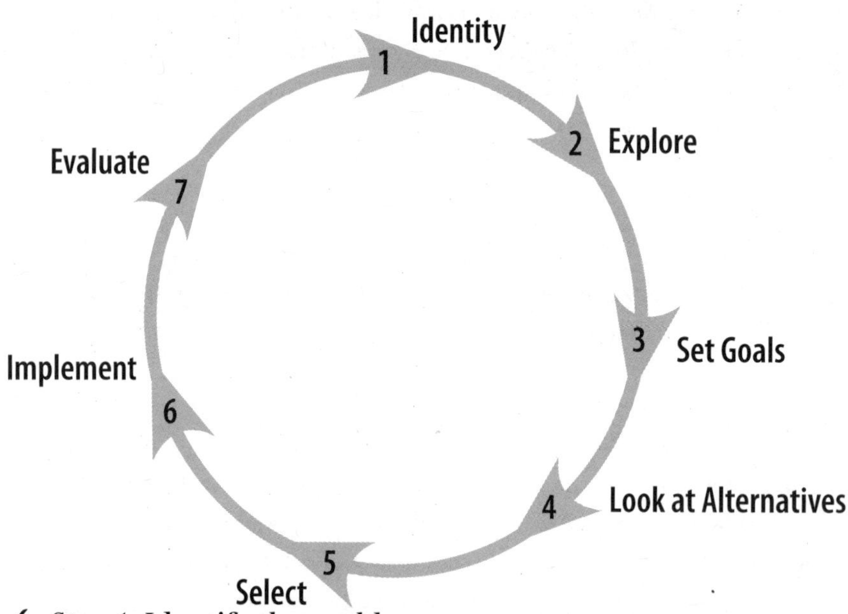

✓ **Step 1. Identify the problem**

The first step you need to take is to identify and name the problem so that you can find an appropriate solution. Sometimes you might be unsure about what the problem is: you might just feel general anxiety or be confused about what is getting in the way of your goals. If it is a personal problem you can ask yourself, your friends or a guidance counselor, "What is the problem which is getting in the way of me achieving my goal." If it is an academic issue you can ask yourself, "What is hindering me from completing this task," and you can consult with a teacher to clarify the issue.

✓ **Step 2. Explore the problem**

When you are clear about what the problem is, you need to think about it in different ways. You can ask yourself questions such as:

» *How is this problem affecting me?*

» *How is it affecting others?*

» *Who else experiences this problem?*

» *What do they do about it?*

» *Seeing the problem in different ways is likely to help you find an effective solution.*

✓ **Step 3. Set goals**

Once you have thought about the problem from different angles you can identify your goals. What is it that you want to achieve? Sometimes you might get so frustrated by a problem that you forget to think about what you want. For example, you might become stressed out about completing a number of assignments on time. This could lead to discouragement, and you may even give up entirely. It is important at this time to consider the question: What is my immediate goal? Do you want to:

» *get over your anxiety?*

» *increase your time management skills?*

» *complete the assignments to the best of your ability?*

» *finish the assignments as soon as possible?*

If you decide your goal is to reduce your stress and anxiety, that will lead to solutions which are different from those linked to the goal of completing your assignments as soon as possible. One goal may lead you to a school counselor for advice, while the other goal may lead you to apply for extensions for your assignments. So working out your goals is a vital part of the problem solving process.

✓ **Step 4. Look at alternatives**

When you have decided what your goal is, you need to look for possible solutions. The more possible solutions you find the more likely it is that you will be able to discover an effective solution. For problems such as how to select a topic for a paper or how to find a part-time job, you can brain-storm for ideas. The purpose of brain-storming is to collect together a long list of possibilities. It does not matter whether the ideas are all useful or practical or manageable: just write down the ideas as they come into your head. Some of the best solutions arise from creative thinking during brain-storming. You can also seek ideas about possible solutions from friends, family, or the internet. The aim is to collect as many alternative solutions as possible.

✓ **Step 5. Select a possible solution**

From the list of possible solutions you can sort out which are most relevant to your situation and which are realistic and manageable. You can do this by predicting outcomes for possible solutions and also checking with other people who may have experience with the same or a similar problem. For example, if you are hunting for part-time jobs, you may first want to develop a list of your skills to direct you to an effective plan. If you are selecting the topic for a paper, you may want to do some library or internet research first.

✓ **Step 6. Implement a possible solution**

Once you have selected a possible solution you are ready to put it into action. You will need to have energy and motivation to do this because implementing the solution may take some time and effort. (If the solution had been easy to find and do, you would have probably already done it.) You can prepare yourself to implement the solution by planning when and how you will do it, whether you talk with others about it, and what rewards you will give yourself when you have done it.

✓ **Step 7. Evaluate**

Just because you have worked your way through the problem solving process it does not mean that, by implementing the possible solution, you automatically solve your problem. So evaluating the effectiveness of your solution is very important. You can ask yourself (and others) :

» *How effective was that solution?*

» *'Did it achieve what I wanted?*

» *What consequences did it have for my situation?*

If the solution was successful in helping you solve your problem and reach your goal, then you know that you have effectively solved your problem. If you feel dissatisfied with the result, then you can begin the steps again.

Viewing problem solving as a cycle may help you recognize that problem solving is a way of searching for a solution which will lead to a further set of different possible solutions, which you can evaluate. If you have solved the problem you have found an effective solution. If you judge the problem has not been solved you can look for, and try, alternative possibilities by beginning the problem solving cycle again.

☛ When to use problem solving

You can use problem solving techniques anytime you have a problem to solve or a goal to achieve. You can use the problem solving model to look for solutions to issues connected with your study, relationships, work or sports. You can take the problem solving steps by yourself, with a friend, or in a group. Problem solving with others is often very effective because you have access to a wide variety of viewpoints and potential solutions. The problem solving model is a useful resource for you to utilize in your personal, academic, and working lives.

☛ Conclusion

Problem solving is a skill and a process which you can learn. You can implement the process to help you solve a problem by following the seven steps outlined in this article. Once you have learned the steps and begun to implement the process, problem solving will be a new skill which you have acquired and can be used at school, at home and in the workplace.

Chapter 10

Team Work and Collaboration Skills

Part I: Teamwork and Collaboration Skills

By Kevin Eikenberry, Kevin Eikenberry Group
Indianapolis, Indiana

Most everyone I talk with wants greater success in some (or many) parts of their life. And however independent you may think you are, no one can achieve as much working alone as they can with the collaborative help of others . . . if that collaboration is truly helpful.

You hopefully have experienced times where a group was really clicking; it's amazing the amount of progress that can be made. However, you've likely also experienced times when working together seemed hard and even counter-productive to getting any result.

Here are seven ways to improve collaboration and to make the work of a group more successful in any situation:

✓ Step One: Have a common purpose

Too often we get the cart before the horse. We have a group of people assembled to do some work and since we are all busy we dive right into the task, often without a clear sense for why the work is being done or what the perfect end result would be. Without a clear and common purpose—the reason for being together that everyone shares—collaboration will never reach anywhere near the level that is possible.

✓ Step Two: Develop concrete goals.

The common purpose unites the group, and the goals provide focus and energy. If you want the maximum results from any group, make sure you have concrete goals.

✓ Step Three: Communicate freely.

Collaboration requires communication. Effective collaboration requires open and honest communication about ideas, experiences and opinions. In a group where hierarchy is present, realize that the hierarchy can be a barrier to the free flow of communication, and do what you can to counterbalance it.

✓ Step Four: Combine the best of each person.

Each person brings great strengths in terms of perspective, experience, ideas, skills and much more. Collaboration (and results) will be enhanced when the strengths of each team member are recognized, valued, and used.

✓ Step Five: Create open-mindedly.

Collaboration is an act of creation. You bring people together to find synergy—the sum being greater than the contribution of each individual. Collaboration will be enhanced when people feel comfortable about sharing their ideas, and worry less about whose idea gets implemented. Not coincidentally, as you master the first four points, this step gets easier.

✓ Step Six: Circulate accountability.

Someone may be the team leader, and that is fine. But greater collaboration will come when everyone feels responsible, when everyone is comfortable and "allowed" to take a leadership role or take the lead in making something happen. The most collaborative groups have a leader, but are filled with people ready to do what it takes to achieve results.

✓ Step Seven: Compete externally.

It is hard to collaborate when you feel competition within the group. Competition for power, position, ideas and more all get in the way of collaborative success. With a clear purpose and goals, people can be clear on what they are trying to accomplish and how to do that in service of the team's success, not their personal success.

Consider these seven items like a checklist. While all are required for the best collaboration, look for the one that a group you are on is doing well (and support that at even greater levels), and recognize one that the group could improve on (and do what you can to help make that happen).

These "Seven C's" will help you navigate the waters of working with others. The group might be a true working team, or it might be a group gathered for a one-time event to solve a problem or complete a task. In any case the more of these C's that are working for you, the more enjoyable and successful working with others will be.

Publisher Note: Kevin Eikenberry is the head of Kevin Eikenberry Group, a professional speaking, training, and consulting team. Their website is *www.kevineikenberry.com.*

Part II: Collaboration Skills Checklist

The Prep Center, Intermediate School District 287
Plymouth, Minnesota

How well do you collaborate with other students or co-workers? Are you able to draw out the best from others? Below is a simple self-discovery survey where you can appraise your personal skills at effective collaboration. Use the following continuum:

1= I have trouble with this
2= I do this reasonably well
3= I see this as a strength of mine.

<u>Do not write your answers in the book.</u> Use a separate piece of paper and learn if you are already a good collaborator or where you need improvement.

1	2	3	I look for common points of agreement
1	2	3	I listen deeply to others
1	2	3	I often check to see if I understand the speaker
1	2	3	I often compliment others
1	2	3	I think before I speak
1	2	3	I am OK with different points-of-view
1	2	3	I usually ask people to tell me more
1	2	3	I ask questions that encourage the speaker
1	2	3	I don't take differences of opinion personally
1	2	3	I don't attack the person, rather I focus on the issue
1	2	3	I am attuned to the time restraints of others
1	2	3	I maintain a sense of humor, even when the going gets tough
1	2	3	I don't need to be right all the time

Part II

Chapter 11

Primary Life Skills

Daniel R. Goldenson, Publisher, Starting Out, Inc.
William H. Foster, Ph.D., Dean and Professor, Muskie School of Public Service, University of Southern Maine

Introduction

The Partnership for 21st Century Skills is a national organization seeking to bring the latest skill sets into the educational system. This organization is working with educational, business, community, and government leaders across America to bring materials about these skills into the classroom. Life and career skills are a critical part of their focus.

This chapter will examine the five life skill areas that the Partnership has identified—skills that are used throughout life, in working, social, and family environments.

- ✓ **Flexibility and Adaptability**
- ✓ **Initiative and Self-Direction**
- ✓ **Social and Cross-Cultural Skills**
- ✓ **Productivity and Accountability**
- ✓ **Leadership and Responsibility**

Part I: Flexibility and Adaptability

In all group settings, but most commonly in employment situations, managers are always looking for employees who are flexible and adaptable, since working roles change over time as a business grows, responds to competition, creates new products, and identifies new markets. Adaptability enables us to respond to and embrace change.

One of the most effective ways of building flexibility and adaptability skills is by giving small groups a series of different life problems to tackle, asking them to come up with practical solutions.

Flexibility and adaptability involve responding to change, such as in a new school, neighborhood, or job, or accepting the need for personal change in a new situation or relationship.

Example: *On a camping trip in the wilderness, flexibility and adaptability are especially important, since we encounter unexpected situations. For example, if a tent becomes damaged, we may have to build a shelter out of branches and leaves, or we may have to hike a long distance to find water.*

Part II: Initiative and Self-Direction

The Partnership for 21st Century Skills has identified six aspects of initiative and self-direction, skills which set us apart from others or enable us to work effectively on our own. They include the following:

- **Monitoring one's own understanding and learning needs.**
  Are you understanding the material you are studying? Do you need a further explanation or clarification? Do you need a tutor to help you with difficult concepts? Are you learning the right information for the job you are about to take? Do you need to take a special course or gain certification in a specific area? Each of these situations requires taking charge of your own learning needs. This approach requires initiative and self-direction.

  Example: *You are taking a computer course and find that the instructor is moving* *too quickly. What do you do? Ask if the instructor can give you extra time or find a tutor or older student to explain difficult concepts. When you monitor your own needs you will know when you are progressing and when you need further assistance. Never hesitate to ask questions, discuss ideas with others, and seek the advice of those who are more experienced.*

- **Going beyond basic mastery of skills and/or curriculum to explore and expand one's own learning and opportunities to gain expertise.**

  To expand your own knowledge or skills, and to set yourself apart from others in a competitive environment—whether in school, at work, or in another group situation—you must take initiative and put together the educational or training solutions that will enable you to succeed. Taking on this task for yourself requires self-direction and a personal commitment to control your own educational path.

  Example: *You may start in an entry-level job and realize that if you gain certain additional skills, such as obtaining a commercial driver's license, a first aid certification, an associates degree, or a real estate license you can take a major step up in your career path. Looking for ways to advance your career by obtaining additional training demonstrates strong personal initiative, a quality that every employer seeks.*

- **Demonstrating initiative to advance skill levels towards a professional level.**

  The more personal initiative you take to advance your skills and career path, the more likely it is that you will be a success. There is always more to learn, more opportunities to seek out, and more assistance you can find to advance your career. Ask questions, take jobs or apprenticeships where you will learn new skills, take college or adult education courses, or enroll in a career training school, community college, or four-year college with a real commitment to succeed.

  Example: *To become a manager, a supervisor, a teacher or professor, or a company CEO, you need to show even more personal initiative. Assess how a stronger education, coupled with valuable experience, can bring you to a professional level of expertise in your field, and find ways to realize such a goal. Often you can take courses in the evening or part-time and still continue working at your current job.*

☛ **Defining, prioritizing and completing tasks without direct oversight.**
Tackling any problem or completing any task, no matter how simple or complicated, first involves understanding and defining that problem or task. What task or larger goal are you trying to complete? Should it be divided into parts so you can tackle it more easily? Should certain steps be given priority over others? Can you organize your efforts into orderly steps so you can achieve our result in a methodical way?

Examples: *If you are applying for college or a training program, you will want to plan the application process carefully, leave plenty of time to gather information, allow enough time to compose and proof-read any written material, and possibly include other examples of your work, such as a design portfolio, prior work experiences, or strong recommendations.*

In a similar way, applying for a job requires defining the type of job you are seeking, conducting a thorough search of opportunities, and then preparing a resume that is suited for the job you are seeking. Tasks like these are conducted for your personal benefit, and should be tackled independently since training programs or employers are interested in your own submission, not the work of others.

Part II

☛ **Utilizing time efficiently and managing workload.**
Time management skills are among the most important life skills we can develop, since almost every task we undertake has a time component or deadline. Given time limitations, we must learn to plan how to complete tasks over time and not at the last minute.

Example: I*n the academic world, research and writing a paper is a large task that requires strong time management skills. Often it is useful to set up a calendar of completion dates for each stage of the project: background research and note-taking, writing the rough draft, completing the final draft, proof-reading and spell-checking, and presentation. In a mail order business the employees must figure out how to get all the daily packages out on time using different shipping methods. This process may entail setting up an assembly line where one person brings the items to a packing station, another person does the packaging, and a third person determines the postage.*

- **Demonstrating commitment to learning as a lifelong process.**
  We learn throughout our lives, although school or college seem to represent a more concentrated period of learning. Because life is constantly changing, we are always facing new opportunities to learn and master additional skills. Learning is interesting and rewarding, and always leads to new opportunities and a fuller life.

  Example: *You have become a teacher in an elementary school, but now think you would like to be a school counselor. This new goal will involve further learning but will take you to a new career plateau. At many junctures of one's life there are opportunities to change careers, learn new hobbies or sports, join new organizations, and meet new and interesting people. All along the way, the learning process continues and brings numerous personal, social, and financial benefits.*

Part III: Social and Cross-Cultural Skills

In school, at work, and in different social situations you will be dealing with people of different backgrounds, cultural experiences, and points of view. This type of diversity in group situations is a valuable asset, as it leads to new and unexpected friendships, new ideas, new experiences, new ways to look at problems, and often new attitudes or opinions.

The Partnership for 21st Century Skills has identified three skill areas that make our tasks and jobs more interesting and more productive:

- **Working appropriately and productively with others.**
  Although there are many tasks you may need to perform alone, such as writing an article or repairing a piece of machinery, numerous activities and occupations involve working closely and effectively with others. Learning to utilize the skills and talents of each member of a group makes the entire group far more effective than the sum of its parts.

  Example: *Consider designing and decorating a room. Although you could take on this task along, you may benefit far more by combining the talents of different people. Some people are especially good designers, knowing how to combine colors, fabrics, furnishings,* *and wall decorations in a pleasing fashion. Others know how to construct furniture, hang wallpaper, paint or refinish, or install floor covering. Putting together an entire team will often bring about a better result than drawing on your own personal abilities.*

- **Leveraging the collective intelligence of groups when appropriate.**
  Leveraging often means getting more out of a group task than adding the input of each member. Each member may know a part of a solution, but when all the parts are put together, the result may be an extremely valuable discovery or solution.

  Example: *If a group of people want to help a poor farming community build a new water supply system, the task will take many different work efforts: drilling for water or finding a fresh water source, piping the water to a central location, and setting up a method for community members to use the new fresh water supply. But how can this effort be leveraged for a greater result? Once the water supply is provided, the community members can improve growing conditions and increase the output of their farms, which leads to higher incomes and better living conditions. The group has found that the sum of the member skills has produced a far greater result than the initial task involved.*

- **Bridging cultural differences and using differing perspectives to increase innovation and the quality of work.**
  People from different backgrounds often have different ways of handling tasks or accomplishing certain goals. Some groups and cultures may have more advanced technologies, equipment, or training while others have not had the benefit of educational innovation. When people with diverse backgrounds address the same task or problem, they often can come up with innovative new solutions, just because of the diversity of the group.

  Example: *Schools approach cultural differences with special programs, such as English as a Second Language, often trying to provide the extra effort needed to blend- the capabilities of a group of diverse students. Cultural differences have a profound impact on artistic creations, on the way we design and decorate our homes, and on the types of functional and decorative items we place around us. Innovative ideas emerge from the interaction of people of different backgrounds, and the interplay of their differing perspectives.*

Part II

Part IV: Productivity and Accountability

Here are two aspects of productivity and accountability that we face frequently in our lives:

- **Setting and meeting high standards and goals for delivering quality work on time.**
  Everyone sets standards or goals. Sometimes these standards are set by others, and we have to follow them, and sometimes we set our own standards and goals and work to reach them. In either case, we are concerned about quality and time: how well a task is accomplished and how quickly can we deliver the result. Improving the performance of tasks within time constraints leads to higher productivity. And each person or group member becomes responsible or accountable for a part of the end result.

  Example: *Schools, offices, factories, and groups are always concerned about productivity. They constantly want to know: Is everyone learning the new skills? Can we teach more quickly, more effectively or with better teaching aids? Can office workers get jobs done more efficiently by using newer computers or different software? Can a factory turn out more cars by designing assembly line improvements? Can the company increase its profit if everyone is more focused?*

- **Demonstrating diligence and a positive work ethic, such as being punctual and reliable.**
  A positive attitude toward work is the key ingredient in producing a good result. If we care about our courses, our jobs, and our other responsibilities, we will be more successful than if we are passive or disinterested. Reliability and punctuality become important personal traits that help us do a good job and be recognized by others that we are productivity and successful.

  Example: *Workers who show up on time can usually get a job finished far more quickly than if they arrive at differing times and are not available to work together. A painter who arrives without his assistant may not be able to set up a scaffolding, so his work is delayed. An instructor who arrives fifteen minutes late has wasted many hours of the entire group, and he or she may not have enough time to complete the lesson.*

Part V: Leadership and Responsibility

Sometimes we classify individuals in a group as "leaders" and "followers." The leaders seem to take charge or volunteer first or answer questions first. The followers stand back and make their move after others have spoken or acted.

Building leadership and responsibility skills involves a learning process. We are not born to fall in one category or the other. We can decide for ourselves if we want to lead or follow.

Here are four guidelines that help define leadership and responsibility, whether in school, at work, or in other social settings:

- **Using interpersonal and problem-solving skills to influence and guide others toward a goal.**
  Building skills and learning to solve problems through experience help pave the way for leadership roles. Those who draw on their skill sets and their body of life experiences are able to influence a group and guide it toward a goal or objective.

  Example: *The person who has learned how to write a paper or how to repair an engine is in a perfect position to share those skills with others in a group. Problem-solving skills are partly about "approach" and partly about "knowledge." If you have built a staircase, assembled a bicycle, or baked a cake, you can probably follow a set of instructions for many tasks, and bring others into the process.*

- **Leveraging strengths of others to accomplish a common goal.**
  Some people have better specific skills, talents, or experience than others. Everyone in a group does not have to be an expert at everything. A leader can assign different tasks depending upon individual ability, and still end up completing a complicated project.

  Example: *You join an organization to provide food to the needy in your community, and everyone wants to provide as much food as possible to the largest number of people.*

A leader will see this goal as an opportunity to assign different tasks to different people so that the sum of all the efforts will result in the most productive food operation. Some people may want to grow vegetables in a large garden. Others may want to collect canned goods at schools. And still others may want to obtain unsold food from restaurants or supermarkets. These different efforts involve organization and leadership, but the result will be very satisfying.

- **Demonstrating integrity and ethical behavior.**
  In public and private life, both high integrity and ethical behavior are critical to the smooth working of a society, an organization, and a family.

  Example: *Elderly people are sometimes not treated well in group or nursing homes, and their relatives may not visit very often to see how they are treated. Nurses and managers who treat people well even if they are not being supervised by family members show high integrity and set a high standard of ethical behavior. On the other hand, staff members who lower their standard of care if the resident cannot speak or respond or if family members are absent show a poor level of integrity and ethical behavior.*

- **Acting responsibly with the interests of the larger community in mind.**

  Example: *Business leaders in the past few years have often shown a lack of integrity and ethical behavior, ultimately destroying large companies, large banks, and even some of the footings of our economic system. Along the way, their compromises and misdeeds were not always apparent, and seemed to go on unnoticed. For example, mortgages were given to almost anybody, whether or not the person had the ability to repay the mortgage. Such short-term decisions ultimately destroyed many banks and investment companies.*

Part III

Family and Personal Relationships

Chapter 12

Building Strong Family Relationships

Developed by the Oregon State University Extension Service and the Starting Out! Research Group

Part I: The Family as the Cornerstone of Society

- **Our society thrives on strong families.**
  Our family teaches us how to function in the world. It should provide love and warmth to all of its members. A strong family gives its members the support they need to make it through life's toughest spots.

- **Strong families have good communication.**
  Strong families have open lines of communication—where all family members feel heard and respected. One of the best ways to strengthen your family is to increase your listening skills and those of other family members. Until we can hear each other, we cannot build strong relationships.

Part II: Good Communication is a Starting Point

- **To build strong family relationships, listen actively to each other.**
  - *Give the person your full attention, turn off the TV, or put down what you are doing.*
  - *Focus on what the person is telling you—rather than thinking about your reaction or*

response to what is being said. (There will be time for that.)

- *Listen for how the other person is feeling and relay back to them what you think they were saying and how they are feeling. "I hear you saying that you don't like your sister. You look pretty mad. Did something happen?"*
- *Resist giving advice or your reaction until you are certain you have fully understood what the person was saying to you.*

☛ **Use "I" messages rather than "You" messages when talking.**

"I" messages are more difficult because they require us to be clear about our own thoughts and feelings. They, however, increase the chances that our message will be heard and decrease the chances that a fight will begin.

"I don't like all this fighting. It upsets me to see the two of you not getting along." Rather than "What's wrong with the two of you? You're making me crazy! Can't you ever get along?"

Teach everyone in your family to talk with "I" messages as much a possible. You are much more likely to resolve problems when the focus is on behaviors and how those behaviors are affecting you or the family.

"You" messages should be discouraged because they often lead to bad feelings and increased fighting. "You" messages seldom resolve the problem.

☛ **Encourage all family members to share their thoughts and feelings.**

Strong families allow all family members—no matter how young or small—to talk about their thoughts and feelings. This does not mean that members are not respectful of one another, but rather that feelings and ideas are respected. Everyone should be expected to express themselves in appropriate ways—such as with "I" messages. When people feel heard and respected, they feel better about themselves, are more open to solving problems, and are more likely to allow others to express themselves.

Part III: Spending Time with Your Family

☛ **Strong families spend time together.**

In today's busy world it can be difficult for families to find time to be together. All relationships need attention—and this includes the family as a whole.

Family rituals can offer a set time for families to get together and give each other the attention that is needed. A family ritual is simply a time that is set aside on a regular basis for a family to get together. This can mean having dinner together, celebrating a holiday together, going to church together, or just going for a walk together every week. It is important that the family ritual be predictable and that other activities are not allowed to upset it.

Family rituals help define who is in our family and who we are as a family. It allows time for the family to get together, to share experiences with one another, and to reconnect with each other. Knowing that the family will have time together can help us deal with those times when we are apart. Even though parents may work, children can know that each evening, each weekend (or whenever works for your family) they will have some "special time" with you.

Part IV: Treat Your Children as Special

☛ **Every child is special and every child needs some special time when he can have his parent all to himself.**

Giving your child some "special time" helps develop a close relationship with your child. Consider setting aside some time—perhaps 15 minutes—for each child each week. (Better yet, 15 minutes each day, if that is possible.) Make it a predictable ritual so that the child can depend on it and look forward to this time with you. Be sure that this "special time" is not easily interrupted by other activities. For example, don't answer the phone during this time.

Allow your child to help you decide how to spend this time. You could read books, sing songs, go for a walk, play a game—or whatever your child enjoys. The more you are able to spend "special time" with your child the stronger your relationship will be.

☛ **Look for opportunities to connect with your child.**

Although setting aside time with your child is important, also look for small moments that you can use to connect with your child. You can make up stories together while doing chores, talk about concerns while on the way to the grocery store, read a book together while waiting for dinner to finish. We often think we have to wait for our "special time" but all these small moments help us stay connected in between the more scheduled times.

Part V: Dealing with Conflict

- **Strong families handle their conflict fairly.**
  All families have conflict—it's a natural part of human relationships. Strong families are able to work through fights and disagreements by focusing on the problems, rather than by "tearing each other down."

- **Stay focused on the behavior or problem.**
  Use "I" messages to express your thoughts and feelings about the problem. For example, if you and your child are arguing about bedtime, you could say "I get angry when you continue to argue with me even after I've told you my decision. I want you to go to bed now." instead of "You never listen to me. Go to bed now or I'll spank you."

- **Stay focused on the present problem.**
  Do not bring up old issues and problems. These only distract from the present issue. You can discuss them later.

- **Respect each other's right to safety.**
  Fights should never become violent. When people are so angry that they feel like hitting one another or throwing things, then the discussion should be stopped. Agree to get together to talk again after everyone has had a chance to calm down.

- **Use your problem solving skills to create new solutions to the problem and teach your kids to think of ways to resolve conflict.**
  It is not useful to fight about what isn't working. Instead, focus on what has worked in the past or what could work now.

Part VI: Building Bonds of Trust

- **Strong families develop trust.** Strong, healthy families recognize the importance of developing trust. Trust is the glue that holds relationships together.

Some ways to develop trust in your family are:

- *Give your child opportunities to earn your trust. Let her do small tasks around the house and praise her for doing it on her own.*
- *Show your child that you can be trusted. Children need to know that they can count on what their parents say. Follow through with the things you promise to do.*
- *Allow people in your family to make amends. We all make mistakes. Teach your child to forgive and allow yourself to forgive others. Holding on to past hurts often only hurts us.*
- *Teach everyone how to say "I'm sorry." Taking responsibility for our good and our bad behaviors is important and helps to develop trust. People learn to trust that they can be loved even though they are not perfect.*

Part VII: Parenting From a Distance

You can be a good parent even if you are far away.

Building a bridge to your children while you are still incarcerated is a difficult but important task. Consider the following:

- *Your child or children will be upset and embarrassed that you are in jail or prison. This is a natural reaction.*
- *Your child or children will find it difficult to understand that you committed a serious crime. This is a natural reaction.*
- *Your child or children may not want to have any contact with you because of what you have done. This is a natural reaction.*

The job of building a bridge to your children and re-establishing your role as a parent from a distance is a task that will not only improve the life and happiness of your children, but will add greatly to your life and mood while you remain incarcerated.

Consider these steps that will enable you to embrace your children and maintain your parental bond:

- *Write to your spouse or significant other and keep them in your life if that is possible.*
- *Write to your children and explain that although you have made serious mistakes, you are dealing with them and paying your debt to society through your incarceration. Ask your children to write you letters.*

- *Show an interest in your children's lives. Ask about their activities, their friends, and their achievements. Don't forget their birthdays and other holidays even though you are not present. Send along notes as frequently as you can to each of your children, and consider this one of your "duties" while in prison. Your kids will have busy lives and may not write very often, but that doesn't mean that you shouldn't write them. Don't forget. You are their parent.*
- *Encourage your children to take the right path and to get a good education so they can succeed.*
- *Explain to your family what you are learning in prison, and what you plan to do when you get out. Give them hope that you will return as a better person.*
- *Encourage your children to visit you by telling them how much you miss them and how eager you are to see them. Let them know how much you care about them.*

Chapter 13

Mentors, Advisors, and Role Models

Starting Out! Research Group

Strong mentoring relationships can help ex-offenders increase their odds for success after release.

Ministers, employers, social workers, and community volunteers can become valuable connections during the difficult process of transitioning from incarceration to the independence and responsibility of life outside the prison walls.

In Burlington, Vermont, an organization called Mercy Connections has partnered with another organization called Vermont Works for Women to create a mentoring program to support women making the transition from Vermont's correctional facilities to life in the community. The program guides women through numerous difficult decisions relating to family, housing, employment, and health, and services as a key catalyst for successful reintegration.

The United Way in West Michigan recruits volunteers in the community to mentor ex-offenders as part of a team that provides support for overcoming obstacles and making positive changes.

In Franklin, Tennessee, Corner Men Ministries exists as a "Ministry of Mentoring" to ex-offenders. They recruit, train, match, and provide on-going ministry support to volunteer mentors and their mentees. The program provides training through a curriculum on parenting, fatherhood, and goal-setting. Volunteers go into the prisons to prepare offenders for their release, and then follow up upon their release.

What Mentoring Can Do For You

A mentor can be anybody whom you respect and who is willing to spend time with you and counsel you about your reintegration process, family problems, and employment needs. He or she can be a minister or church volunteer, which is quite common; a supervisor at a job; a member of a veterans organization; or a caring individual in your community who participates in one of the many fraternal organizations and lodges, such as Masons, Knights of Columbus, or the American Legion.

A mentor is a concerned, accepting friend and advisor who meets with you to provide support and encouragement. A mentor, either individually or as part of a mentor group, typically meets with you, the mentee, at a location in the community approximately once a week or at a minimum twice each month.

Individuals released from a correctional facility, or who are on probation or parole, often have limited support systems and can benefit greatly from a mentor or advisor. Upon release, one needs help with housing, employment, transportation, family problems, and other basic needs. Adjustment to family responsibilities is especially challenging, and sometimes family mentoring is provided in addition to individual mentoring.

A good mentor does not have to be a trained professional, although experience working with ex-offenders can be very helpful. Many times it is just a caring person to talk to with a different perspective and someone who can encourage your efforts to make progress. Organized mentoring programs normally train their volunteers so they will be more equipped to take on the challenges of mentoring ex-offenders.

How Mentoring Works

Volunteer mentors should be the same gender as the mentee. A preliminary meeting is held with the mentee and mentor at which time guidelines that promote healthy communication, boundaries, and expectations are established. It is best to have mentors and mentees meet at a volunteer organization, a church, or a public location such as a park or restaurant.

Mentors give their mentees a window on "normal" life, and their meetings can involve discussions of work, health, family issues, and recreation. A friendship of this kind can also enable an ex-offender to be less upset with setbacks that come up.

A mentor can become your "advocate," by assisting you in finding jobs, housing, and other resources. Once he or she gets to know you, your mentor can sometimes speak on your behalf and assure others that you have turned over a new leaf and are pursuing a purposeful life.

How to Find a Mentor

Some communities have mentoring programs for ex-offenders, but most do not. For this reason you may need to find your own mentor. Here are some ideas that may help you:

✓ Contact one or more ministers in your town and ask them if they have time to work with you as a mentor. If there is a mentoring program in the community, they will know about it.

✓ Contact the closest Volunteers of America office in your home area. Many VOA programs are involved in re-entry activities, and you may be able to find a mentor.

✓ Ask your corrections counselor if there are any mentoring programs where you live. One avenue is to locate a prisoner advocacy group in your community.

✓ If you like and respect your boss, ask him or her to give you a little time periodically to guide you with your decisions and problems. Good advice and suggestions can often be conveyed in a matter of minutes, but may be just what you need to solve a problem.

✓ Check with organizations like Big Brothers and Big Sisters of America, the local office of the Salvation Army, and fraternal and service organizations.

✓ Americorps, the national service organization, has mentoring programs in some communities. Find out if there is an Americorps program in your city or state.

Looking for Role Models: Join a Support Group

All of us know people whom we respect and admire. Sometimes we know them personally, but often they are public figures in sports, business, or public life. Role models can also be everyday people, or even other ex-offenders who have been successful with their transition from incarceration.

Find out how others have handled their reintegration problems, how they have found jobs and helpful employers, and how they tackled other personal challenges.

Support groups exist in many communities for people with different problems. Many revolve around people with the same illness, such as cancer, depression, or alcoholism. You may want to join one, such as Alcoholics Anonymous, since you will be in the company of others with similar problems who are trying to straighten out their lives. Observe how other members approached their problems, and try to follow their examples.

Chapter 14

Understanding Intimate Partner Violence

Centers for Disease Control and Prevention
National Center for Injury Prevention and Control

What is Intimate Partner Violence (IPV)?

Intimate partner violence (IPV) is abuse that occurs between two people in a close relationship. The term "intimate partner" includes current and former spouses and dating partners. IPV exists along a continuum from a single episode of violence to ongoing battering.

IPV includes four types of behavior:

- ✓ Physical abuse is when a person hurts or tries to hurt a partner by hitting, kicking, burning, or other physical force
- ✓ Sexual abuse is forcing a partner to take part in a sex act when the partner does not consent.
- ✓ Threats of physical or sexual abuse include the use of words, gestures, weapons, or other means to communicate the intent to cause harm.
- ✓ Emotional abuse is threatening a partner or his or her possessions or loved ones, or harming a partner's sense of self-worth. Examples are stalking, name-calling, intimidation, or not letting a partner see friends and family.

Often, IPV starts with emotional abuse. This behavior can progress to physical or sexual assault. Several types of IPV may occur together.

Why is IPV a Public Health Problem?

Many victims do not report IPV to police, friends, or family. Victims think others will not believe them and that the police cannot help.

- **Each year...**

  Women experience about 4.8 million intimate partner related physical assaults and rapes.

  Men are the victims of about 2.9 million intimate partner related physical assaults.

- **Intimate Partner Violence resulted in 1,544 deaths in 2004. Of these deaths, 25% were males and 75% were females.**

- **The cost of IPV was an estimated $5.8 billion in 1995.**
  Updated to 2003 dollars, that's more than $8.3 billion. This cost includes medical care, mental health services, and lost productivity (e.g., time away from work).

Part III

How does Intimate Partner Violence Affect Health?

IPV can affect health in many ways. The longer the abuse goes on, the more serious the effects on the victim. Many victims suffer physical injuries. Some are minor like cuts, scratches, bruises, and welts. Others are more serious and can cause lasting disabilities. These include broken bones, internal bleeding, and head trauma.

Not all injuries are physical. IPV can also cause emotional harm. Victims often have low self-esteem. They may have a hard time trusting others and being in relationships. The anger and stress that victims feel may lead to eating disorders and depression. Some victims even think about or commit suicide.

IPV is linked to harmful health behaviors as well. Victims are more likely to smoke, abuse alcohol, use drugs, and engage in risky sexual activity.

Who is At Risk for Intimate Partner Violence?

Several factors can increase the risk that someone will hurt his or her partner. However, having these risk factors does not always mean that IPV will occur.

☛ Risk factors for perpetration (hurting a partner):

- ✓ *Using drugs or alcohol, especially drinking heavily*
- ✓ *Seeing or being a victim of violence as a child*
- ✓ *Not having a job, which can cause feelings of stress*

How Can We Prevent Intimate Partner Violence?

☛ The goal is to stop IPV before it begins.

Strategies that promote healthy dating relationships are important. These strategies should focus on young people when they are learning skills for dating. This approach can help those at risk from becoming victims or offenders of IPV.

☛ We need good role models.

Both men and women can work with young people to prevent IPV. Adults can help change social norms, be role models, mentor youth, and work with others to end this violence. For example, by modeling nonviolent relationships, men and women can send the message to young boys and girls that violence is not okay.

☛ Getting Help Before It's Too Late

Traditionally, women's groups have addressed IPV by setting up crisis hotlines and shelters for battered women. These are very important avenues for help and you should know about them if IPV threatens your family.

Communities offer emergency assistance to families experiencing domestic violence. Don't permit IPV to go on. Call the police if you are being attacked. Get help from social service agencies and shelters so you are not subjected to further IPV.

Chapter 15

Sexual Health and Responsible Sexual Behavior

The Surgeon General, U.S. Department of Health and Human Services

We, as a nation, must address the significant public health challenges regarding the sexual health of our citizens. In recognition of these challenges, promoting responsible sexual behavior is included among the Surgeon General's Public Health Priorities and is also one of the Healthy People 2010 "Leading Health Indicators for the Nation." While it is important to acknowledge the many positive aspects of sexuality, we also need to understand that there are undesirable consequences as well, such as alarmingly high levels of sexually transmitted disease (STD) and HIV/AIDS infection, unintended pregnancy, abortion, sexual dysfunction, and sexual violence.

In the United States:

1. STDs infect approximately 12 million persons each year;
2. 774,467 AIDS cases, nearly two-thirds of which were sexually transmitted, have been reported since 1981;
3. An estimated 800,000 to 900,000 persons are living with HIV;
4. An estimated one-third of those living with HIV are aware of their status and are in treatment, one-third are aware but not in treatment, and one-third have not been tested and are not aware;

5. An estimated 40,000 new HIV infections occur each year;
6. An estimated 1,366,000 induced abortions occurred in 1996;
7. Nearly one-half of pregnancies are unintended;
8. An estimated 22 percent of women and two percent of men have been victims of a forced sexual act; and
9. An estimated 104,000 children are victims of sexual abuse each year.

Each of these problems carries with it the potential for lifelong consequences—for individuals, families, communities, and the nation as a whole.

There are serious disparities among the populations affected. The economically disadvantaged, racial and ethnic minorities, persons with different sexual identities (gay, lesbian, bisexual, and transgendered), disabled persons, and adolescents often bear the heaviest burden.

Persons of all ages and backgrounds are at risk and should have access to the knowledge and services necessary for optimal sexual health.

Sexual health is connected with both physical and mental health, and that it is important throughout a person's entire lifespan, not just the reproductive years.

Individuals and communities have a responsibility to protect sexual health. The responsibility of well-informed adults as educators and role models for their children cannot be overstated.

Issues around sexuality can be difficult to discuss—because they are personal and because there is great diversity in how they are perceived and approached.

Sexuality encompasses more than sexual behavior. The many aspects of sexuality include not only the physical, but the mental and spiritual as well, and that sexuality is a core component of personality. Sexuality is a fundamental part of human life.

For the many thousands of persons living with HIV/AIDS in this country

- We realize that you are not the enemy.
- The enemy in this epidemic is the virus, not those infected with it.
- You need our support and encouragement.
- You need to help stop the spread of this illness.
- Be responsible in your own behavior and help others become aware of the need for responsible behavior in their sexual lives.
- Working together, we can make a difference.

We need to appreciate the diversity of our culture, engage in mature, thoughtful, and respectful discussion, be informed by the science that is available to us, and invest in continued research. This is a call to action. We cannot remain complacent. Doing nothing is unacceptable. Our efforts not only will have an impact on the current health status of our citizens, but will lay a foundation for a healthier society in the future.

Digging Deeper

Centers for Disease Control (CDC): Sexual Health

http://www.cdc.gov/sexualhealth/

A major feature of the CDC's sexual health page is preventing the spread of HIV/AIDS and other sexually transmitted diseases. There is also information regarding prevention of sexual violence and how to get help if you are a victim. Other topics include reproductive health and birth control.

Columbia University's Go Ask Alice: Sexual Health

http://www.goaskalice.columbia.edu/Cat7.html

This website puts all of its information into question and answer format. Since questions come from ordinary people, they cover a variety of details that you may have never thought to ask or been afraid to ask. Browse the different categories, or submit a question of your own.

Medline Plus: Sexual Health

http://www.nlm.nih.gov/medlineplus/sexualhealth.html

From anatomy to diseases, from wellness to sexuality, this page covers a lot of information. Read the latest news, or look up a specific condition or symptoms. There is also a search function to help you locate a sexual health provider in your area. If you don't find the answers to all your questions, try looking at one of the related topics listed on the right side of the page.

Chapter 16

Putting Together Your Personal Support Network

The Urban Institute and Other Sources

Having understanding and supportive family members, friends who want you to succeed, and community support groups that take an interest in your welfare can all help to make your transition back into society a success. Together, these caring and helpful individuals and groups around you can become your own **personal support network.**

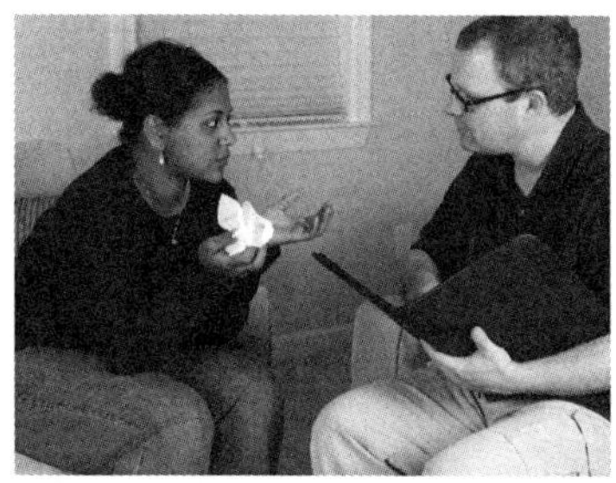

The Benefits of Family Support

Most prisoners believe that family support is an important factor in helping them stay out of prison. Prior to release, over half of Illinois and Maryland Returning Home respondents reported that family support would be an important factor in helping them avoid returning to prison. After release, nearly three-quarters of Illinois and Maryland respondents felt that family support had been an important factor in avoiding prison. In a focus group, participants in Pennsylvania's Community Orientation and Reintegration (COR) Program cited family reunification as a major need in their re-entry process. Prisoners in a Rhode Island focus group reported heavy reliance on their families for both emotional and financial support following their release.

Family Support Helps Reduce Recidivism

Strong family support before prison may reduce the likelihood of recidivism. Respondents in the Illinois Returning Home study who reported more positive family relationships were less likely to be reconvicted, while those with negative family relationships were more likely to be reconvicted or reincarcerated. Further, respondents in the Maryland Returning Home study with closer family relationships and strong family support were less likely to have used drugs since their release.

Family Support Helps Employment Prospects

Close family relationships may improve employment outcomes for returning prisoners. Respondents in the Maryland Returning Home study who had closer family and intimate partner relationships and stronger family support were more likely to be employed after release. In Illinois, respondents who had an intimate partner after release reported having been employed for more weeks on average (30 percent more) than those without a partner.

Friends Who Care About You

Close friends who care about you can help keep you focused on the important job of re-building your life after incarceration. They can help you with transportation needs, employment contacts and referrals, and staying away from the temptations of alcohol and drugs.

On the other hand, old acquaintances or friends you may have made in jail or prison are probably people who will not be helpful, and may lead you back to your old ways. If you want to keep out of prison, avoid those individuals and hang-outs that may expose you to criminal activity.

Support Groups You Can Join

Every community, but especially larger population areas, has numerous support and advocacy groups that are interested in helping you succeed with your re-entry. They are especially eager to see that you don't commit new crimes and return to prison.

☛ Here are some ways to find worthwhile support groups:

✓ *Ask your counselor or probation officer for the names and addresses of support groups such as Alcoholics Anonymous and groups meeting at local churches.*

✓ *Get a list of telephone hotlines for your area that offer referrals to drug programs, mental health programs, domestic violence resources, and other assistance groups.*

✓ *Check the Yellow Pages for social service organizations in your city or community, many of which offer free assistance.*

✓ *Visit the Department of Health and/or Human Services in your city for lists of support groups and types of assistance for re-entering offenders.*

✓ *Visit the federal government website, www.reentry.gov, and check out the section with map links to resources in every state.*

Your Employment Help Network

Building a network of contacts and places to go for employment is vital to your successful re-entry to society. Start with the closest CareerOneStop office which is operated by the federal and state government and which can provide advice, training assistance, and job listings.

Part III

Your Faith-Based Support Network

For many ex-offenders, establishing or re-establishing connections with a church or church-run organization can offer many benefits. Find someone who can serve as your mentor or spiritual advisor, and begin spending some time helping others in your community to demonstrate that you want to "give back" to the society that has already paid for your incarceration. Make yourself a positive role model for young people by telling them about your experiences and the bleak reality of prison life.

Adult Education and Training Support

If you want to build or improve skills to get a better job, seek out adult education classes that are offered in your community, locate apprenticeship opportunities, and find out how you can get further training in any field. The CareerOneStop office nearest you can help you find these worthwhile programs. While you improve your education and skill level, you will make new friends who will take an interest in you and your success.

Recreational Outlets for Support

Join the YMCA, the YWCA, adult leagues, or other programs in your community and participate in sports and recreational activities that will improve the quality of your life.

Be Your Own Booster

Above all, have faith in yourself and your ability to succeed in society. Don't be negative or discouraged. Use your energy to get ahead, solve problems, and convince others that you are a productive member of society. There are no limits to the possibilities for your ultimate success if you develop the right attitudes and a solid work ethic.

Part IV

Education & Training

Chapter 17

Education Pays Big Dividends

U.S. Census Bureau
U.S. Department of Commerce

Does going to school pay off? Most people think so. Currently, almost 90 percent of young adults graduate from high school and about 60 percent of high school seniors continue on to college the following year. People decide to go to college for many reasons. One of the most compelling is the expectation of future economic success based on educational attainment.

The U.S. Census Bureau and the Bureau of Labor Statistics collect annual data to demonstrate the economic value of an education; that is, the added value of a high school diploma or college degree.

Adults with advanced degrees earn four times more than those with less than a high school diploma, according to recent tabulations released by the U.S. Census Bureau.

Detailed tables, available in a Census report entitled Educational Attainment in the United States, 2006, show that adults 18 and older with a master's, professional, or doctoral degree earned an average of $79,946, while those with less than a high school diploma earned about $19,915.

The study also shows that in 2005 adults with a bachelor's degree earned an average of $54,689, while those with a high school diploma earned $29,448.

The table below, based upon 2006 data, shows how higher educational attainment translates into both higher salary levels and lower unemployment rates:

Education and Training Pays (2006)

Educational Attainment	Unemployment Rate	Median Weekly Earnings
Doctoral Degree	1.4%	$1,441
Professional Degree	1.1%	$1,474
Master's Degree	1.7%	$1,140
Bachelor's Degree	2.3%	$962
Associate Degree	3.0%	$721
Some College	3.9%	$674
High School Grad	4.3%	$595
Some High School	6.8%	$419

Source: U.S. Bureau of Labor Statistics (www.bls.gov)

Other Benefits of Higher Education

College graduates also enjoy benefits beyond increased income. A report published by the Institute for Higher Education Policy reviews the individual benefits that college graduates enjoy, including:

- Higher levels of saving
- Increased personal/professional mobility
- Improved quality of life for their offspring
- Better consumer decision making
- More hobbies and leisure activities

Source: Institute for Higher Education Policy

Part IV

Digging Deeper

KnowHow2Go.org

http://www.knowhow2go.org/

Geared to students at different levels, this user-friendly website provides step-by-step explanations of how to prepare for college. KnowHow2Go resources are also available for many individual states by clicking on a map of the United States, while other states post their own links. This multi-media site was developed by the American Council on Education and other partners.

Students.gov

http://www.students.gov/STUGOVWebApp/Public

As the official U.S. government website for college students and their families, this rich resource provides extensive information on planning your education, selecting schools, internships, student jobs, career development, financing your education, and military service funding. Because of the many valuable links, it is one of the very best places to start your research.

CollegeBoard.com: Plan for College

http://www.collegeboard.com/student/plan/index.html

The College Board website provides an excellent starting point for students planning for college. Providing very specific Junior and Senior Action Plans, with testing and application calendars, the site also emphasizes necessary skill building, effective study habits, and other components of academic success.

Chapter 18

The Educational Menu: Training for Every Need

Starting Out!® Research Group

These days, students often feel pressured to consider college when they would prefer following a different educational route. Other students cannot afford college or feel they are not qualified. And some students are simply looking for a shorter-duration, focused training program as a stepping stone to a hands-on technical occupation, a union trade, or a service-oriented field.

Dozens of interesting careers can be successfully entered with an associate degree or a one- or two-year training program rather than a four-year education. On-the-job training for many can be as rewarding and productive as classroom courses, and can provide an income while learning a new trade or occupation. Others prefer to enter military service and later reap the educational rewards offered under the GI Bill.

This article examines each of the types of educational or training options that are available for students instead of four-year college commitments, including two-year colleges; community colleges; armed forces training; private career, correspondence and vocational schools; government-sponsored adult training programs, apprenticeships, and the Jobs Corps. At the end of each profile we have provided a "Digging Deeper" section offering web links to other excellent sources of information.

Part I: Two-Year Colleges

According to the 2004 U.S. Census Population Survey, graduates of two-year colleges who received an associate degree earned, on average, $46,000 annually, compared with high school diploma recipients, who received $34,000 in income. For the same reporting year, the National Center for Educational Statistics (NCES) reported that the cost of an associate degree was nearly $9,000 less than that of a four-year institution.

There are other revealing statistics about two-year colleges. For example, students who enroll in a public, two-year college increase the likelihood that they will move on to a four-year college for a bachelor's degree. The NCES also reported that 47 percent of undergraduates during the 2003-2004 academic year received financial aid.

What are the characteristics of junior, two-year colleges? According to Research and Markets, a major market research reporting source, "junior colleges may be independently organized (public or non-public), part of a school district, or part of an independently organized system of junior colleges. Junior colleges offer college transfer courses and programs (including the first two years of college instruction); vocational, technical and semi-professional occupational programs; and general education programs. In addition, junior colleges confer associate degrees, certificates or diplomas below the baccalaureate level, and may also be known as community colleges."

Digging Deeper

U.S. Two-Year Colleges

http://www.cset.sp.utoledo.edu/twoyrcol.html

Using a map of the United States, this University of Toledo website offers over 1,000 state-by-state listings of two-year colleges. Unfortunately, some of the schools do not have proper hyperlinks, so you may have to search for the school by name and state on www.google.com.

NCES College Navigator

http://nces.ed.gov/collegenavigator/

The National Center for Educational Statistics offers an excellent college navigator tool which allows the visitor to generate a list of colleges by state or nearby zip code or search for a college by name or by type of institution.

Part II: Community Colleges

Community colleges are a vital part of the post-secondary education delivery system. According to the American Association of Community Colleges (AACC), "they serve almost half (46%) of the undergraduate students in the United States, providing open access to postsecondary education, preparing students for transfer to four-year institutions, providing workforce development and skills training, and offering noncredit programs ranging from English as a second language to skills retraining to community enrichment programs or cultural activities."

There are 1,195 community colleges in the United States, of which 987 are public, 177 are independent, and 31 are located on Indian reservations. Of 11.6 million community college students today, 6.6 million are earning credits, and 40 percent are enrolled full time.

Because community colleges serve students of all ages, the average student age is 29, although 43 percent are 21 or younger. Somewhat over half (59 percent) are women, and 34 percent represent minorities. About 83 percent of part-time community college students are employed, while 50 percent of full-time students work at least part-time.

Financial aid is provided to 47 percent of community college students through federal grants, federal loans, or state aid.

The most noteworthy statistic is the cost of tuition. The average annual tuition plus fees amounts to $2,272, representing one of the best values in education today.

Part III: From Community College to the Workplace

Very large numbers of successful employees begin with community college educations. Here are further statistics from the AACC:

- **Health care:** 50 percent of new nurses and the majority of other new health-care workers are educated at community colleges.
- **International programs:** Close to 100,000 international students attend community colleges, about 39 percent of all international undergraduate students in the United States.
- **Workforce training:** 95 percent of businesses and organizations that employ community college graduates recommend community college workforce education and training programs.
- **Homeland security:** Close to 80 percent of firefighters, law enforcement officers, and Emergency Medical Technicians (EMTs) are credentialed at community colleges.
- **Five hottest community college programs:** registered nursing, law enforcement, licensed practical nursing, radiology, and computer technologies.
- **Earnings:** The average expected lifetime earnings for a graduate with an associate degree are $1.6 million, about $.4 million more than a high school graduate earns.

Digging Deeper

U.S. Community Colleges by State

http://www.utexas.edu/world/comcol/state/

The University of Texas at Austin has compiled an excellent list of community colleges by state and city, with active hyperlinks to take you to the school's homepage on the web.

American Association of Community Colleges

http://www.aacc.nche.edu/

The AACC has an excellent community college finder based upon a map of the United States, with active links to detailed information on the colleges in each state. This is an especially thorough source. In addition, this non-profit organization has many other helpful resources about community colleges and the national programs which it sponsors.

Part IV: Private Career, Correspondence and Vocational Schools

The following article was prepared by the Federal Trade Commission as a guide for consumers seeking reputable career training schools.

Focused Training for Skilled Jobs

Whether you're new to the job market or looking to enhance your skills, a private vocational or correspondence school can be an excellent starting point for furthering your career. These schools train students for a variety of skilled jobs, including automotive technician, medical assistant, hair stylist, interior designer, electronics technician, paralegal, and truck driver. Some schools also help students identify prospective employers and apply for jobs.

While many private vocational and correspondence schools are reputable and teach the skills necessary to get a good job, others may not be as trustworthy.

Their main objective may be to increase profits by increasing enrollment. They do this by promising more than they can deliver.

For example, they may mislead prospective students about the salary potential of certain jobs or the availability of jobs in certain fields. They also may overstate the extent of their job training programs, the qualifications of their teachers, the nature of their facilities and equipment, and their connections to certain businesses and industries.

It's not always easy to spot the false claims that some schools may make, but there are steps consumers can take to make sure that the school they enroll in is reputable and trustworthy.

Do Some Homework

Before enrolling in a vocational or correspondence school, do some homework. Here's how:

- Consider whether you need additional training or education to get the job you want. It's possible that the skills you'll need can be learned "on the job." Look at employment ads for positions that you're interested in and call the employer to learn what kind of experience is important for those positions.
- Investigate training alternatives, such as community colleges. The tuition may be less than at private schools. Also, some businesses offer education programs through apprenticeships or on-the-job training.
- Compare programs. Study the information from various schools to learn what is required to graduate. Ask what you'll get when you graduate—a certificate in your chosen field or eligibility for a clinical or other externship? Are licensing credits you earn at the school transferable? If you decide to pursue additional training and education, find out whether two- or four-year colleges accept credits from any vocational or correspondence school you're considering. If reputable schools and colleges say they don't, it may be a sign that the vocational school is not well regarded.
- Find out as much as you can about the school's facilities. Ask about the types

of equipment—computers and tools, for example—that students use for training and supplies and tools that you, as a student, must provide. Visit the school; ask to see the classrooms and workshops.

- Ask about the instructors' qualifications and the size of classes. Sit in on a class. Are the students engaged? Is the teacher interesting?
- Get some idea of the program's success rate. Ask what percentage of students complete the program. A high dropout rate could mean that students don't like the program. How many graduates find jobs in their chosen field? What is the average starting salary?
- Ask for a list of recent graduates. Ask some about their experiences with the school.
- Find out how much the program is going to cost. Are books, equipment, uniforms, and lab fees included in the overall fee or are they extra?
- If you need financial assistance, find out whether the school provides it, and if so, what it offers. The U.S. Department of Education administers several major student aid programs in the forms of grants, loans, and work-study programs. About two-thirds of all student financial aid comes from these programs. Call the Federal Student Aid Information Center at 1-800-4 FED AID (1-800-433-3243) for a free copy of The Student Guide. It's also available at *www.studentaid.ed.gov/students/attachments/siteresources/FundingEduBeyondHighSchool_0708.pdf*.
- Ask for the names and phone numbers of the school's licensing and accrediting organizations. Check with these organizations to learn whether the school is up to date on its license and accreditation. Licensing is handled by state agencies. In many states, private vocational schools are licensed through the state department of education. Truck driver training schools, on the other hand, may be licensed by the state transportation department. Ask the school which state agency handles its licensing. Accreditation is usually through a private education agency or association, which has evaluated the school and verified that it meets certain requirements. Accreditation can be an important clue to a school's ability to provide appropriate training and education—if the accrediting body is reputable. Your high-school guidance

counselor, principal, or teachers can tell you which accrediting bodies have worthy standards.

- Check with the attorney general's office and the Better Business Bureau in the state where you live and in the state where the school is based, as well as with your county or state consumer protection agency, to see whether complaints have been filed against the school. A record of complaints may indicate questionable practices, but a lack of complaints doesn't necessarily mean that the school is without problems. Unscrupulous businesses or business people often change names and locations to hide complaint histories.

Digging Deeper

Choosing a Career or Vocational School

http://www.ftc.gov/bcp/conline/pubs/services/votech.shtm

The Federal Trade Commission offers excellent advice about choosing a career or vocational school and avoiding scams. The "Do Some Homework" section provides a valuable checklist of steps to take as you search for and compare schools.

Vocational Schools Database, Located by State

http://www.rwm.org/rwm/

Another colorful map of the United States provides hyperlinks to vocational schools in each state. Schools are organized by career field.

CollegeBoard: Career Colleges and Schools

http://www.collegeboard.com/student/csearch/majors_careers/31371.html

The College Board, a non-profit organization known for college services, also provides useful information on career training schools. Use the "Advanced Search" tool to find career programs at two-year colleges which will award an associate degree in the field.

Part V: Armed Forces Training for Civilian Careers

Each of the branches of the armed forces offers extensive, specialized training for the military roles that soldiers pursue during their enlistment. The Army, Navy, Air Force, Marine Corps, and Coast Guard each have their own military occupational specialties (MOS), many of which relate closely to civilian occupations.

All enlistees also take an Armed Services Vocational Aptitude Battery, which helps guide each individual in his or her career planning.

According to the Bureau of Labor Statistics, in an article in spring 2007, entitled Military Training for Civilian Careers, the military has more than 140 occupational specialties, most of which relate to civilian jobs, including jobs in aviation, mechanics, training and organization, computers, construction, food services, healthcare, law enforcement, maintenance, manufacturing, power plant operations, and media services.

In addition to these in-service training opportunities, the armed forces provide excellent educational benefits outside military training for veterans, certain active-duty service personnel, and reservists under the well-known GI Bill.

Digging Deeper

Bureau of Labor Statistics: Military Training for Civilian Careers

http://www.bls.gov/opub/ooq/2007/spring/art02.pdf

An excellent slide presentation at this site provides information about preparing for civilian careers utilizing military knowledge and training.

The GI Bill

http://www.gibill.va.gov

One of the great benefits of military service is the GI Bill, which offers extensive educational and training assistance. This is the website to find out all about the GI Bill and how you can advance your training. Visit the appropriate section covering either active service personnel or reservists to find out how to apply for benefits.

Part VI: Government-Sponsored Adult Training Programs

The Department of Labor's Employment and Training Administration (ETA) funds training programs that teach job skills and provide job placement services for adults who are at least 18 years of age. The programs are administered locally by OneStop Career Centers. The types of training offered by a local training center can vary depending on the job opportunities in the community. To help locate training programs in your area, search for a One Stop Center in your state, visit America's Service Locator, or call ETA's Toll-Free Help Line at 877-US-2JOBS (1-877-889-5267).

DIGGING DEEPER

Department of Labor: Employment and Training Administration

http://www.doleta.gov/

The U.S. Department of Labor Employment and Training Administration provides extensive information on occupational planning and training. Visit the section called "Advancing Your Career" to find resources on self-assessment, finding jobs, job loss, and employee rights.

Career OneStop

http://www.careeronestop.org/

This is the home page of the Department of Labor's national network of OneStop Career Centers, along with extensive resources on all aspects of employment. You can explore careers, launch a job search, examine education and training opportunities, find the closest Career Center, and develop a resume.

Part VII: Apprenticeships

Apprenticeship is a combination of on-the-job training and related instruction in which workers learn the practical and theoretical aspects of a highly skilled occupation. Apprenticesh and/or employer associations.

The Department of Labor's role is to safeguard the welfare of apprentices, ensure equality of access to apprenticeship programs, and provide integrated employment and training information to sponsors and the local employment and training community.

Digging Deeper

U.S. Department of Labor: Apprenticeships

http://www.dol.gov/dol/topic/training/apprenticeship.htm

The Department of Labor's website provides excellent materials on apprenticeships from the Office of Apprenticeship Training for both workers and employers, including how to become an apprentice in a particular field. The National Apprenticeship Program is described in two detailed fact sheets.

National Apprenticeship System

http://www.doleta.gov/OA/nas.cfm

The Department of Labor provides this w website dedicated to the National Apprenticeship System, a program creating uniform standards for operation of apprenticeships, as well as rights and protections for apprentices.

Registered Apprenticeship Website

http://www.doleta.gov/OA/eta_default.cfm

This related Department of Labor website covers registered apprenticeship programs, with information for individuals, employers, and state apprenticeship directors. There is also a searchable apprenticeship program sponsor link to identify apprenticeship by state and county.

Career Voyages: Apprenticeships

http://www.careervoyages.gov/apprenticeship-main.cfm

To find specific apprentice programs, Career Voyages, which is a government website, offers links to such areas as manufacturing, aerospace, automotive, construction, energy, healthcare, homeland security, hospitality, information technology, and transportation. You can also search for state apprenticeship offices and access career videos in hundreds of fields.

Part VIII: Job Corps

Job Corps is the nation's largest and most comprehensive residential education and job training program for at-risk youth, ages 16 through 24. Job Corps combines classroom, practical, and work-based learning experiences to prepare youth for stable, long-term, high-paying jobs. Established in 1964, Job Corps has trained and educated more than 2 million young people to date, serving approximately 62,000 young adults each year.

How Does Job Corps Work?

Job Corps is a no-cost education and vocational training program administered by the U.S. Department of Labor that helps young people get a better job, make more money, and take control of their lives.

At Job Corps, students enroll to learn a trade, earn a high school diploma or GED and get help finding a good job. When you join the program, you will be paid a monthly allowance; the longer you stay with the program, the more your allowance will be. Job Corps provides career counseling and transition support to its students for up to 12 months after they graduate from the program.

Where is Job Corps?

There are currently 122 Job Corps centers located in 48 states, the District of Columbia and Puerto Rico. To support all of the centers, Job Corps also manages outreach, admissions and career transition operations at hundreds of locations nationwide.

Training and Education

The Career Development Services System (CDSS) is Job Corps' approach for providing seamless services to students, including recruitment, education, career training, job assistance and transitional support services after graduation. Upon joining Job Corps, each student works with staff to develop an individualized Personal Career Development Plan (PCDP) to stay on track for success. Students receive hands-on career training in more than 100 occupational areas, including health occupations, construction-related fields, culinary arts, business, and technology-related industries. They can also participate in on-the-job training at real work sites through work-based learning opportunities. In the academic classroom, students have the opportunity to earn a high school diploma or GED and learn employability and independent living skills.

While enrolled in the program, students receive housing, meals, basic medical care, and biweekly living allowances. Job Corps also has a strict zero tolerance policy for drugs and violence. Since Job Corps is a self-paced program and lengths of stay vary, students may remain enrolled for up to two years.

After Graduation

Through employer partnerships, Job Corps places trained graduates who are familiar with industry procedures and equipment with local, regional, and national employers. Employers save time and money by hiring skilled workers who are ready to work immediately. Job Corps has one of the highest job placement rates among the nation's job training programs. Approximately 90 percent of Job Corps graduates go on to careers in the private sector, enlist in the military, or move on to higher education or advanced training programs. Job Corps graduates receive transitional support services, including help locating housing, child care, and transportation, for up to 18 months after they leave the program.

Eligibility

To enroll in Job Corps, students must meet the following requirements:

- Be 16 through 24
- Be a U.S. citizen or legal resident
- Meet income requirements
- Be ready, willing, and able to participate fully in an educational environment

Funded by the United States Congress, Job Corps has been training young adults for meaningful careers since 1964. Job Corps is committed to offering all students a safe, drug-free environment where they can take advantage of the resources provided.

How to Apply

If you're interested in joining the Job Corps program or finding out more about it, call 800–733–JOBS or 800–733–5627. An operator will provide you with general information about the program, refer you to the admissions counselor closest to where you live and mail you an information packet.

Job Corps is administered by the Department of Labor's Office of the Secretary. For information on Job Corps, including eligibility requirements and location of the center nearest you, call 800–733–JOBS.

Digging Deeper

U.S. Department of Labor: Job Corps

http://jobcorps.dol.gov/

Students, prospective employees, employers, and parents can access full information on Job Corps at this Department of Labor website. Prospective participants in Job Corps can get eligibility information at this site or visit one of the Job Corps offices located nationwide.

Part IV

Chapter 19

Pairing Occupations With Education

CareerOneStop
U.S. Department of Labor

CareerOneStop (www.careeronestop.org) is a U.S. Department of Labor-sponsored website that offers career resources and workforce information to job seekers, students, businesses, and workforce professionals to foster talent development in a global economy. It includes:

- America's Career InfoNet (www.careerinfonet.org), which helps individuals explore career opportunities to make informed employment and education choices. The website features user-friendly occupation and industry information, salary data, career videos, education resources, self-assessment tools, career exploration assistance, and other resource that support talent development in today's fast-paced global marketplace.
- America's Service Locator (www.ServiceLocator.org), which connects individuals to employment and training opportunities available at local OneStop Career Centers. The website provides contact information for a range of local work-related services, including unemployment benefits, career development, and educational opportunities.

Every career has a specific set of educational and training requirements, with the more advanced opportunities requiring the greatest amount of training. Nevertheless, many fulfilling jobs can be pursued through apprenticeships, certified training, or technical courses of study. While a college education may be advantageous for many careers, numerous skilled occupations require shorter training programs, many with valuable certification programs.

CareerOneStop is...

- Your source for employment information and inspiration
- The place to find tools to help job seekers, students, businesses and career professionals
- Sponsored by the U.S. Department of Labor

Step One: What level of training are you seeking?

The table below defines each level of training and provides links to specific listings of apprenticeship programs, technical schools, colleges, and military service benefits for further education. This chart should be consulted before you move on to Step Two and examine specific occupations and learn about their educational requirements. Visit the following table online to access the hot links for each category:

http://www.careeronestop.org/EducationTraining/Plan/WhatsAvailable.aspx

Education and Training Options	Definition	Looking for more?
Apprenticeship	An employer's formal training program combining on-the-job learning with technical instruction for a specific trade.	Registered Apprenticeship website
Certifications	An examination or a record of work-related credentials. Issued to an individual by an external organization to communicate a certain level of skill attainment.	Certification Finder
Community College	Institution typically offering two-year or Associate of Arts degree that can transfer to a four-year college or university.	Community College Finder

Part IV

Technical College	One- to two-year training programs in a variety of subject areas. Short-term training also available.	Find technical colleges in the Community College Finder
4-year College or University	Earn a bachelor of arts or bachelor of science degree in your chosen field of study.	Find 4-year colleges in Education and Training Finder
Customized Training	Topic-specific, short-term training designed for a specific employer.	Find customized training links in the Career Resource Library
Internships	Opportunity for hands-on, real work experience. May be required in some college majors, or may be an entry-level internship you apply for after graduating college.	Find internship links in the Career Resource Library
Armed Forces Training	Career and educational guidance, including tuition assistance, scholarships, state assistance, and GI Bill benefits.	Visit Education at www.military.com
Job Corps	A free, Department of Labor program designed for individuals ages 16-24 to obtain training and job skills.	Job Corps Web site
Workforce Investment Act (WIA) Training	Federal program that provides short-term training and education at technical colleges, community colleges, and universities.	Workforce Investment Act (WIA) Eligible Training Provider

Step Two: What are the educational requirements of specific occupations?

Visit the site and review fields of interest or new fields you've never considered. Consider the training you will need to enter these fields.

Step Three: What are the fastest growing occupations and their educational requirements?

The third resource from CareerOneStop.org is a list of the 50 fastest-growing occupations, showing employment growth projections through 2014, state rankings, earnings expectations, and educational and training requirements. We have included the top 20 in the chart below:

No.	Occupation	Employment		Percent Change	Earnings	Training Needed
		2006	2016			
1	Network systems and data communications analysts	261,800	401,600	53%	$$$$	Bachelor's degree
2	Personal and home care aides	767,300	1,155,800	51%	$	Short-term on-the-job training
3	Home health aides	787,300	1,170,900	49%	$	Short-term on-the-job training
4	Computer software engineers, applications	506,800	732,500	45%	$$$$	Bachelor's degree
5	Veterinary technologists and technicians	71,200	100,400	41%	$$	Associate degree
6	Personal financial advisors	176,200	248,400	41%	$$$$	Bachelor's degree
7	Makeup artists, theatrical and performance	2,100	3,000	40%	$$$	Postsecondary vocational award
8	Medical assistants	416,900	564,600	35%	$$	Moderate-term on-the-job training
9	Veterinarians	62,200	84,000	35%	$$$$	First professional degree
10	Substance abuse and behavioral disorder counselors	83,300	112,000	34%	$$$	Bachelor's degree
11	Skin care specialists	38,200	51,300	34%	$$	Postsecondary vocational award
12	Financial analysts	220,600	295,200	34%	$$$$	Bachelor's degree
13	Social and human service assistants	338,700	452,600	34%	$$	Moderate-term on-the-job training
14	Gaming surveillance officers and gaming investigators	8,700	11,600	34%	$$	Moderate-term on-the-job training

15	Physical therapist assistants	60,300	79,800	32%	$$$	Associate degree
16	Pharmacy technicians	285,000	376,400	32%	$$	Moderate-term on-the-job training
17	Forensic science technicians	13,100	17,100	31%	$$$	Bachelor's degree
18	Dental hygienists	167,000	217,200	30%	$$$$	Associate degree
19	Mental health counselors	99,800	129,800	30%	$$$	Master's degree
20	Mental health and substance abuse social workers	122,300	158,800	30%	$$$	Master's degree

Digging Deeper

U.S. Department of Education/Student Portal

http://www.ed.gov/students/landing.jhtml

The U.S. Department of Education offers a well-organized student-based site for educational planning. The College Navigator helps you research colleges based upon location, programs, tuition, distance learning opportunities, and evening courses. The most useful link at this site is the "Portal for Student Aid," allowing you to set up your own password-protected account to store the information you locate and to apply for federal tuition assistance.

College Board: Find the Right Colleges for You

http://collegesearch.collegeboard.com/search/index.jsp

The College Board provides a user-friendly search tool to locate and compare just under 4,000 colleges and universities. The "College Matchmaker" enables you to search by location, type of campus setting, majors and academics, and costs. The "College QuickFinder" accesses detailed profiles when the user submits the name of the institution. You can easily set up your own secure account to manage the college search process.

Chapter 20

Financing Your Education

U.S. Department of Education

Student financial aid is available from a wide variety of sources, including the federal government, individual states, and directly from colleges and universities, as well as from numerous other public and private agencies and organizations. Whatever the source, all forms of college aid fall into four basic categories:

1. **Grants.**

   Gift aid from grants does not have to be repaid and is generally awarded based at least partially on financial need.

2. **Work Study.**

   The Federal Work-Study Program (FWS) is a federally funded source of financial assistance used to offset financial education costs. Students earn money by working and attending school. The money does not have to be repaid.

3. **Loans.**

   Loans are borrowed and must be repaid with interest. As a general rule, educational loans have far more favorable terms and interest rates than traditional consumer loans.

4. **Scholarships.**

   Offered by schools, local/community organizations, private institutions and trusts, scholarships do not have to be repaid and are generally awarded based on specific criteria.

Steps to Finding Student Aid

- ✓ Be prepared to fill out applications explaining your career interests and educational goals. How did your career interests evolve? Did someone inspire you? Read the advice at FinAid.org.
- ✓ Check state and community scholarships, including large employers, fraternal and religious organizations, unions, professional associations, and community service organizations. Visit the state agency links we have provided under "Digging Deeper."
- ✓ Search for federal scholarships at StudentAid.ed.gov
- ✓ Explore college scholarships at the schools of your choice.
- ✓ Use FastWeb.com or other scholarship search engines such as at CollegeBoard.com to build a list of other possible scholarships for which you are eligible.
- ✓ Check the college savings plan in your state at the link we have provided.
- ✓ Prepare submissions carefully: transcripts, test scores, essays, family financial information, letters of recommendation, proof of eligibility, scholarship forms, and career/major selections. Write clearly and spell-check your application.

Digging Deeper

U.S. Department of Education: Federal Assistance

http://www.studentaid.ed.gov

The U.S. Department of Education has a wealth of information on choosing, applying for, and paying for education after high school. This information, along with applications for federal financial assistance, is posted online at this site or you can call 1-800-433-3243. On the left margin you can access all of the federal student aid programs, while on the right you can set up a secure account and actually apply for assistance. Click on the FAFSA link, follow the simple instructions, and start your application.

State Education and Assistance Agencies: Click on the Map

http://www.ed.gov/about/contacts/state/index.html

After examining federal sources, you should check with your own state's department of education at this webpage, which provides a convenient map of the United States. After clicking on a particular state, you will find information on financial aid and loan programs.

College Savings Plan Network

http://www.collegesavings.org/index.aspx

For families seeking college loan assistance, this helpful site will connect you with tax-advantaged college savings plans—called "529 Plans"—around the country. Use the top link to "My State's 529 Plan" to find out how it works. While you can compare plans between states, and sometimes it is worth going out of state, the general rule is that your own state will offer the most attractive terms and tax treatment.

FastWeb: The Scholarship Search Engine

http://www.fastweb.com/

Developed by Monster.com, this personal, free log-in site will give direct access to thousands of scholarships, including a feature that matches scholarships to your personal profile. The site also offers help in finding internships and jobs. FastWeb is the most widely used site for students seeking financial aid.

Smart Student Guide to Financial Aid

http://www.finaid.org

Judged to be one of the most useful websites on financial aid, FinAid has excellent short articles on all of the types of financial assistance and statistical tables, as well as sections devoted to student loans, scholarships, savings plans, and military assistance. The major links are listed separately in this "Digging Deeper" section.

Armed Forces Benefits for Education

http://education.military.com/education-home/

Another Monster.com site, Military.com offers extensive resources for members of the armed services, including this important section on educational assistance under the GI Bill. Check out the "Money for School" links on the left column, and then use the GI Bill Search Engine in the upper right to find out how to finance your education with government benefits. The site is rich in content covering schools and colleges, other types of military benefits, and additional valuable information features.

Part V

Getting Into the Job Market

Chapter 21

Searching for a New Job

Starting Out! Research Group

This chapter provides a comprehensive guide to the entire process of finding a job after incarceration, including important preparatory steps before re-entry, followed by more extensive contacts and recommendations to use once you are on your own.

Part I: Seven Steps to Follow Before Release

☛ Research Different Types of Jobs and Careers

Think about different career fields that might appeal to you for future work and also might draw upon your skills, experience, and training. The best place to go is the homepage of the CareerOneStop system at: *www.careeronestop.org*. By using the scroll-down menu on the upper right side of the site you can access numerous valuable information sources, including videos at Career Voyages.

☛ Prepare Yourself for the Job Market

Employers require that you provide information about your training, skills, and experience so they can evaluation your qualifications for a particular job. The accepted method of summarizing this information is on a personal resume. Visit Chapter 24 and learn how to prepare a resume and accompanying cover letter.

Take advantage of any job and education opportunities in prison. This will develop your skills and improve your employability and therefore your chances of finding a good job upon your release.

☛ Compile an Employment Folder

An employment folder should be prepared that holds not only your personal information and documents, but all of your research and contact information once you start your job search. The employment folder should include copies of your resume, social security card, birth certificate, high school diploma or GED certificate, vocational certificates or college diplomas, and a transcript from each school you have attended (including prison schools). Remember to bring extra copies for use during interviews, and to keep the originals with you in your folder.

As you collect information about jobs and employers in your home area, you can place it in this same folder for future reference.

☛ Complete Your Resume and Cover Letter

If you do not have a resume, prepare one as described in Chapter 24, or using a similar format. Resumes should be neat and preferably typed without spelling errors. Be sure to have someone proof-read your resume and make suggestions for improvements.

☛ Practice Interview Skills and Filling Out Applications

The Starting Out! Re-Entry Workbook provides a sample Employment Application Form. Practice filling this out so you will be prepared when you receive applications in the mail or from employers you later visit. Again, proof-read your application so that you avoid spelling errors and poor punctuation. Get help from others if necessary. Read Chapter 25 to learn how to handle an interview.

☛ Build a List of Possible Employers and Job Prospects

Using as many of the following methods as possible, build a large list of possible employers and jobs in the community or city where you live. Here are some suggestions on ways to find this information:

- ✓ **Ask your family and friends** on the outside to give you lists of companies and organizations that are advertising for new employees in your community. Have them cut out newspaper ads and listings and send them to you.
- ✓ **Call the CareerOneStop Office** in or near your home town. You can find the closest one by calling 1-877-US2-JOBS (1-877-872-5627) or by visiting *http://www.servicelocator.org*. Ask for a list of the largest area employers, such as manufacturing companies, warehouses, hospitals, hotels, large restaurants, or other organizations that might offer reliable and steady jobs. Keep your skills and education in mind as you specify possible types of employment.
- ✓ **Using the internet, visit your home state job bank** listed at *http://www.careeronestop.org*. There is a link on the right side of this opening page. This is an excellent source of current job openings.
- ✓ **Call town and city personnel offices** where you live and ask about job openings that match your skills, such as road work, maintenance, landscaping, office or clerk positions, public works, etc. You can also research town and city jobs online by going to the website of the city and searching for "employment."
- ✓ **Read Chapter 23 on "Employers Friendly Toward Past Offenders"** to get ideas for further job leads.

☛ Send Out Resumes and Make Calls

When you are 60 days or so from release, you should **mail resumes and cover letters** to employers whose addresses you have compiled.

Plan to follow up with these same employers by telephone or in person and request an interview when you are released.

Remember that employers are looking for people who know what they want to do, who have skills, and who want a career with their organization. Keep in mind that a significant number of ex-offenders have been employed in construction, retail, hospitality, food service, transportation, and warehousing jobs. Don't forget to consider employers who hire staff for hotels, colleges, hospitals, and apartment building owners/managers.

Part II: Employers Do Hire Ex-Offenders

Assume employers will hire you if you are a good match for their needs. One survey of more than 1200 employers reported that only eight percent said they would not hire an ex-offender. Since 92 percent of employers will consider hiring you, feel free to look for work from any legitimate source. Limiting yourself to employers that you believe hire ex-offenders can also limit your wages and job prospects. You should try to find employers who are a good match for your skills, experience, and career goals.

Your job search should include **all potential employers**. According to Richard Bolles' popular employment book, "What Color Is Your Parachute," some of the best ways to find a job are:

✓ **Asking for job-leads** from family members, friends, and people in the community. This common approach has a 33 percent success rate.

✓ **Knocking on the door** of any employer, factory, or office that interests you, whether they are known to have a vacancy or not, has a 47 percent success rate.

✓ **Using the internet or telephone** Yellow Pages has a 69 percent success rate. First, identify topics or fields of interest in the town or city where you will live upon release. Then, call up organizations listed in these categories to ask if they are hiring for types of position you are seeking. Be confident and polite, and ask if you can speak with the personnel manager.

✓ **Remember, the two most critical factors** to a successful job search are positive attitude and persistence. You are marketing a product, yourself, and you have to believe in yourself in order to land that job. Also, like any sales situation, you have to make plenty of contacts. Treat your employment search like a job and spend at least eight hours a day at it. Employers will not usually come looking for you so you have to get out to meet them.

Part III: State and Federal Jobs for Ex-Offenders

Ex-offenders have no special status when applying for state and federal jobs. The application and selection procedures for state jobs follows state guidelines, and federal jobs follow the rules and guidelines of the Office of Personnel Management (OPM).

☛ State Jobs

To find out about state jobs, contact the Department of Human Resources in the state where you plan to release. You can also find out about jobs with most states' governments on the internet at www.state.__.us. Fill in the blank with the two letter postal code for the state. For example, Virginia would be www.state.va.us. Though this works for most states, it does not work for all. If it doesn't, simply do an internet search for your state name; this should bring you to the homepage. State jobs may also be posted at the local CareerOneStop Office and each state's contact information can be found in the blue pages of the telephone book.

Although each state's website is different, you can find job information by entering "jobs" in the "search" box for any given state website.

Another shortcut is to go to *www.job-hunt.org* and enter your state name at the top.

☛ Federal Jobs: www.USAjobs.gov

The Office of Personnel Management (OPM) announces most federal jobs on their website at *www.usajobs.gov.* You can also call the OPM automated telephone system, an interactive voice response telephone system, at 478-757-3000 or TDD 478-744-2299. Job seekers can access current job vacancies, employment information fact sheets, applications, forms, and even apply for some jobs. Many federal agencies have job information telephone numbers located in the blue pages of the telephone book. Federal job postings are also available from the nearest CareerOneStop office.

Part IV: CareerOneStop Centers: Training, Jobs, and Guidance

☛ Locating the Closest CareerOneStop Office

The CareerOneStop System in your state offers employment and training assistance. Visit your closest state CareerOneStop office to learn how this program can help you get ahead. To find the closest office, call 1-877-348-0502 or go online and locate *www.servicelocator.org/*.

☛ Types of Assistance Available at CareerOneStop:

1. *Listings of federal, state, and local job openings*
2. *Jobs bulletin board, job vacancy books, and periodicals*
3. *Computer access for internet / job search websites and resume preparation*
4. *Skills testing and individualized employment interest assessment*
5. *Labor market information on top industries: Jobs in demand or on the decline*
6. *Up-to-date equipment and technology available for job searches including fax, copier, typewriter, paper, supplies, and telephone*
7. *Pre-Employment Training*
8. *Vocational / Career Exploration*
9. *Workshops and Job Fairs*
10. *GED Preparation*
11. *Job Specific Skills Training*
12. *On-the-Job Training*

Part V: Job Corps

Job Corps is a **free** education and training program that helps young people learn a career, earn a high school diploma or GED, and find and keep a good job. For eligible youth at least 16 years of age, Job Corps provides the all-around skills needed to succeed in a career and in life. To learn more, visit Job Corps on the web at *www.jobcorps.gov.*

If you or someone you know is interested in joining Job Corps, call 800-733-JOBS or 800-733-5627 where an operator will provide you with general information about Job Corps, refer you to the admissions counselor closest to where you live, and mail you an information packet.

Part VI: Job Programs for Veterans

Three important programs that can help veterans are offered through the U.S. Department of Labor. Below is a description of each program and points of contact:

☛ Veterans Employment and Training Service (VETS)

The mission statement for VETS is to provide veterans and transitioning service members with the resources and services to succeed in the 21st century workforce by maximizing their employment opportunities, protecting their employment rights, and meeting labor-market demands with qualified veterans today.

Information about job assistance for veterans can be found at CareerOneStop Centers and on the web at *http://www.dol.gov/vets/*.

The federal government's "Hire Vets First" program can only help ex-offenders who have honorable discharges.

☛ Veterans Workforce Investment Program (VWIP)

The Veteran's Workforce Investment Program (VWIP) was created recently through funding from the U.S. Department of Labor. VWIP is a statewide program that addresses the unique needs of veterans seeking employment, training, job counseling, and related services and to develop and promote maximum employment opportunities for eligible veterans. For information, ask your local CareerOneStop Center or a local office of the Veterans Administration.

☛ Homeless Veterans' Reintegration Program (HVRP)

The purpose of the Homeless Veterans' Reintegration Program (HVRP) is to provide services to assist in reintegrating homeless veterans into meaningful employment within the labor force and to stimulate the development of effective service delivery systems that will address the complex problems facing homeless veterans. Ask your CareerOneStop or Veterans' Administration office about this program and whether it is available in your community.

Part VII: Physical and Mental Disability Employment and Training Services

☛ Disabilities Are Not a Barrier to Employment

Physical and mental disability employment and training services are available at One-Stop Career Centers and through other federal partners. The Disability Employment and Initiatives Unit of the Employment and Training Administration helps identify policies and provides technical assistance to address barriers to work for people with disabilities.

The President's Committee on Employment of People with Disabilities provides additional services, including a job recruitment program for people with disabilities, and a career exploration program for high school students with disabilities. A toll-free number for the Job Accommodations Network (800-526-7234) provides information on the employment provisions of the Americans with Disabilities Act.

☛ Ticket to Work Program

The Ticket-to-Work and Work Incentive Improvement Act of 1999 provides an opportunity for people who receive social security disability benefits to work. It provides training and employment opportunities for disabled individuals while allowing them to continue to receive social security benefits. Call toll 866-968-7842, or866-833-2967 (TTY). Preferably, visit the internet at *www.yourtickettowork.com.*

Part VIII: Native American Employment and Training Services

The Workforce Investment Act contains provisions aimed at supporting employment and training activities for Indian, Alaska Native, and Native Hawaiian individuals. The Department of Labor's Division of Indian and Native American Programs (DINAP) funds grant programs that provide training opportunities at the local level for this target population. To find the program nearest you, look for a grant program in your state, contact your local One-Stop Center, or call ETA's toll-free help line at 877-872-5627 (TTY: 877-889-5267).

Part IX: Senior Workers Employment Program

The Senior Community Service Employment Program (SCSEP) is a part-time employment program for low-income persons age 55 or over. Program participants work at community and government agencies and are paid the federal or state minimum wage, whichever is higher. They may also receive training, and can use their participation as a bridge to other employment positions which are not supported with federal funds. The program is administered by the Department of Labor's Employment and Training Administration (ETA).

Part X: Apprenticeship

Apprenticeship is a combination of on-the-job training and related instruction in which workers learn the practical and theoretical aspects of a highly skilled occupation. Apprenticeship programs can be sponsored by individual employers, joint employer and labor groups, and/or employer associations.

The Department of Labor's role is to safeguard the welfare of apprentices, ensure equality of access to apprenticeship programs, and provide integrated employment and training information to sponsors and the local employment and training community. Information about apprenticeship programs can be obtained from your local One-Stop Career Center, from union locals listed in the white pages of the telephone book, or from the following internet site: *http://bat.doleta.gov/bat.cfm*. This site allows you to search by state and county to find apprenticeship programs and their sponsors.

Part XI: Employer Work Opportunity Tax Credit (WOTC)

The WOTC is one tool in a diverse toolbox of flexible strategies designed to help move people from welfare into gainful employment and obtain on-the-job experience. It joins other tax credits, education, and workforce training programs that help American workers with barriers to employment prepare for good jobs; ease their transition from job to job; benefit from the creation of effective regional economic development strategies; and create high performance workplaces.

Ask CareerOneStop personnel about participating employers in your area that may be interested in tax breaks if they hire you.

Part XII: Federal Employee Bonding Program

The federal bonding program is designed to help a job applicant get and keep a job. The program issues Fidelity Bonds and is sponsored by the U.S. Department of Labor. A fidelity bond is a business insurance policy that protects the employer in case of any loss of money or property due to employee dishonesty. To be eligible for the bond, the employer must schedule a date to start work. The Employment Service local office then requests The McLaughlin Company in Washington, DC, to issue to the employer a Fidelity Bond insurance policy covering the worker.

Chapter 22

Breaking the Barriers to Employment

U.S. Department of Justice, Bureau of Prisons, Employment Information Handbook

Ex-offenders face barriers to employment. Barriers to employment may include: stigma and bias, drug and alcohol problems, a lack of continuous work history, and poor education.

Despite these barriers, it's important to persevere. Finding a job will bring many positive things to your life, such as self-confidence, as well as an income to help you create the home and life you want.

What should I do to prepare for release?

You should start preparing for release as early in your sentence as possible. This should include an assessment of your career objectives, completion of all education and vocational training programs offered by the prison, resolution of any substance abuse issues that you may have, and development of a realistic post release plan.

☛ Create a Plan

Many people who prepare for release are unrealistic about what they are going to do and lack a workable plan. One example is a person who has no business experience and plans to start a business instead of finding employment. To successfully open a business you must have a business plan and start-up capital, but only about half of all new businesses survive after four years. While your long term goal may be to start a business, a job may be a more realistic immediate post-release objective.

☛ Have the Right Paperwork

It is also important to remember that companies are required to verify your citizenship before they can hire you. The Immigration and Naturalization Service requires employers to complete a Proof of Identity form for new hires to prove they are eligible to work in the United States. Documents that are considered acceptable forms of identity include your passport, social security card, birth certificate, and driver's license. After you leave prison is not the time to discover that you do not have a copy of your social security card and birth certificate.

☛ Make an Employment Folder

Many employers require that you provide information about the training, skills, and experience that they are looking for. An employment folder that contains your personal information and documents is a good way to do this. The employment folder should include copies of your resume, social security card, birth certificate, high school diploma or General Educational Development certificate, vocational certificates or college diplomas, and a transcript from each school you have attended (include prison schools). Remember to bring extra copies for use during interviews, and to keep the originals with you in your folder.

☛ Prepare a Resume

If you do not have a resume, prepare one using the resources in this book and online. When you are 60 days or so from release, you should mail resumes and cover letters to employers whose addresses you obtain from the telephone book yellow pages or other sources. You should request an application form in your letter. Plan to follow up with these same employers by telephone or in person and request an interview when you are released. If you do not have access to the yellow pages, you may want to ask a friend, relative, or even your parole officer to send you 10–20 addresses from the yellow pages.

☛ **Stay Hopeful**

Remember that employers are looking for people who know what they want to do, who have skills, and who want a career with their company. Keep in mind that a significant number of ex-offenders have been employed in construction, retail, accommodation, food service, transportation and warehousing jobs. Don't forget to consider employers who hire staff for hotels, colleges, hospitals, and apartment building owners/managers.

If you have access to the internet, it is a good source for local and national employment information. To explore your career options, visit *www.careervoyages.gov*.

Job training programs

One way to improve your chances of getting a good job is to participate in a job training program. You will learn valuable skills, have something to add to your resume, and may even find a mentor or reference.

☛ **Employment and Training Administration**

The Department of Labor's Employment and Training Administration (ETA) funds adult training programs that teach job skills and provide job placement services for adults who are at least 18 years of age. The programs are administered locally by One Stop Career Centers. The types of training offered by a local training center can vary depending on the job opportunities in the community. To help locate training programs in your area, search for a One Stop Center in your state at America's Service Locator (*www.servicelocator.org*) or call ETA's Toll-Free Help Line at 1-877-872-5627 (TTY: 1-877-889-5267). You can also visit ETA online at *www.doleta.gov.*

☛ **Senior Community Service Employment Program**

The Senior Community Service Employment Program (SCSEP) is a part-time employment program for low-income persons age 55 or over. Program participants work at community and government agencies and are paid the federal or state minimum wage, whichever is higher. They may also receive training, and can use their participation as a bridge to other employment positions which are not supported with federal funds. The program is administered by the Department of Labor's Employment and Training Administration (ETA); learn more at *www.doleta.gov/SENIORS/*.

☛ **Apprenticeship**
Apprenticeship is a combination of on-the-job training and related instruction in which workers learn the practical and theoretical aspects of a highly skilled occupation. Apprenticeship programs can be sponsored by individual employers, joint employer and labor groups, and/or employer associations. The Department of Labor's role is to safeguard the welfare of apprentices, ensure equality of access to apprenticeship programs, and provide integrated employment and training information to sponsors and the local employment and training community. Information about apprenticeship programs can be obtained from One-Stop Career Centers listed in the blue pages of your telephone book, from union locals listed in the white pages of the telephone book, or from the following internet site: *www.doleta.gov/atels_bat*.

Look into release gratuities for federal prisoners

The Release Gratuities, Transportation, and Clothing program is offered primarily to sentenced federal prisoners who are being released. Additionally, the court may direct the United States Marshals Service (USMS) to afford similar gratuities to pretrial detainees housed in Bureau of Prisons (BOP) facilities who are arrested, but not indicted, indicted but not convicted, or who are released to probation. Although the BOP will ordinarily afford pretrial detainees with adequate clothing upon release, monetary release gratuities paid to pretrial detainees are the exclusive responsibility of the USMS. Designated federal inmates released from BOP institutions will be provided clothing, transportation to their release destinations, and appropriate funds (up to $500) based upon an inmate's release needs and budgetary and statutory limitations.

Release gratuities are intended to be a means to supplement inmates' "other" resources upon release from prison, and to help them readjust back into the community. They are not intended to provide for an inmate's entire release needs. Therefore, inmates should be encouraged to save funds for release (such as industrial and performance pay and outside receipts) in their respective trust fund accounts or independent savings accounts. To request a release gratuity, inmates should meet with their Unit Team.

For further information, please review Program Statement 5873.06, Release Gratuities, Transportation, and Clothing: *www.bop.gov/policy/progstat/5873_006.pdf*. Some concerns relating to a release gratuity fall specifically within the BOP's Administrative Remedy Program, Title 28 C.F.R. § 542. For information on this, go to *www.bop.gov/DataSource/execute/dsPolicyLoc* and select P.S. 1330.16 from the 1000 Series. Inmates are encouraged to raise any release gratuity concerns throughout the release process.

Job search tips

Dealing with potential employers is never an easy task for people with criminal records. Ex-offenders who lie on a job application may get hired, but then fired if their record becomes known. Those who are honest may feel like they never even get a chance. Although there are no magic formulas for dealing with this sensitive situation, the following hints may be helpful. See your release preparation coordinator for more information.

Make a "To Do List" every day and outline daily activities to look for a job.

- ✓ Apply for jobs early in the day. This will make a good impression and give you time to complete applications, have interviews, take tests, etc.
- ✓ Call employers to find out the best times to apply. Some companies take applications only on certain days and times during the week.
- ✓ Write down all employers you contact, the date of your contacts, people you talk to, and special notes about your contacts.
- ✓ Apply at several companies in the same area when possible. This saves time and money.
- ✓ Be prepared. Have a "master application" and resumes, pens, maps and job information with you all the time. Who knows when a "hot lead" will come your way.
- ✓ Follow up leads immediately. If you find out about a job late in the day, call right then! Don't wait until the next day.

Check Points

- ✓ Look for job openings with employers who need your job skills.
- ✓ Networking. Tell everyone you know you're looking for a job. Ask about openings where your friends work.
- ✓ State Employment Service Offices provide help to find jobs and other services, such as career counseling. Look for one near you by searching at *www.servicelocator.org.*
- ✓ Local public libraries have books on occupations and sometime post local job announcements.
- ✓ Community colleges and trade schools sometimes offer counseling and job information to students and the general public. Locate on near you by visiting *www.utexas.edu/world/univ* and clicking one of the community college links.
- ✓ Faith-based organizations sometimes offer employment services or provide job search help.
- ✓ Government sponsored training programs offer direct placement or short-term training and placement for qualified applicants. Check the yellow pages under Job Training Programs or Government Services. You can also do a search for different programs at *www.careeronestop.org* and click on "Education and Training."
- ✓ Journals and newsletters for professionals or trade associations often advertise job openings in their fields. Ask for these at the public library. You can also browse the Career Finder at *www.startingout.com*; each career profile includes links to professional associations.

Be Aware of Other Resources for Ex-Offenders

Federal programs are generally designed to help people who need work, housing, public assistance, and other services. While each program has different standards for participation with low income being the most common requirement, there are no federal programs exclusively for ex-offenders.

Most assistance programs are administered locally by community agencies. You can find the addresses for them in the local telephone book's blue pages and on the internet. One of the first stops you should make is to the state employment service office to help you with job leads. Their local addresses are located in the blue pages of the telephone book or at *www.servicelocator.org*. You may want to ask the state employment service about job search assistance, federal bonding, employer tax incentives, job training, and Workforce Investment Act-sponsored training, as well.

If you are a non-federal offender in a state or local correctional institution, you should ask education services staff for information about community, state, and private programs to help ex-offenders as well as local faith-based organizations. Assistance may also be available from local faith-based organizations.

Your local library may offer public access to the internet and provide employment information specific to your community. If there is a One-Stop Career Center in your area (find out at *www.servicelocator.org*), be sure to visit it for job leads, training, and other services that can help you and your family. Always explain your situation when you visit any assistance services agencies and, if they cannot be of assistance, do not forget to ask for a referral to another agency or private organization that may be able to help you.

Veterans should contact their local veterans affairs office for assistance. The VA has a wide range of programs that can be helpful, including rehabilitation services. The Internet website for the VA is *www.va.gov*, or you can contact their national toll free number at 800-827-1000. Local VA offices are also listed in the government pages of the telephone book. Note: Only veterans with honorable or general discharges are eligible to receive services.

A Real-Life Example

Our Place newsletter: Finding Our Place Spring 2005, excerpt from interview
(www.ourplacedc.org/pages/pubs.html)

TPW: Through all of this you were able to hang in there. When you first came home you had no job, no money, nothing.

AO: The first job I had was at a mall in one of those studios that take glamour shots [they make you over and photograph you]. I was the oldest person there and I was only 23-years-old. And guess what they were paying me? Seven dollars an hour [laughing]!

Do you know the lady actually had the nerve to fire me from that b.s. job [laughing]? She said I wasn't moving fast enough [we're both laughing now]!

TPW: When you got fired from there what happened?

AO: You know another thing that hurt me about my mother? My mother is a manager at a temporary employment agency. It should have been no problem for me to have a job. She wouldn't give me a job. She eventually did but it took a really long time.

TPW: Why do you think that was?

AO: Maybe she still thought that I was the old me. But Tracy, she saw me and talked to me when she visited me. Couldn't she tell from talking to me? I don't know, maybe she thought I was just running game [fooling] on her.

TPW: Sometimes it's just scary to take a chance on a person.

AO: How could she give all the strangers a chance and not give me a chance? Any one of those people she hired could have messed up on the job. She took a risk everyday with them but wouldn't give me a chance. I was like, 'Come on help me out here. Be here for me.' She eventually did, but I had to go through a lot first.

TPW: In spite of her not being there for you, you didn't give up. What kept you holding on?

AO: God. I was in the hole [segregation] and I was reading a pamphlet that was inside the Bible [that's all there was to read]. The pamphlet had a prayer in it that said something about, 'Please forgive who and what I have been.' I've done so many things to people. I loved money, but the way I was getting it [selling drugs] kept me out in the street all day and most of the night. A time came when women were just as important to me as money, so I figured out a way to get the money faster and easier so I would have time to be with the women. I started robbing people.

TPW: But something changed.

AO: I got into the church. I really started listening to the message. I got serious and it seemed like God was trying to tell me something. It was like He put me in a situation because I was living such a destructive life—so he could get my attention. I have a purpose and the way I was going I was going to mess it all up. I finally realized that I don't want to live like that anymore. There's so much I want out of life that my old lifestyle would prevent me from getting. Yeah, I was getting money but there was just too much other stuff that came with the way I was getting it. I just made up my mind that I can be successful in a legitimate way.

TPW: You got fired from the one job. How did you end up working for Metro?

AO: Before I started at Metro my mother placed me on a job because she got in a bind. She needed to fill a position in the dietary department of a hospital at the last minute and couldn't find anyone else so she called me. After that came the Metro job.

TPW: Tell me about that. It's not easy to get into Metro is it?

AO: Everybody I talk to thinks that it's hard but it was no problem for me at all. A friend told me Metro was having a job fair. I went, filled out an application. I was given a date to take a test. I took the test. I got a date for an interview. I was honest with the lady – told her where I had been [in my life] and where I am trying to go. Metro doesn't have a problem hiring people who have a record.

TPW: She may have been impressed by the fact that you are so young to have been through all you've been through and to have made a decision to turn your life around. Many people can't make the decision to do something different until they've put themselves through many hard times.

AO: I took a physical and a urine test and I was given a date to start training. I guess it was just my time.

TPW: Now you have a career at Metro and you live in a nice house with a roommate. What are your plans for your future?
AO: I want to get into real estate. I want to own something that will give me some income. I want to own my own home. I just want to do the things that most people

want to do. I want to have a successful career doing something I'm happy with. Even though Metro pays very well – I never wanted to be a bus driver when I grew up. It's okay for the moment but it's just a stepping stone for me. For real, I can see myself doing something like what Our Place does because I'm passionate about helping other people who are in bad situations. I know what it's like to feel like nobody's there for you . . . just to be out there on your own trying to make it.

TPW: What would you say to other women coming home to start a new life?

AO: If you are thinking the same way when you come home, that you were thinking when you went in [to prison] you are not going to make it. It starts with changing your thought patterns. You have to make a conscious decision to want something different, that you are going to do something different. Just don't give up. No matter how rough it gets, don't give up! It takes foot work. Nothing is going to be handed to you out here. If you are looking for an easy ride you are going to be disappointed. You have to be willing to struggle, and if you've been locked up and you made it through, you already know how to struggle. Persevere.

Digging Deeper

Ex-Offender Job Search Resources

http://www.akronlibrary.org/internetresources/bg/exoff.pdf

In this document, the Akron-Summit County Public Library in Akron, Ohio has put together a wide variety of resources that would be helpful to people in all states. Find out about job search and employment books and websites, as well as educational opportunities, self-help resources, and housing and medical assistance. You can also find contact information for non-profit organizations and agencies that work with former inmates.

Ex-Offender Employment Resources

http://www.bop.gov//inmate_programs/itb_references.jsp

This webpage provides links to major federal agencies that offer employment information and assistance to ex-offenders. Explore these websites and find out about job training, employer tax credits, student aid, and more.

Ex-Offender Employment Information Handbook

http://www.bop.gov/inmate_programs/emp_info_handbk.pdf

Don't be intimidated by the size of this document! It is full of helpful information on a variety of employment-related topics. From information about employment programs to job search tips and a sample resume, you will find a lot of resources to help you fin a job. In addition, there is information about non-job-related subjects, such housing, voting rights, education, and how to get a driver's license.

National Transitional Jobs Network: Find a Transitional Jobs Program

http://www.transitionaljobs.net/FindTJ/FindaTJPrgm.html

Transitional jobs are short-term, subsidized jobs that help people gain work experience, learn technical skills, and earn a paycheck. Participants in this program also receive support and mentoring. This page can help you find a program near you with its interactive map.

The Wizard of Jobs: Ex-Felon Resources

http://www.thewizardofjobs.net/exfelons.html

Here you will find an alphabetical list of links to a variety of ex-offender resources. There are links to federal and state resources, as well as programs and non-profits. Also included are helpful articles on related topics. Browse the list, and see which resources can help you.

Chapter 23

Employers Friendly Toward Past Offenders

U.S. Department of Justice, Bureau of Prisons,
Ex-Offender Employment Resources
Our Place D.C.

Are there employers who hire ex-offenders?

Assume employers will hire you if you are a good match for their needs. One survey of more than 1200 employers report that only eight percent said they would not hire an ex-offender. Since 92 percent of employers will consider hiring you, feel free to look for work from any legitimate source. Limiting yourself to employers that you believe hire ex-offenders can also limit your wages and job prospects. You should try to find employers who are a good match for your skills, experience, and career goals.

Your job search should include **all potential employers**. According to Richard Bolles' popular employment book, *What Color Is Your Parachute*, some of the best ways to find a job are:

» *Asking for job-leads from family members, friends, and people in the community has a 33 percent success rate.*

» *Knocking on the door of any employer, factory, or office that interests you, whether they are known to have a vacancy or not, has a 47 percent success rate.*

» *Using the phone book's yellow pages to identify subjects or fields of interest to you in the town or city where you will release, and then calling up the employers listed in that field to ask if they are hiring for the type of position you can do and do well, has a 69 percent success rate.*

Remember, the two most critical factors to a successful job search are attitude and persistence. You are marketing a product, yourself, and you have to believe in the product (you) in order to land that job. Also, like any sales situation, you have to market the product (you) and make sure that you make plenty of contacts. Treat your employment search like a job and spend at least 8 hours a day at it. Employers will not usually come looking for you so you have to get out to meet them.

Special government incentive programs for employers

The federal government has a number of programs that offer incentives to employers who hire ex-offenders. Be sure to mention these to potential employers, if your record is discussed at your interview.

- **Employer tax credit programs**

  The Work Opportunity Tax Credit (WOTC), authorized by the Small Business Job Protection Act of 1996 (P.L.104-188), is a federal tax credit that encourages employers to hire targeted groups of job seekers by reducing employers' federal income tax liability by as much as $2,400 per qualified new worker or $1,200 if working 400 hours or more per qualified summer youth. Learn more about WOTC at *http://www.doleta.gov/business/incentives/opptax/*.

  The new employee must belong to a target group. The target group is defined in the law and the One Stop Career Center can assist you in determining your eligibility.

All new adult employees must work a minimum of 120 (or up to a maximum of 400) hours; summer youth must work at least 90 days between May 1 and September 15 before the employer is eligible to claim the tax credit. The tax credit for new hires employed 400 or more hours (or 180 days), is 35 percent of qualified wages for the first year of employment and 50 percent for the second year. Qualified wages are capped at $10,000 per year. Wages include tax-exempt amounts received under accident or health plans as well as educational assistance and dependent assistance programs.

To receive certification that a new employee qualifies for this tax credit, the employer must:

✓ Complete the one page IRS Form 8850 by the day the job offer is made;

✓ Complete the one page ETA Form 9061 or Form 9062:

- » *if the new employee has already been conditionally certified as belonging to a WOTC target group, complete the bottom of ETA Form 9062 (and sign and date it) that he or she has been given by a State Employment Security Agency or participating agency.*
- » *if the new employee has not been conditionally certified, the employer and/or the new employee must fill out and complete, sign and date ETA Form 9061.*
- » *Mail the signed IRS and ETA forms to the employer's State Employment Security Agency. The IRS form must be mailed within 21 days of the employee's employment start date.*

Further instructions and links to the mentioned forms can be found at *www.doleta.gov/business/incentives/opptax.*

☛ Federal bonding program

The federal bonding program is designed to help a job applicant get and keep a job. The program issues Fidelity Bonds and is sponsored by the U.S. Department of Labor. A fidelity bond is a business insurance policy that protects the employer in case of any loss of money or property due to employee dishonesty. To be eligible for the bond, the employer must schedule a date to start work. The Employment Service local office then requests The McLaughlin Company in

Washington, DC, to issue to the employer a Fidelity Bond insurance policy covering the worker.

For further information call or write to Ron Rubbin, Federal Bonding Program, 1725 DeSales Street, NW, Suite 700, Washington, DC 20036. Telephone: 1-877-872-5627, or contact your state bonding coordinator. To find your state bonding coordinators, go to *www.bonds4jobs.com* and click on "Directory of State Bonding Coordinators."

- **Unicor bonding program**

  A new program, initiated in February, 2006 provides a $5,000 fidelity bond for employed ex-federal prisoners who worked in Federal Prison Industries (UNICOR) for at least six months during incarceration. For additional information, contact the UNICOR bonding specialist at 202-305-3872 or write to *rxking@bop.gov*. You can also go to *www.unicor.gov* and click on "Inmate Transition Program," where there is information on the UNICOR bonding program as well as other useful information for former inmates.

DIGGING DEEPER

Ex-Offender Employment Resources, Bureau of Prisons, Department of Justice

http://www.bop.gov//inmate_programs/itb_references.jsp

This webpage provides links to major federal agencies that offer employment information and assistance to ex-offenders. Explore these websites and find out about job training, employer tax credits, student aid, and more.

Ex-Offender Employment Information Handbook

http://www.bop.gov/inmate_programs/emp_info_handbk.pdf

Don't be intimidated by the size of this document! It is full of helpful information on a variety of employment-related topics. From information about employment programs to job search tips and a sample resume, you will find a lot of resources to help you fin a job. In addition, there is information about non-job-related subjects, such housing, voting rights, education, and how to get a driver's license.

Hiring Ex-Offenders Can Benefit Companies

http://www.bizjournals.com/pacific/stories/2004/08/02/smallb1.html

This article talks about the benefits to employers of hiring a former inmate, such as access to tax credits and bonding programs. These examples could be useful during a job interview, as employers may not realize that hiring you offers the added bonus of federal benefits, in addition to a new employee.

The Federal Bonding Program

http://www.bonds4jobs.com/highlights.html

This website describes the details of the Federal Bonding Program, which provides bonds that guarantee the honesty of a new employee for the first six months of employment. You can seek bonding for yourself by following the instructions on the "Seeking Bonding?" page. This program is free for both employers and employees.

Chapter 24

Building a Resume and Writing an Effective Cover Letter

CareerOneStop
U.S. Department of Labor

After you have found some jobs that interest you, the next step is to apply for them. You will almost always need to complete resumes or application forms and cover letters. Later, you will probably need to go on interviews to meet with employers face to face.

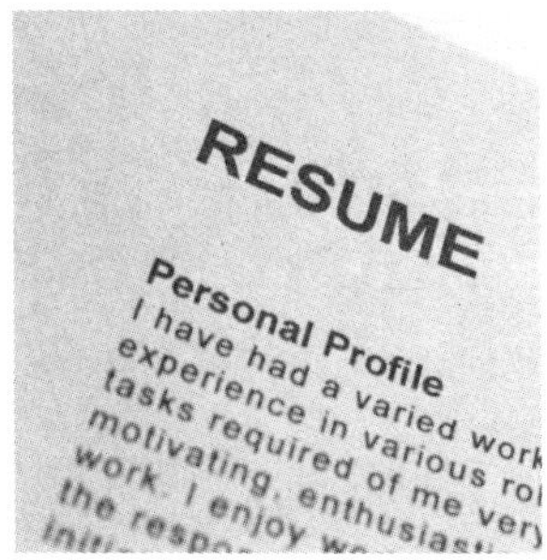

Resumes and Application Forms

Resumes and application forms give employers written evidence of your qualifications and skills. The goal of these documents is to prove—as clearly and directly as possible—how your qualifications match the job's requirements. Do this by highlighting the experience, accomplishments, education, and skills that most closely fit the job you want.

Gathering Information

Resumes and application forms both include the same information. As a first step, gather the following facts:

- **Contact Information:** Including your name, mailing address, e-mail address (if you have one you check often), and telephone number.
- **Job Sought or Career Objective:** Type of work or specific job you are seeking or a qualifications summary, which describes your best skills and experience in just a few lines.

- **Education:** Including school name and its city and state, months and years of attendance, highest grade completed or diploma or degree awarded, and major subject or subjects studied. Also consider listing courses and awards that might be relevant to the position. Include a grade point average if you think it would help in getting the job.

- **Experience, Paid and Volunteer:** For each job, include the job title, name and location of employer, and dates of employment. Briefly describe your job duties and major accomplishments. In a resume, use phrases instead of sentences to describe your work; write, for example, "Supervised 10 children" instead of writing "I supervised 10 children."

- **Special Skills:** You might list computer skills, proficiency in foreign languages, achievements, and membership in organizations in a separate section.

- **References:** Be ready to provide references if requested. Good references could be former employers, coworkers, teachers, or anyone else who can describe your abilities and job-related traits. You will be asked to provide contact information for the people you choose.

Throughout the application or resume, focus on accomplishments that relate most closely to the job you want. You can even use the job announcement as a guide, using some of the same words and phrases to describe your work and education.

Look for concrete examples that show your skills. When describing your work experience, for instance, you might say that you increased sales by 10 percent, finished a task in half the usual time, or received three letters of appreciation from customers.

Choosing a Format

After gathering the information you want to present, the next step is to put it in the proper format. In an application form, the format is set. Just fill in the blanks. But make sure you fill it out completely and follow all instructions. Consider making a copy of the form before filling it out, in case you make a mistake and have to start over. If possible, have someone else look over the form before submitting it.

In a resume, there are many ways of organizing the information you want to include, but the most important information should usually come first. Most applicants list their past jobs in reverse chronological order, describing their most recent employment first and working backward. But some applicants use a functional format, organizing their work experience under headings that describe their major skills. They then include a brief work history that lists only job titles, employers, and dates of employment. Still other applicants choose a format that combines these two approaches in some way. Choose the style that best showcases your skills and experience.

Whatever format you choose, keep your resume short. Many experts recommend that new workers use a one-page resume. Avoid long blocks of text and italicized material. Consider using bullets to highlight duties or key accomplishments.

Before submitting your resume, make sure that it is easy to read. Are the headings clear and consistently formatted with bold or some other style of type? Is the type face large enough? Then, ask at least two people to proofread the resume for spelling and other errors, and make sure you use your computer's spell checker.

Scannable Resumes and Electronic Submissions

Keep in mind that many employers scan resumes into databases, which they then search for specific keywords or phrases. The keywords are usually nouns referring to experience, education, personal characteristics, or industry buzz words. Identify keywords by reading the job description and qualifications in the job ad; use these same words in your resume. For example, if the job description includes customer service tasks, use the words "customer service" on your resume. Scanners sometimes misread paper resumes, which could mean some of your keywords don't get into the database. So, if you know that your resume will be scanned, and you have the option, e-mail an electronic version. If you must submit a paper resume, make it scannable by using a simple font and avoiding underlines, italics, and graphics. It is also a good idea to send a traditionally formatted resume along with your scannable resume, with a note on each marking its purpose.

Keep Your Resume Up to Date

It is a good practice to keep your resume up-to-date at all times, adding relevant information as you move along your career path. For example, if you take a special course, attend a seminar, or receive a new certification, be sure to add these important facts to your resume. Naturally, keep track of the dates you work for each employer, and the duties you performed. Also, update your list of references of people who know you best.

Writing an Effective Cover Letter

Chances are, if you have developed a resume that fits your needs, you are ready to prepare an effective cover letter. Here, the rules are very simple:

- ✓ Prepare a short, typed business format letter
- ✓ Explain what you are applying for
- ✓ Show interest and some knowledge of the employer
- ✓ Indicate that your resume is attached
- ✓ Spell-check your final letter

We have included a sample cover letter after the sample resumes, as a general guide. Feel free to vary the style, be friendly, and ask for a response.

Sample Resumes and Cover Letter

Three sample resumes and one cover letter have been included after the "Digging Deeper" section, representing three stages of resume submission:

- right out of high school, no experience;
- right out of high school or college, limited experience; and
- after college with some part-time job experience.

Focus on the example that most closely relates to your situation. Good luck with your job search!

Digging Deeper

CareerOneStop: Resumes, Cover Letters, and Interviews

http://www.careeronestop.org/ResumesInterviews/ResumesInterviews.aspx

Offering more than just resume and cover letter writing instructions, this section of CareerOneStop also explains how to post resumes on job boards, includes resume and interview check lists, provides templates for both cover letters and resumes, and gives in-depth explanations on how to prepare for interviews.

College Board: Resume Writing 101

http://www.collegeboard.com/student/plan/high-school/36957.html

Offering solid advice on resume writing, especially for college graduates, this site identifies how to get started, what should be included, and how it should be presented. Organization, writing style, and choice of words are useful covered topics, along with a group of websites that offer additional resume preparation assistance.

How to Write a Cover Letter

http://www.ccs.neu.edu/co-op/Manual/Coverletters.html

This website, which comes from Northeastern University, offers advice on structuring and writing an effective cover letter. It is often necessary to tailor cover letters to each individual company or opportunity, because you will want to stress different information depending upon the nature of the employer, position opening, and skills required. Try to show the end product to a friend or advisor to ensure that your letter is effective.

I. Resume - High School Graduate - No Work Experience

Your First Name, Initial, Last Name
Street Address
City, State Zip Code
Home Telephone
Cell Phone Number
E-Mail (if any)

Job or Career Objective

I am applying for the warehouse inventory control position, or any similar opportunity in warehousing and distribution.

Education

Name of High School, City, State, 2002–2006

Part-Time Experience

Sunoco Gas Station, After School, September 2004–June 2006
Pumped gas, cleaned windshields, washed cars

School Activities and Achievements

Co-captain of soccer team, Most Improved Player
Best Shop Project, 2006

Volunteer Experience

Big Brother/Big Sisters
Assistant coach, Little League

Interests and Activities

Building and flying model gas engine airplanes

Computer Skills

Microsoft Word

II. Resume - High School or College Graduate - Limited Experience

Your First Name, Initial, Last Name
Street Address
City, State Zip Code
Home Telephone
Cell Phone Number
E-Mail (if any)

Job or Career Objective

I am applying for the automobile mechanic position.

Education

Name of High School, City, State, 2002–2006
County Community College, Automotive Engine Certificate Program, 2005–2006

Experience

Sunoco Gas Station, after school, September 2001–June 2005
Pumped gas, cleaned windshields, washed cars

Foreign Car Dealership, Junior Mechanic, Part-Time, July 2005–June 2006
Foreign Car Dealership, Junior Mechanic, Full-Time, June 2006 to present

Leadership Experience

Co-captain of soccer team, Most Improved Player
Best Shop Project, 2006

Volunteer Experience

Big Brother/Big Sisters
Assistant coach, Little League

Interests & Activities

Building and flying model gas engine airplanes

Computer Skills
Microsoft Word

III. Resume - College Grad - Limited Job Experience

Judith T. Jones

Current Address:	Permanent Address:
125 Davis Hall	125 Apple Road
Cornell University	Cambridge, MA 02138
Ithaca, NY 14853	Home Phone
Cell Phone	
E-Mail: jt123@cu.edu	

OBJECTIVE: Quality control position in manufacturing

EDUCATION: B.S. Mechanical Engineering. Expected graduation, May 2007

Cornell University

GPA: 3.3/4.0

Earning and financing 50% of college education and expenses

Partial scholarship

COMPUTER SKILLS:

Software:		Languages	
AutoCAD	MiniTab	Fortran	PowerC
TK Solve Mathematica		Visual Basic	C++

EXPERIENCE: Camp Counselor, Camp Wavus, Nobleboro, ME, 2004, 2005
Acoustics Lab Assistant, MIT, Summer 2006
-Tested new equipment
-Learned about acoustical materials for concert halls
-Took field measurements in three concert halls
-Used new software to evaluate acoustical characteristics

ACTIVITIES: Student Engineers Council, VP, 2005–2006
College Marching Band, 2005–2007
Co-Captain, girls' high school soccer team, 2003

AVAILABILITY: September 2007, following summer trip to South America with Habitat for Humanity

IV. Sample Cover Letter

Judith T. Jones
125 Apple Road
Cambridge, MA 02138
Cell Phone Number
EMail Address

March 17, 2007

Mr. Robert R. Williams
Personnel Director
High-Speed Manufacturing Company
10 Mile Street
Quincy, MA 02169

Dear Mr. Williams:

I read about your quality control department opening in the Boston Globe during Spring Break a few days ago, and would like to apply for this position. I will be available by June 1, 2007.

In May I expect to receive my B.S.M.E. degree from Cornell University, and I have taken several courses in manufacturing, plant operations, and quality control. Last summer I had a great job at the Acoustics Lab at MIT testing new equipment, taking acoustical measurements, and using the latest evaluation software.

I am especially interested in working in a manufacturing environment dealing with high-technology products. I understand that your company produces various types of sensors.

Please feel free to contact me with questions on my cell phone or by e-mail. I can also return to Quincy for an interview at any time. Enclosed is my resume.

Thank you very much for your consideration.

Sincerely,

Judith T. Jones

Chapter 25

The Job Interview

Adapted from the *Harvard University Job Manual*
Harvard University

Introduction

Throughout your career you will be interviewed by some people who are skilled interviewers and by others who are not. There is no one "right" way to interview, and no matter what the format, it is your responsibility to do the best you can in each situation.

Being well prepared will increase your self-confidence, which in turn will improve your performance in the interview. Below are the steps worth taking to produce the best interview result.

Step 1: Preparing for the Interview

It is difficult to overemphasize the importance of being well prepared for a job interview. Your degree of preparation speaks volumes about your interest level and the way you will work at assigned responsibilities. In addition to increasing your confidence, solid preparation will provide you with the foundation that will allow you to give articulate answers and ask pertinent questions.

To make the best case for your candidacy for a particular job, you need to be prepared with information about yourself AND about the job, organization, and field. It is virtually impossible to make a case for a match if you are informed about only one side of the equation.

Step 2: Researching Yourself: Developing the Story You Want to Tell

Begin to think about yourself as a job candidate by asking yourself a series of questions:

- ✓ What are my skills and strengths?
- ✓ What are my accomplishments?
- ✓ What motivates me to do my best work?
- ✓ In which environments do I thrive?
- ✓ What are my values?
- ✓ What are the most important things an employer needs to know about me?

Remember: Most likely, interviewers will begin by asking questions directly from your resume.

Step 3: Researching the Employer: The Other Side of the Equation

Complete your preparation by finding out as much as you can about the specific employer, so that you can both talk knowledgably about where your qualifications intersect with the employer's needs and convey genuine enthusiasm about the opportunity at hand. You need to be able to explain why you want to do this job and why you have chosen this employer, rather than the others in the field. A good interviewer will quickly find out that you know little or nothing about the organization when you can't explain why exactly you want to work there. An interview is also your opportunity to become a person, not just a piece of paper—make the most of it.

Step 4: Putting It All Together

Once you have researched yourself and the specific organization and position for which you are interviewing, you arc ready to think about the most effective way to describe your experiences and assets in language that the employer will recognize, using the vocabulary of the field.

Look closely at the specific job requirements of the position as described in the ad, job description, information session, or informational interview. Use these requirements to create an outline of speaking points for your interview. Match your experiences to these points with concrete examples that illustrate your candidacy. When discussing your skills, try whenever possible to use the same language as the organization uses.

Step 5: Practice, Practice, Practice

Look for opportunities to practice your interviewing skills: role play with roommates, friends, tutors, family—even in front of a mirror. The more experience you have with verbalizing your thoughts, the more effective and polished your presentation will be.

Digging Deeper

Bureau of Labor Statistics: Job Interview Tips

http://www.bls.gov/oco/oco20045.htm

This U.S. Department of Labor site offers practical information on all aspects of the job interview process: preparation, personal appearance, interview guidelines, and important information to bring to the interview. These tips are part of an extensive website covering all aspects of employment and training.

CollegeGrad.com: Interviewing Information

http://www.collegegrad.com/intv/

Highlighted by an online video practice tool, this useful commercial website, which concentrates on job opportunities for college graduates, offers detailed information on such topics as mastering competitive interviews, dressing for success, practice questions you need to answer, possible questions you may ask of the interviewer, interview locations, and interview follow-up suggestions.

Part VI

Employment and the Workplace

Chapter 26

Employment Rights and Responsibilities

U.S. Equal Employment Opportunity Commission

Your Rights

You may be familiar with the word "discrimination," but do you know what it really means? And do you understand how it applies in the context of your job?

To "discriminate" against someone means to treat that person differently, or less favorably, for some reason. Discrimination can occur while you are at school, at work, or in a public place, such as a mall or subway station. You can be discriminated against by school friends, teachers, coaches, co-workers, managers, or business owners.

The Equal Employment Opportunity Commission (EEOC) is responsible for protecting you against one type of discrimination—employment discrimination because of your race, color, religion, sex (including pregnancy), national origin, disability, or age (age 40 or older). Other laws may protect you from other types of discrimination, such as discrimination at school or discrimination at work because of your sexual orientation.

The laws enforced by EEOC protect you against employment discrimination when it involves:

- ✓ Unfair treatment because of your race, color, religion, sex (including pregnancy), national origin, disability, or age (age 40 or older).
- ✓ Harassment by managers, co-workers, or others in your workplace, because of your race, color, religion, sex (including pregnancy), national origin, disability, or age (age 40 or older).
- ✓ Denial of a reasonable workplace change that you need because of your religious beliefs or disability.
- ✓ Retaliation because you complained about job discrimination or assisted with a job discrimination investigation or lawsuit.

Medical Privacy

You have a right to keep any medical information you share with your employer private. Your employer should not discuss your medical information with others, unless they have a need to know the information. The laws enforced by EEOC also strictly limit what an employer can ask you about your health.

Your Responsibilities

- ☛ **Don't Discriminate:**

  You should not treat your co-workers unfairly or harass them because of their race, skin color, national origin, sex (including pregnancy), religion, disability, or age (age 40 or older). For example, you should not tell sexual or racial jokes at work or tease people because they are different from you.

- ☛ **Report Discrimination:**

  You should tell your company about any unfair treatment or harassment. Find out if your company has a policy on discrimination that specifies who you should contact about these issues.

- **Request Workplace Changes:**

  You have a responsibility to tell your company if you need a workplace change because of your religious beliefs or medical condition. Your request does not have to be in writing, but you must provide enough information so your company can determine how to help you.

Digging Deeper

U.S. Equal Employment Opportunity Commission

http://www.eeoc.gov/

Extensive resources on the U.S. Employment Opportunity Commission are provided at the agency's website, including laws, discriminatory practices, covered employers, and procedures for filing a complaint.

The Fair Labor Standards Act

http://www.dol.gov/compliance/laws/comp-flsa.htm

The Fair Labor Standards Act (FLSA), which prescribes standards for the basic minimum wage and overtime pay, affects most private and public employment. It requires employers to pay covered employees who are not otherwise exempt at least the federal minimum wage and overtime pay of one and one-half times the regular rate of pay. For nonagricultural operations, it restricts the hours that children under age 16 can work and forbids the employment of children under age 18 in certain jobs deemed too dangerous. For agricultural operations, it prohibits the employment of children under age 16 during school hours and in certain jobs deemed too dangerous. The act is administered by the Employment Standards Administration's Wage and Hour Division within the U.S. Department of Labor.

Occupational Safety & Health Act (OSHA)

http://www.osha.gov/

OSHA's mission is to assure the safety and health of America's workers by setting and enforcing standards; providing training, outreach, and education; establishing partnerships; and encouraging continual improvement in workplace safety and health.

Family and Medical Leave Act

http://www.dol.gov/esa/whd/fmla/

This newer legislation grants family and temporary medical leave under certain circumstances as set forth in the act. Visit this site to learn how this legislation works.

Americans With Disabilities Act (ADA)

http://www.usdoj.gov/crt/ada/adahom1.htm

Individuals with disabilities have benefited greatly from this law, which provides extensive personal benefits and requires workplace accommodations for those with physical handicaps. This site presents detailed information on the ADA.

Bureau of Labor Statistics

http://www.bls.gov/

Within the U.S. Department of Labor, this agency collects and publishes extensive information on employment in the United States. The website offers information on inflation and consumer spending; wages, earnings, and benefits; productivity; safety and health; occupations; demographics; and unemployment.

Chapter 27

Questions and Answers About the Minimum Wage

Wage and Hour Division
U.S. Department of Labor

Minimum wage laws in the United States are complicated and have many exceptions and variations, as explained below. To make things more confusing, there is a federal minimum wage, yet each state sets its own minimum wage level, which may be the same, higher or even lower. In general, where federal and state law have different minimum wage rates, the higher standard normally applies. This section deals principally with the federal minimum wage, but information for each state is included in the "Digging Deeper" section.

What is the federal minimum wage?

Under the Fair Labor Standards Act (FLSA), the federal minimum wage for covered nonexempt employees is $6.55 per hour effective July 24, 2008 and $7.25 per hour effective July 24, 2009. Many states also have minimum wage laws. Where an employee is subject to both the state and federal minimum wage laws, the employee is entitled to the higher minimum wage rate.

Various minimum wage exceptions apply under specific circumstances to workers with disabilities, full-time students, youth under age 20 in their first 90 consecutive calendar days of employment, tipped employees, and student-learners.

What is the minimum wage for workers who receive tips?

An employer may pay a tipped employee not less than $2.13 an hour in direct wages if that amount plus the tips received equal at least the federal minimum wage, the employee retains all tips, and the employee customarily and regularly receives more than $30 a month in tips. If an employee's tips combined with the employer's direct wages of at least $2.13 an hour do not equal the federal minimum hourly wage, the employer must make up the difference.

Some states have minimum wage laws specific to tipped employees. When an employee is subject to both the federal and state wage laws, the employee is entitled to the provisions of each law which provide the greater benefits.

Must young workers be paid the minimum wage?

A minimum wage of $4.25 per hour applies to young workers under the age of 20 during their first 90 consecutive calendar days of employment with an employer, as long as their work does not displace other workers. After 90 consecutive days of employment or the employee reaches 20 years of age, whichever comes first, the employee must receive a minimum wage of $6.55 per hour effective July 24, 2008 and $7.25 per hour effective July 24, 2009.

Other programs that allow for payment of less than the full federal minimum wage apply to workers with disabilities, full-time students, and student-learners employed pursuant to sub-minimum wage certificates. These programs are not limited to the employment of young workers.

What minimum wage exceptions apply to full-time students?

The Full-time Student Program is for full-time students employed in retail or service stores, agriculture, or colleges and universities. The employer that hires students can obtain a certificate from the Department of Labor which allows the student to be paid not less than 85% of the minimum wage. The certificate also limits the hours that the student may work to 8 hours in a day and no more than 20 hours a week when school is in session and 40 hours when school is out, and requires the employer to follow all child labor laws. Once students graduate or leave school for good, they must be paid $6.55 per hour effective July 24, 2008 and $7.25 per hour effective July 24, 2009. There are some limitations on the use of the full-time student program. For information on the limitations or to obtain a certificate, contact the Department of Labor Wage and Hour Southwest Region Office at 525 S. Griffin Square, Suite 800, Dallas, TX, 75202, telephone: 972–850–2603.

What minimum wage exceptions apply to student learners?

This program is for high school students at least 16 years old who are enrolled in vocational education (shop courses). The employer that hires the student can obtain a certificate from the Department of Labor which allows the student to be paid not less than 75 percent of the minimum wage for as long as the student is enrolled in the vocational education program.

Digging Deeper

Federal Minimum Wage Laws

http://www.dol.gov/esa/whd/flsa/

This website within the U.S. Department of Labor provides up-to-date information on the federal minimum wage and its applicability to workers. For those workers who are not covered by federal minimum wage laws, there are individual state laws. The minimum wage changes from time to time and is set by Congress.

State Minimum Wage Laws

http://www.dol.gov/esa/minwage/america.htm

Each state establishes and enforces its own minimum wage laws. This website offers a map of the United States for access to the program coverage in each individual state.

Chapter 28

All About Social Security

Understand The Benefits
Social Security Administration

Social Security: A Simple Concept

Social Security reaches almost every family, and at some point will touch the lives of nearly all Americans.

Social Security helps not only older Americans, but also workers who become disabled and families in which a spouse or parent dies. Today, more than 163 million people work and pay Social Security taxes and more than 49 million people receive monthly Social Security benefits.

Most of our beneficiaries are retirees and their families—about 34 million people.

But Social Security was never meant to be the only source of income for people when they retire. Social Security replaces about 40 percent of an average wage earner's income after retiring, and most financial advisors say retirees will need about 70–80 percent of their work income to live comfortably in retirement. To have a comfortable retirement, Americans need much more than just Social Security. They also need private pensions, savings, and investments.

The Social Security Administration wants you to understand what Social Security can mean to you and your family's financial future. This brief article explains the basics of the Social Security retirement, disability, and survivors insurance programs.

How Social Security Works

The current Social Security system works like this: when you work, you pay taxes into Social Security. The tax money is used to pay benefits to:

- People who already have retired;
- People who are disabled;
- Survivors of workers who have died; and
- Dependents of beneficiaries.

The money you pay in taxes is not held in a personal account for you to use when you get benefits. Your taxes are being used right now to pay people who now are getting benefits. Any unused money goes to the Social Security trust funds, not a personal account with your name on it.

The Future of Social Security

Social Security is a compact between generations. For more than 70 years, America has kept the promise of security for its workers and their families. But now, the Social Security system is facing financial problems, and action is needed to make sure that the system is sound when today's younger workers are ready for retirement.

Here is why the level of benefits that Social Security will be able to pay in the future is uncertain. Today there are about 38 million Americans age 65 or older. Their Social Security retirement benefits are funded by today's workers and their employers, who jointly pay Social Security taxes—just as the money they paid into Social Security was used to pay benefits to those who retired before them. Unless action is taken to strengthen Social Security, in just 10 years we will begin paying more in benefits than we collect in taxes. Without changes, by 2041 the Social Security trust funds will be exhausted. By then, the number of Americans 65 or older is expected to have doubled. There will not be enough younger people working to pay all of the benefits scheduled for those who are retiring. At that point, there will be enough money to pay only about 74 cents for each dollar of benefits that retirees are scheduled to receive. We will need to resolve these issues to make sure Social Security will provide a foundation of protection for future generations as it has done in the past.

Your Social Security Taxes

The Social Security taxes you and other workers pay into the system are used to pay for Social Security benefits.

You pay Social Security taxes on your earnings up to a certain amount. That amount increases each year to keep pace with wages. In 2008, that amount was $102,000.

Medicare Taxes

You pay Medicare taxes on all of your wages or net earnings from self-employment. These taxes are used for Medicare coverage.

Your Social Security Number

Your link with Social Security is your Social Security number. You will need it to get a job and to pay taxes. We use your Social Security number to track your earnings while you are working and to track your benefits after you are getting Social Security.

Do not carry your Social Security card unless you need to show it to your employer. You should be careful about giving someone your Social Security number. Identity theft is one of the fastest growing crimes today. Most of the time identity thieves use your Social Security number and your good credit to apply for more credit in your name. Then they use the credit cards to buy things for themselves, and they do not pay the bills.

Your Social Security number and our records are confidential. If someone else asks us for information we have about you, we will not give any information without your written consent, unless the law requires or permits it.

Getting a Social Security Card

To get a Social Security number or a replacement card, visit www.ssa.gov. You must prove your U.S. citizenship or immigration status, age, and identity. For a replacement card, proof of your U.S. citizenship and age are not required if they are already listed in the system.

Only certain documents can be accepted as proof of U.S. citizenship. These include your U.S. birth certificate, U.S. passport, U.S. consular report of birth, Certificate of Naturalization, or Certificate of Citizenship. If you are not a U.S. citizen, different rules apply for proving your immigration status. Acceptable proofs of identity would include current documents showing your name, identifying information, and, preferably, a recent photograph, such as a driver's license, a state-issued non-driver identification card, or a U.S. passport.

Digging Deeper

Social Security Administration

http://www.ssa.gov

The Social Security Administration provides an extensive website with detailed information on all aspects of Social Security, including your Social Security record of earnings, retirement information and dates, Medicare, Medicaid, Supplemental Security Income (SSI), and survivor benefits. Social Security benefits are underwritten by contributions from both the employer and employee who pay into a trust fund for coverage of future applicants.

Public Agenda: The Future of Social Security

http://www.publicagenda.org/citizen/issueguides/social-security

There is an active national debate on the future of Social Security because the trust fund is not growing fast enough to ensure benefits for future generations. This public interest website explores these issues, along with various approaches to revitalize Social Security.

Chapter 29

Understanding Your Paycheck Deductions

Internal Revenue Service
Starting Out!® Research Group

Where Did All the Money Go?

You have just started a new job and have been handed your first pay check. You are shocked! Where did all the money go? Why has so much been deducted from your check? The "bad news" is standard payroll deductions: state and federal income taxes, Social Security, unemployment insurance, and other items, as described in this section. The "good news" is that all of these deductions have an important purpose for you and your future. Read on.

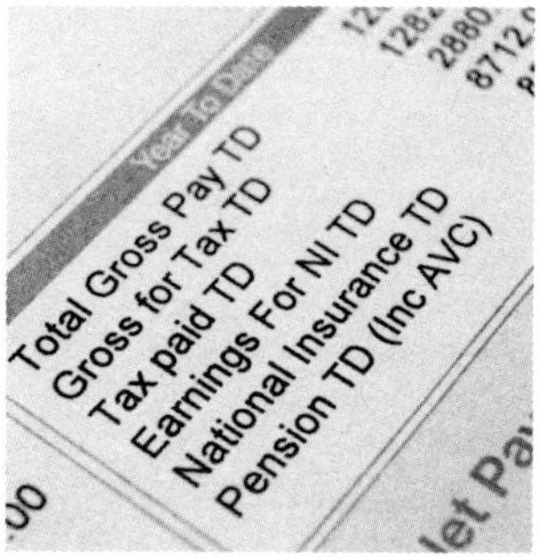

Gross Income

Gross wages or salary represents the amount of money you were hired for, whether it is an hourly rate or salaried rate.

- **Hourly Workers:**

  For typical hourly employees, your gross wages are based upon the number of hours you work multiplied by your hourly rate. For example, if your hourly rate is $15.00 and you work a 35-hour week, multiply $15 x 35 to get $525.00, which is your gross weekly pay. Your gross annual wages are calculated by multiplying this number by the number of weeks you work in a year, such as 52, which would be $27,300. Keep in mind that some people work different numbers of hours per week and may work fewer than 52 weeks a year. Some employees may be entitled to overtime pay if they work more than the standard number of hours each week. Hourly workers are termed "non-exempt" employees because they are not exempt from the provisions of the Fair Labor Standards Act (FLSA). Employees who fall within this category must be paid at least the federal minimum wage for each hour worked and given overtime pay of not less than one and one-half times their hourly rate for any hours worked beyond 40 each week.

- **Salaried Workers:**

  Salaried workers, called "exempt employees," are normally paid a set amount per year and are not paid for overtime. Exempt positions are excluded from minimum wage, overtime regulations, and other rights and protections afforded non-exempt workers. Employers must pay a salary rather than an hourly wage for a position for it to be exempt. Typically, only executive, supervisory, professional, or outside sales positions are exempt positions.

Net Income or "Take Home Pay"

Your gross income, less all taxes and other deductions, constitutes your net income, or "take home pay."

What are the Standard Deductions?

There are a number of standard or base deductions that everyone who claims an income must pay. These are as follows:

- Federal Income Tax—This is the tax that is charged to you based on income, and is calculated from various tables that can be viewed at the site of the Internal Revenue Service (http://www.irs.gov). The more you earn, the higher the income bracket you are in, and hence the higher the amount of tax that is withhold from your pay check.

- Social Security and Medicare (Federal Insurance Contributions Act (FICA))—FICA contributions fund Social Security retirement and health benefits under Medicare, normally after age 65, and unemployment compensation. The Social Security and Medicare deductions are adjusted by the federal government from time to time. In 2008 the social security deduction was 6.20% and the Medicare portion was 1.45%, totaling a combined FICA deduction of 7.65%. There is also an annual cap on the amount of earnings subject to these taxes. In 2008, the cap was $102,000.

- State Income Taxes—State income taxes vary considerably between states, and certain states do not impose a personal income tax. However, for those states that have an income tax, a deduction is taken based upon the rate schedule of the state.

- State Unemployment and Disability Deductions—Some states require employees to contribute to state unemployment and disability income funds.

- City, Local, and/or County Taxes—In some states there are deductions of city or local taxes, such as in New York City, but many states do not have such deductions.

Other Common Payroll Adjustments

- Health Insurance—In some workplaces, employees contribute a portion of the cost of healthcare, and then this deduction is also listed on your pay stub.

- Retirement Plan Deductions—Some employers offer retirement plans as a benefit of employment or permit deductions for employee-paid plans, such as Individual Retirement Accounts, or IRAs. Your employer will explain such plans and options to you.

- Union Dues—The dues paid to a union are usually taken out of your paycheck with each pay period.

Digging Deeper

Internal Revenue Service

http://www.irs.gov

Charged with the collection and enforcement of federal income taxes, the IRS website is filled with information about filing tax returns, obtaining forms, compliance, common questions and answers, privacy statutes, and other resources. The tab covering "Individuals" has special information on the Alternative Minimum Tax (AMT), which is designed to collect a minimum amount from individuals with many tax deductions. Taxpayer rights are also explained at this location.

U.S. Department of Labor

http://www.dol.gov/

Wages, benefits, unemployment insurance, and other topics which relate closely to taxes can be found on the homepage of the U.S. Department of Labor. Links are also available to the rich occupational resources available from this federal agency, including the *Occupational Outlook Handbook.*

Chapter 30

Unemployment and Disability Insurance: The Safety Net

U.S. Department of Labor
Social Security Administration

If you lose your job or become temporarily or permanently disabled, you are normally eligible for insurance compensation which is paid to you instead of your paycheck. These unemployment or disability benefits are made possible because of small deductions that are taken out of everybody's pay.

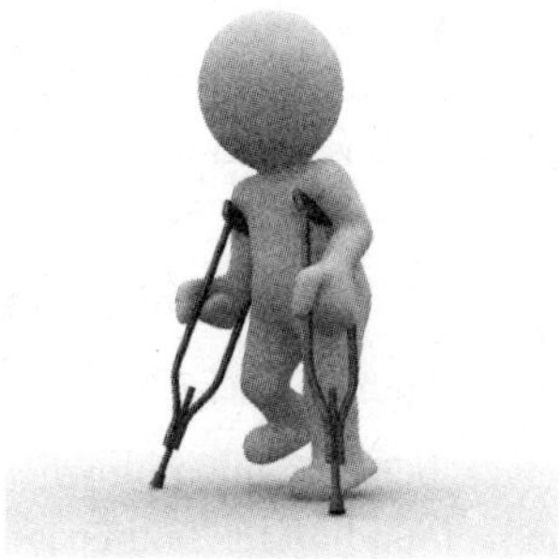

Unemployment Benefits

In general, the Federal-State Unemployment Insurance Program provides unemployment benefits to eligible workers who are unemployed through no fault of their own (as determined under state law), and meet other eligibility requirements of state law. Unemployment insurance payments (benefits) are intended to provide temporary financial assistance to unemployed workers who meet the requirements of state law.

Each state administers a separate unemployment insurance program within guidelines established by federal law. Eligibility for unemployment insurance, benefit amounts, and the length of time benefits are available are determined by the state law under which unemployment insurance claims are established.

Disability Benefits Under Social Security

Disability is a subject you may read about in the newspaper, but not think of as something that might actually happen to you. But your chances of becoming disabled are probably greater than you realize.

Studies show that a 20-year-old worker has a 30 percent chance of becoming disabled before reaching retirement age.

While we spend a great deal of time working to succeed in our jobs and careers, few of us think about ensuring that we have a safety net to fall back on should we become disabled. This is an area where Social Security can provide valuable help to you.

Digging Deeper

Department of Labor: Federal Unemployment Insurance

http://ows.doleta.gov/unemploy/

The federal government and each state government operate together to provide unemployment insurance for workers who lose their jobs. This website from the U.S. Department of Labor provides information on weekly claims in the United States, benefits, duration of benefits, and possible extensions, and state service centers.

State Unemployment Programs

http://www.servicelocator.org/OWSLinks.asp

Individual state unemployment insurance programs, including their coverage and worker eligibility, can be found by clicking on an individual state on the U.S. map provided at this website.

Social Security Disability Benefits

http://www.ssa.gov/disability/

Aside from providing retirement benefits, the Social Security System also provides disability benefits to workers and families. This website from the Social Security Administration explains these benefits, including Supplemental Security Income for low-income workers, which pays benefits on the basis of financial need.

DisabilityInfo.gov: The Federal Government Disability Website

http://www.disabilityinfo.gov

Directed at individuals with disabilities, their families, and employers, this site is a collaboration of 22 separate federal agencies, each with programs or information related to disabilities. The tabs in the red bar at the top of the site address disability information related to employment, education, housing, transportation, health, technology, and community life.

Part VII

Managing Your Mental and Physical Health

Chapter 31

Understanding Drug Abuse and Addiction

National Institute on Drug Abuse

Misunderstandings and Myths

Many people do not understand why individuals become addicted to drugs or how drugs change the brain to foster compulsive drug abuse. They mistakenly view drug abuse and addiction as strictly a social problem and may characterize those who take drugs as morally weak. One very common belief is that drug abusers should be able to just stop taking drugs if they are only willing to change their behavior. What people often underestimate is the complexity of drug addiction—that it is a disease that impacts the brain and because of that, stopping drug abuse is not simply a matter of willpower. Through scientific advances we now know much more about how exactly drugs work in the brain, and we also know that drug addiction can be successfully treated to help people stop abusing drugs and resume their productive lives.

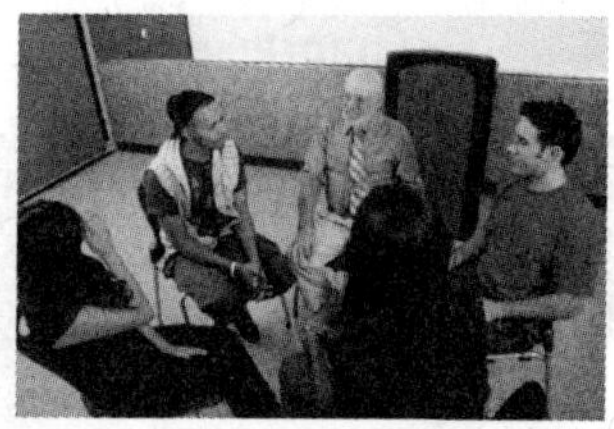

The Burden of Drug Abuse and Addiction

Drug abuse and addiction are a major burden to society. Estimates of the total overall costs of substance abuse in the United States—including health- and crime-related costs as well as losses in productivity—exceed half a trillion dollars annually. This includes approximately $181 billion for illicit drugs, $168 billion for tobacco, and $185 billion for alcohol. Staggering as these numbers are, however, they do not fully describe the breadth of deleterious public health—and safety—implications, which include family disintegration, loss of employment, failure in school, domestic violence, child abuse, and other crimes.

What Is Drug Addiction?

Addiction is a chronic, often relapsing brain disease that causes compulsive drug seeking and use despite harmful consequences to the addicted individual and to those around him or her.

Drug addiction is a brain disease because the abuse of drugs leads to changes in the structure and function of the brain. Although it is true that for most people the initial decision to take drugs is voluntary, over time the changes in the brain caused by repeated drug abuse can affect a person's self control and ability to make sound decisions, and at the same time send intense impulses to take drugs.

Counteracting Addiction's Powerful Grip

It is because of these changes in the brain that it is so challenging for a person who is addicted to stop abusing drugs. Fortunately, there are treatments that help people counteract addiction's powerful disruptive effects and regain control.

Research shows that combining addiction treatment medications, if available, with behavioral therapy is the best way to ensure success for most patients. Treatment approaches that are tailored to each patient's drug abuse patterns and any co-occurring medical, psychiatric, and social problems can lead to sustained recovery and a life without drug abuse.

Similar to other chronic, relapsing diseases, such as diabetes, asthma, or heart disease, drug addiction can be managed successfully. And, as with other chronic diseases, it is not uncommon for a person to relapse and begin abusing drugs again. Relapse, however, does not signal failure—rather, it indicates that treatment should be reinstated, adjusted, or that alternate treatment is needed to help the individual regain control and recover.

What Happens to Your Brain When You Take Drugs?

Drugs are chemicals that tap into the brain's communication system and disrupt the way nerve cells normally send, receive, and process information. There are at least two ways that drugs are able to do this: (1) by imitating the brain's natural chemical messengers, and/or (2) by overstimulating the "reward circuit" of the brain.

Nearly all drugs, directly or indirectly, target the brain's reward system by flooding the circuit with dopamine. Dopamine is a neurotransmitter present in regions of the brain that control movement, emotion, motivation, and feelings of pleasure. The overstimulation of this system produces euphoric effects in response to the drugs. This reaction sets in motion a pattern that "teaches" people to repeat the behavior of abusing drugs.

Why do Some People Become Addicted, While Others Do Not?

No single factor can predict whether or not a person will become addicted to drugs. Risk for addiction is influenced by a person's biology, social environment, and age or stage of development. The more risk factors an individual has, the greater the chance that taking drugs can lead to addiction. For example:

- **Biology.**

  The genes that people are born with—in combination with environmental influences—account for about half of their vulnerability to addiction. Additionally, gender, ethnicity, and the presence of other mental disorders may influence risk for drug abuse and addiction.

- **Environment.**

  A person's environment includes many different influences—from family and friends to socioeconomic status and quality of life in general. Factors such as peer pressure, physical and sexual abuse, stress, and parental involvement can greatly influence the course of drug abuse and addiction in a person's life.

☛ **Development.**

Genetic and environmental factors interact with critical developmental stages in a person's life to affect addiction vulnerability, and adolescents experience a double challenge. Although taking drugs at any age can lead to addiction, the earlier that drug use begins, the more likely it is to progress to more serious abuse. And because adolescents' brains are still developing in the areas that govern decision making, judgment, and self-control, they are especially prone to risk-taking behaviors, including trying drugs that can lead to abuse.

Prevention Is the Key

Drug addiction is a preventable disease. Results from research funded by the National Institute on Drug Abuse have shown that prevention programs that involve families, schools, communities, and the media are effective in reducing drug abuse. Although many events and cultural factors affect drug abuse trends, when youths perceive drug abuse as harmful, they reduce their drug taking. It is necessary, therefore, to help youth and the general public to understand the risks of drug abuse, and for teachers, parents, and healthcare professionals to keep sending the message that drug addiction can be prevented if a person never abuses drugs.

Digging Deeper

National Institute on Drug Abuse (NIDA)

http://www.drugabuse.gov/NIDAHome.html

NIDA has quick links to information geared towards students, parents and teachers, health professionals, and researchers. There is information about specific drugs and the latest news and research. You can also visit one of the other NIDA sites. For example, at teens.drugabuse.gov you'll find true stories, games to test your knowledge of drugs and their effects on your body, and answers to frequently asked questions. You can even submit your own question there, and receive an emailed response. Other NIDA topical sites include issues such as inhalants, club drugs, smoking, and steroids.

Medline Plus: Drug Abuse

http://www.nlm.nih.gov/medlineplus/drugabuse.html

Here is Medline Plus' drug abuse page, which has information on the harmful effects of a number of illegal drugs, as well as the consequences of abusing prescription drugs. Look up fact sheets on individual drugs, or read overviews, research articles, and treatment information. There are also links to drug abuse treatment facilities and programs.

Substance Abuse and Mental Health Services Administration (SAMHSA)

http://www.samhsa.gov/

The SAMHSA homepage is literally packed with information. Links to treatment centers and helplines are found near the top of the page, which also features the latest headlines. You can also browse for information by topic or view highlighted programs and campaigns. Publications include topics such as treatment programs, figuring out if you have a substance abuse problem, and National Addiction Recovery Month.

Chapter 32

Mental Illness: Fact and Fiction

National Institute of Mental Health, Substance Abuse and Mental Health Services Administration

Mental Illness in America

Mental illnesses are very common. They are also widely misunderstood. People with mental illnesses are frequently stigmatized by others who think it's an uncommon condition. The truth is, mental illness can happen to anybody.

An estimated 26.2 percent of Americans ages 18 and older—about one in four adults—suffer from a diagnosable mental disorder in a given year. When applied to the 2004 U.S. Census residential population estimate for ages 18 and older, this figure translates to 57.7 million people. Even though mental disorders are widespread in the population, the main burden of illness is concentrated in a much smaller proportion—about 6 percent, or 1 in 17—who suffer from a serious mental illness. In addition, mental disorders are the leading cause of disability in the U.S. and Canada for ages 15-44. Many people suffer from more than one mental disorder at a given time. Nearly half (45 percent) of those with any mental disorder meet criteria for 2 or more disorders.

Mental Health Myths and Facts

Arm yourself with the facts, then use your knowledge to educate others and reach out to those around you with mental illness. Understanding and support are powerful, and they can make a real difference in the life of a person who needs them.

Myth: *There's no hope for people with mental illnesses.*

Fact: There are more treatments, services, and community support systems than ever before, and more are in the works. People with mental illnesses lead active, productive lives.

Myth: *I can't do anything for a person with mental illness.*

Fact: You can do a lot, starting with how you act and speak. You can create an environment that builds on people's strengths and promotes understanding. For example:

Don't label people with words like "crazy," "wacko," or "loony" or define them by their diagnosis. Instead of saying someone is "a schizophrenic," say he or she "has schizophrenia." Don't say "a schizophrenic person;" say "a person with schizophrenia." This is called "people-first" language, and it's important to make a distinction between the person and the illness.

» Learn the facts about mental health and share them with others, especially if you hear something that isn't true.

» Treat people with mental illnesses with respect and dignity, just as you would anybody else.

» Respect the rights of people with mental illnesses and don't discriminate against them when it comes to housing, employment, or education. Like other people with disabilities, people with mental health problems are protected under federal and state laws.

Myth: *People with mental illnesses are violent and unpredictable.*

Fact: Actually, the vast majority of people with mental health conditions are no more violent than anyone else. People with mental illnesses are much more likely to be the victims of crime. You probably know someone with a mental illness and don't even realize it.

Myth: *Mental illnesses don't affect me.*

Fact: Mental illnesses are surprisingly common; they affect almost every family in America. Mental illnesses do not discriminate—they can affect anyone.

Myth: *Mental illness is the same as mental retardation.*

Fact: These are different conditions. Mental retardation is characterized by limitations in intellectual functioning and difficulties with certain daily living skills. In contrast, people with mental illnesses—health conditions that cause changes in a person's thinking, mood, and behavior—have varied intellectual functioning, just like the general population.

Myth: *Mental illnesses are brought on by a weakness of character.*

Fact: Mental illnesses are a product of the interaction of biological, psychological, and social factors. Social influences, like the loss of a loved one or a job, can also contribute to the development of various mental health problems.

Myth: *People with mental illnesses cannot tolerate the stress of holding down a job.*

Fact: All jobs are stressful to some extent. Anybody is more productive when there's a good match between the employee's needs and the working conditions, whether or not the worker has a mental health problem.

Myth: *People with mental health needs, even those who have recovered, tend to be second-rate workers.*

Fact: Employers who have hired people with mental illnesses report good attendance and punctuality as well as motivation, good work, and job tenure on par with or greater than other employees. Studies by the National Institute of Mental Health (NIMH) and the National Alliance for the Mentally Ill (NAMI) show that there are no differences in productivity when people with mental illnesses are compared to other employees.

Myth: *Once people develop mental illnesses, they will never recover.*

Fact: Studies show that most people with mental illnesses get better, and many recover completely. Recovery refers to the process in which people are able to live, work, learn, and participate fully in their communities. For some individuals, recovery is the ability to live a fulfilling and productive life. For others, recovery implies the reduction or complete remission of symptoms. Science has shown that hope plays an integral role in an individual's recovery.

Myth: *Therapy and self-help are a waste of time. Why bother when you can just take a pill?*

Fact: Treatment varies depending on the individual. A lot of people work with therapists, counselors, friends, psychologists, psychiatrists, nurses, and social workers during the recovery process. They also use self-help strategies and community supports. Often they combine these with some of the most advanced medications available.

Myth: *Children don't experience mental illnesses. Their actions are just products of bad parenting.*

Fact: A report from the President's New Freedom Commission on Mental Health showed that in any given year five to nine percent of children experience serious emotional disturbances. Just like adult mental illnesses, these are clinically diagnosable health conditions that are a product of the interaction of biological, psychological, and social factors.

Myth: *Children misbehave or fail in school just to get attention*

Fact: Behavior problems can be symptoms of emotional, behavioral, or mental problems, rather than merely attention-seeking devices. These children can succeed in school with appropriate understanding, attention, and mental health services.

What is Depression?

Depression is a serious medical illness; it's not something that you have made up in your head. It's more than just feeling "down in the dumps" or "blue" for a few days. It is feeling "down" and "low" and "hopeless" for weeks at a time.

☛ Signs and Symptoms of Depression

- *Persistent sad, anxious, or "empty" mood*
- *Feelings of hopelessness, pessimism*
- *Feelings of guilt, worthlessness, helplessness*
- *Loss of interest or pleasure in hobbies and activities that were once enjoyed*

Treatment

A variety of treatments including medications and short-term psychotherapies have proven effective for depression. You can learn about these treatments from your healthcare provider or clinic.

Other Common Mental Health Conditions

There are dozens of different mental health conditions that affect people, and there is help at hand for all of them. Other common mental health conditions include anxiety disorders, attention-deficit disorder, Alzheimer's disease, autism, bipolar disorder, disruptive behavior, domestic violence, eating disorders, obsessive-compulsive disorder, panic disorder, phobias (fears), self-harm disorders, and stress.

Getting Help: How to Locate Services in Your Community

If unsure where to go for help, talk to someone you trust who has experience in mental health—for example, a doctor, nurse, social worker, or religious counselor. Ask their advice on where to seek treatment. If there is a university nearby, its departments of psychiatry or psychology may offer private and/or sliding-scale fee clinic treatment options. Otherwise, check the Yellow Pages under "mental health,"

"health," "social services," "crisis intervention services," "hotlines," "hospitals," or "physicians" for phone numbers and addresses. In times of crisis, the emergency room doctor at a hospital may be able to provide temporary help for a mental health problem, and will be able to tell you where and how to get further help.

Help Is Available

Listed below are the types of people and places that will make a referral to, or provide, diagnostic and treatment services.

- ✓ Family doctors
- ✓ Mental health specialists, such as psychiatrists, psychologists, social workers, or mental health counselors
- ✓ Religious leaders/counselors
- ✓ Health maintenance organizations
- ✓ Community mental health centers
- ✓ Hospital psychiatry departments and outpatient clinics
- ✓ University- or medical school-affiliated programs
- ✓ State hospital outpatient clinics
- ✓ Social service agencies
- ✓ Private clinics and facilities
- ✓ Employee assistance programs
- ✓ Local medical and/or psychiatric societies

Immediate Crisis Help

If you are thinking about harming yourself or attempting suicide, tell someone who can help right away:

- ✓ Call your doctor's office.
- ✓ Call 911 for emergency services.
- ✓ Go to the nearest hospital emergency room.
- ✓ Call the toll-free, 24-hour hotline of the National Suicide Prevention Lifeline at 800-273-TALK (800-273-8255) to be connected to a trained counselor at a suicide crisis center nearest you.

Ask a family member or friend to help you make these calls or take you to the hospital.

Family Members and Friends in Crisis: What to Do

If you have a family member or friend who is suicidal, do not leave him or her alone. Try to get the person to seek help immediately from an emergency room, physician, or mental health professional. Take seriously any comments about suicide or wishing to die. Even if you do not believe your family member or friend will actually attempt suicide, the person is clearly in distress and can benefit from your help in receiving mental health treatment.

Chapter 33

Smoking and Tobacco Use

U.S. Centers for Disease Control and Prevention

Health Effects of Cigarette Smoking

Smoking harms nearly every organ of the body, causing many diseases and reducing the health of smokers in general. The adverse health effects of cigarette smoking account for an estimated 438,000 deaths, or nearly 1 of every 5 deaths, each year in the United States. More deaths are caused each year by tobacco use than by all deaths from human immunodeficiency virus (HIV), illegal drug use, alcohol use, motor vehicle injuries, suicides, and murders combined.

☛ Cancer

Cancer is the second leading cause of death and was among the first diseases causually linked to smoking.

Smoking causes about 90 percent of lung cancer deaths in men and almost 80 percent of lung cancer deaths in women. The risk of dying from lung cancer is more than 23 times higher among men who smoke cigarettes, and about 13 times higher among women who smoke cigarettes, compared with people who have never smoked.

Smoking causes cancers of the bladder, oral cavity, pharynx, larynx (voice box), esophagus, cervix, kidney, lung, pancreas, and stomach, and causes acute myeloid leukemia.

Rates of cancers related to cigarette smoking vary widely among members of racial/ethnic groups, but are generally highest in African-American men.

☛ Cardiovascular Disease (Heart and Circulatory System)

Smoking causes coronary heart disease, the leading cause of death in the United States. Cigarette smokers are two to four times more likely to develop coronary heart disease than nonsmokers.

Cigarette smoking approximately doubles a person's risk for stroke.

Cigarette smoking causes reduced circulation by narrowing the blood vessels (arteries). Smokers are more than 10 times as likely as non-smokers to develop peripheral vascular disease.

Smoking causes abdominal aortic aneurysm.

☛ Respiratory Disease and Other Effects

Cigarette smoking is associated with a tenfold increase in the risk of dying from chronic obstructive lung disease. About 90 percent of all deaths from chronic obstructive lung diseases are attributable to cigarette smoking.

Cigarette smoking has many adverse reproductive and early childhood effects, including an increased risk for infertility, pre-term delivery, stillbirth, low birth weight, and sudden infant death syndrome (SIDS).

How to Quit

You CAN quit smoking. Quitting smoking has immediate as well as long term benefits for you and your loved ones. The resources listed under "Digging Deeper" discuss the benefits of quitting and provide helpful guidance.

For additional support in quitting, including free quit coaching, a free quit plan, free educational materials, and referrals to local resources, call **1–800–QUIT–NOW** (1–800–784–8669); TTY 1–800–332–8615.

Secondhand Smoke

Secondhand smoke, also known as environmental tobacco smoke, is a complex mixture of gases and particles that includes smoke from the burning cigarette, cigar, or pipe tip (sidestream smoke) and exhaled mainstream smoke.

Secondhand smoke contains at least 250 chemicals known to be toxic, including more than 50 that can cause cancer.

☛ Health Effects of Secondhand Smoke Exposure

Secondhand smoke exposure causes heart disease and lung cancer in nonsmoking adults.

Non-smokers who are exposed to secondhand smoke at home or work increase their heart disease risk by 25–30 percent and their lung cancer risk by 20–30 percent.

Breathing secondhand smoke has immediate harmful effects on the cardiovascular system that can increase the risk of heart attack. People who already have heart disease are at especially high risk.

Secondhand smoke exposure causes respiratory symptoms in children and slows their lung growth.

Secondhand smoke causes sudden infant death syndrome (SIDS), acute respiratory infections, ear problems, and more frequent and severe asthma attacks in children.

There is no risk-free level of secondhand smoke exposure. Even brief exposure can be dangerous.

Smokeless Tobacco

The two main types of smokeless tobacco in the United States are chewing tobacco and snuff. Chewing tobacco comes in the form of loose leaf, plug, or twist. Snuff is finely ground tobacco that can be dry, moist, or in sachets (tea bag-like pouches). Although some forms of snuff can be used by sniffing or inhaling into the nose, most smokeless tobacco users place the product in their cheek or between their gum and cheek. Users then suck on the tobacco and spit out the tobacco juices, which is why smokeless tobacco is often referred to as spit or spitting tobacco. Smokeless tobacco is a significant health risk and is not a safe substitute for smoking cigarettes.

☛ Health Effects

Smokeless tobacco contains 28 cancer-causing agents (carcinogens). It is a known cause of human cancer, as it increases the risk of developing cancer of the oral cavity. Oral health problems strongly associated with smokeless tobacco use are leukoplakia (a lesion of the soft tissue that consists of a white patch or plaque that cannot be scraped off) and recession of the gums.

Smokeless tobacco use can lead to nicotine addiction and dependence.

Adolescents who use smokeless tobacco are more likely to become cigarette smokers.

Digging Deeper

Centers for Disease Control and Prevention (CDC): Smoking and Tobacco Use

http://www.cdc.gov/tobacco/basic_information/index.htm

The CDC offers a wide range of information on the topic of smoking. You can learn about the health effects of tobacco products, including secondhand smoke, as well as the tobacco industry and marketing. The Quit Smoking page is very helpful, with helplines, smoking cessation materials, and step-by-step advice to help you quit. The "Within 20 Minutes of Quitting" poster is very interesting, showing you how your health begins to improve, even just 20 minutes after your last cigarette.

1-800–QUIT–NOW

http://1800quitnow.cancer.gov/Default.aspx

1–800–QUIT–NOW is a free service that can help you quit smoking or chewing tobacco. It offers a helpline, as well as links to resources in your state. In addition, you can read the QUIT NOW Challenge Blogs, to learn about other people's true experiences.

I QUIT! What to Do When You're Sick of Smoking, Chewing, or Dipping

http://www.cdc.gov/tobacco/quit_smoking/how_to_quit/00_pdfs/IQuit.pdf

A booklet that will help you quit all tobacco products by taking you step-by-step through the quitting process. There are suggestions to help you deal with the cravings and to keep smoking out of your life for good.

Question and Answers About Smoking Cessation

http://www.cancer.gov/cancertopics/factsheet/Tobacco/cessation

This fact sheet from the National Cancer Institute talks about the chemicals that can be found in tobacco and the health problems caused by smoking. There's a discussion of the immediate and long term benefits of quitting, as well as the different methods and medications to help someone quit. Finally, there is contact information for a number of different smoking cessation programs and government offices.

Tobacco Cessation—You Can Quit Smoking Now!

http://www.surgeongeneral.gov/tobacco/

The U.S. Surgeon General's website offers you the latest information to help you quit smoking. Print out the information PDFs, or read the latest reports and press releases.

Nicotine Addiction

http://smoking.drugabuse.gov/

This website emphasizes the dangers of tobacco use: the medical consequences and the effects of addiction. Read the latest news and research and find resources to help you quit. There is also an event calendar, with meetings, seminars, and symposiums on different tobacco-related topics.

Smokefree.gov

http://www.smokefree.gov/

Smokefree.gov is a website dedicated to helping you quit smoking. The Quit Smoking page—which can be downloaded in PDF format and printed out—has information on why to quit, preparing to quit, and staying quit. This includes advice on managing cravings, medicines that can help, withdrawal symptoms you might get, and why quitting is so hard. In addition, there are links to Expert Help and brochures you can print out.

Chapter 34

Alcohol and Public Health

U.S. Centers for Disease Control and Prevention

Introduction

Alcohol use is very common in our society. Drinking alcohol has immediate effects that can increase the risk of many harmful health conditions. Excessive alcohol use, either in the form of heavy drinking (drinking more than two drinks per day on average for men or more than one drink per day on average for women), or binge drinking (drinking five or more drinks during a single occasion for men or four or more drinks during a single occasion for women), can lead to increased risk of health problems such as liver disease or unintentional injuries.

According to national surveys, over half of the U.S. adult population drank alcohol in the past 30 days. Approximately 5 percent of the total population drank heavily while 15 percent of the population binge drank. Our national surveys previously defined binge drinking as five or more drinks for both men and women. From 2001 to 2005, there were approximately 79,000 deaths annually attributable to excessive alcohol use. In fact, excessive alcohol use is the third leading lifestyle-related cause of death for people in the United States each year.

Alcohol Terms

☛ The Standard Measure of Alcohol

In the United States, a standard drink has about half an ounce (13.7 grams or 1.2 tablespoons) of pure alcohol. Generally, this amount of pure alcohol is found in:

- » *12 ounces of regular beer or wine cooler.*
- » *8 ounces of malt liquor.*
- » *5 ounces of wine or 1.5 ounces of 80-proof distilled spirits or "liquor" (gin, rum, vodka, whiskey).*

☛ Levels and Patterns of Drinking

- » *Heavy drinking–For women, more than one drink per day on average. For men, more than two drinks per day on average.*
- » *Binge drinking–For women, more than three drinks during a single occasion. For men, more than four drinks during a single occasion.*

☛ Excessive Drinking

This term includes heavy drinking, binge drinking, or both. Most people who binge drink are not alcoholics or alcohol dependent.

☛ Alcohol Abuse

- » *Alcohol abuse is a pattern of drinking that results in harm to one's health, interpersonal relationships, or ability to work. Manifestations of alcohol abuse include:*
- » *Failure to fulfill major responsibilities at work, school, or home.*
- » *Drinking in dangerous situations, such as drinking while driving or operating machinery.*
- » *Legal problems related to alcohol, such as being arrested for drinking while driving or for*

Part VII

physically hurting someone while drunk.

» *Continued drinking despite ongoing relationship problems that are caused or worsened by drinking.*

» *Long term alcohol abuse can turn into alcohol dependence.*

☛ Alcohol Dependence

Dependency on alcohol, also known as alcohol addiction and alcoholism, is a chronic disease. The signs and symptoms of alcohol dependence include:

» *A strong craving for alcohol.*

» *Continued use despite repeated physical, psychological, or interpersonal problems.*

» *The inability to limit drinking.*

» *Physical illness when one stops drinking.*

» *The need to drink increasing amounts of alcohol to feel its effects.*

Who Should Not Drink at All?

There are some persons who should not drink any alcohol, including those who are:

✗ Pregnant or trying to become pregnant.

✗ Taking prescription or over-the-counter medications that may cause harmful reactions when mixed with alcohol.

✗ Under the age of 21.

✗ Recovering from alcoholism or unable to control the amount they drink.

✗ Suffering from a medical condition that may be worsened by alcohol.

✗ Driving, planning to drive, or participating in other activities requiring skill, coordination, and alertness.

Immediate Health Risks of Excessive Alcohol

Excessive alcohol use has immediate effects that increase the risk of many harmful health conditions. These immediate effects are most often the result of binge drinking and include:

- ✗ **Unintentional injuries,** including traffic injuries, falls, drownings, burns and unintentional firearm injuries.
- ✗ **Violence,** including intimate partner violence and child maltreatment. About 35 percent of victims report that offenders are under the influence of alcohol. Alcohol use is also associated with two out of three incidents of intimate partner violence. Studies have also shown that alcohol is a leading factor in child maltreatment and neglect cases and is the most frequent substance abused among these parents.
- ✗ **Risky sexual behaviors,** including unprotected sex, sex with multiple partners, and increased risk of sexual assault. These behaviors can result in unintended pregnancy or sexually transmitted diseases.
- ✗ **If pregnant,** miscarriage, stillbirth, and a combination of physical and mental birth defects that last throughout life.
- ✗ **Alcohol poisoning,** a medical emergency that results from high blood alcohol levels that suppress the central nervous system and cause loss of consciousness, low blood pressure and body temperature, coma, respiratory depression, and death.

Long Term Health Risks

Over time, excessive alcohol use can lead to the development of chronic diseases, neurological impairments, and social problems. These include but are not limited to:

- ✗ **Neurological problems,** including dementia, stroke, and neuropathy.
- ✗ **Cardiovascular problems,** including myocardial infarction, cardiomyopathy, atrial

fibrillation, and hypertension.

- ✗ **Psychiatric problems,** including depression, suicidality, and anxiety.
- ✗ **Social problems,** including unemployment, lost productivity, and family problems.
- ✗ **Cancer of the mouth, throat, esophagus, liver, prostate for men, and breast for women.** In general, the risk of cancer increases with increasing amounts of alcohol.
- ✗ **Liver diseases,** including:
    - » *Alcoholic hepatitis which is inflammation of the liver that can progress to cirrhosis.*
    - » *Cirrhosis is scarring of the liver that prevents this vital organ from functioning properly. This condition often leads to complete liver failure, and is among the 15 leading causes of all deaths in the United States.*
    - » *Alcohol use by those with Hepatitis C virus (HCV) can cause the infection to worsen. Alcohol may also interfere with the medications used to treat HCV.*
    - » *Other gastrointestinal problems, including pancreatitis and gastritis.*

DIGGING DEEPER

Medline Plus: Alcoholism

http://www.nlm.nih.gov/medlineplus/alcoholism.html

This page starts out with a definition of alcoholism, and then provides links to more in-depth information further down the page. You can learn how to diagnose alcoholism and about treatment and rehabilitation options. View the latest research on the topic, as well as statistics on alcohol use and alcohol-related illness and death.

Medline Plus: Alcohol and Youth

http://www.nlm.nih.gov/medlineplus/alcoholandyouth.html

Kids who start drinking are putting themselves in a risky situation, being more likely to be victims of violence, do poorly in school, and struggle with alcohol addiction throughout their lives. This page has resources geared specifically toward teenagers and kids. There is information to help them stay sober, but also what can be done when a parent is an alcoholic.

Stop Underage Drinking

http://www.stopalcoholabuse.gov/

The focus of this website is to, as the title states, stop underage drinking. There are a number of resources for parents and educators, as well as youth, including a number of downloadable publications. You can find a great of information on the effects of alcohol, including an online quiz that tests your knowledge. There are also resources to help you drink responsibly or quit if you are addicted.

The Cool Spot

http://www.thecoolspot.gov/

While geared toward youth, anyone can get a "reality check" about the seriousness of drinking too much. You can learn about the short term and long term health effects of alcohol, as well as the social problems that can arise. A very important aspect of this site is the information on resisting peer pressure, letting you know that you have a right to say no. Remember, friends wouldn't make you do something you don't want to do.

Chapter 35

What to Know About Sexually-Transmitted Diseases

National Institutes of Health

What are Sexually Transmitted Diseases (STDs)?

STDs, also called sexually transmitted infections or STIs, are diseases that you get by having intimate sexual contact—that is, having sex (vaginal, oral, or anal intercourse)—with someone who already has the disease. Every year, STDs affect more than 13 million people.

What are the different types of STDs?

Researchers have identified more than 20 different kinds of STDs, which can fall into two main groups:

☛ STDs caused by bacteria

These diseases can be treated and often cured with antibiotics. Some bacterial STDs include: chlamydia, gonorrhea, trichomoniasis, and syphilis.

☛ STDs caused by viruses

These diseases can be controlled, but not cured. If you get a viral STD, you will always have it. Some viral STDs include: HIV/AIDS, genital herpes, genital warts, human papilloma virus (HPV), hepatitis B virus, and cytomegalovirus.

What are the symptoms of STDs?

The symptoms vary among the different types of STDs. Some examples of common symptoms include:

- ✓ *Unusual discharge from the penis or vagina*
- ✓ *Sores or warts on the genital area*
- ✓ *Burning while urinating*
- ✓ *Itching and redness in the genital area*
- ✓ *Anal itching, soreness, or bleeding*

If you are having any of these symptoms or think you might have an STD, talk to your health care provider.

Testing for STDs If You're Sexually Active

☛ For women:

At a minimum, get a Pap smear—a simple procedure that collects cells from your cervix to test for cancer or precancerous changes. This type of cancer can arise as a result of a human papillomavirus (HPV) infection—a common STD. Pap smears are recommended for women who are age 21 and older or no later than three years after a woman's first intercourse. If you're a woman between age 30 and 69, you may only need a Pap smear every two to three years if you've had three normal Pap smears in a row and have had no new sexual partners.

☛ For men:

Centers for Disease Control and Prevention (CDC) guidelines don't suggest routine STD screening if you don't have any symptoms, unless your sexual practices include having sex with men.

If you are a man who has sex with men, annual screening for HIV, syphilis, chlamydia and gonorrhea is recommended. HIV and syphilis can be life-threatening if untreated, and chlamydia and gonorrhea can put you at greater risk of acquiring HIV and other STDs.

☛ For men and women:

Also see your doctor for STD testing if you have any signs such as genital sores, including fluid-filled blisters, ulcerations or warts, or if you have unusual discharge from your penis or vagina. If you're a woman, abdominal pain or fever along with unusual discharge may indicate pelvic inflammatory disease (PID)—an STD-related condition that can cause infertility.

The Federal Centers for Disease Control and Prevention (CDC) also encourages voluntary HIV testing, at least once, as a routine part of medical care if you are an adolescent or adult between the ages of 13 to 64. The CDC advises yearly HIV testing if you are at high risk of infection, for example if you've had unprotected sex with more than one sexual partner since your last screening.

How can STDs be prevented?

The only way to ensure that you won't get infected is to stop having sex. This means avoiding all types of intimate sexual contact.

If you are sexually active, you can reduce your risk of getting STDs by practicing "safe sex." This means:

- ✓ *Using a condom for vaginal, oral, and anal intercourse—every time*
- ✓ *Knowing your partner and his/her STD status and health*
- ✓ *Having regular medical check-ups, especially if you have more than one sexual partner*

Where to Get Information and Help

If you think you may have a sexually-transmitted disease, it is important to get medical help. Visit a clinic, emergency ward, or a private physical to get examined and treated. Then, try to avoid risky behaviors that will expose you to STDs again.

Chapter 36

Preventing High Blood Pressure and High Cholesterol

National Cholesterol EducationProgram, National Heart, Lung, and Blood Institute

Part I: Controlling High Blood Pressure

You can take steps to prevent high blood pressure by adopting a healthy lifestyle. These steps include maintaining a healthy weight; being physically active; following a healthy eating plan that emphasizes fruits, vegetables, and low-fat dairy foods; choosing and preparing foods with less salt and sodium; and, if you drink alcoholic beverages, drinking in moderation. In this section you will learn more about healthy lifestyle habits for preventing and controlling high blood pressure.

1. Healthy Eating Plan

Research has shown that following a healthy eating plan can both reduce the risk of developing high blood pressure and lower an already elevated blood pressure.

For an overall eating plan, consider the DASH eating plan. “DASH” stands for “Dietary Approaches to Stop Hypertension,” a clinical study that tested the effects of nutrients in food on blood pressure. Study results indicated that elevated blood pressures were reduced by an eating plan that emphasizes fruits, vegetables, and low-fat dairy foods and is low in saturated fat, total fat, and cholesterol. The DASH eating plan includes whole grains, poultry, fish, and nuts and has reduced amounts of fats, red meats, sweets, and sugared beverages.

2. Reduce Salt and Sodium in Your Diet

A key to healthy eating is choosing foods lower in salt and sodium. Most Americans consume more salt than they need. The current recommendation is to consume less than 2.4 grams (2,400 milligrams[mg]) of sodium a day. That equals 6 grams (about 1 teaspoon) of table salt a day. The 6 grams include all salt and sodium consumed, including that used in cooking and at the table. For someone with high blood pressure, the doctor may advise eating less salt and sodium, as recent research has shown that people consuming diets of 1,500 mg of sodium had even better blood pressure lowering benefits. These lower-sodium diets also can keep blood pressure from rising and help blood pressure medicines work better.

3. Maintaining a Healthy Weight

Being overweight increases your risk of developing high blood pressure. In fact, blood pressure rises as body weight increases. Losing even 10 pounds can lower blood pressure—and it has the greatest effect for those who are overweight and already have hypertension.

Being overweight or obese are also risk factors for heart disease. They increase your chance for developing high blood cholesterol and diabetes—two more major risk factors for heart disease.

Part VII

4. Being Physically Active

Being physically active is one of the most important steps you can take to prevent or control high blood pressure. It also helps reduce your risk of heart disease. It doesn't take a lot of effort to become physically active.

5. Limiting Alcohol Intake

Drinking too much alcohol can raise blood pressure. It also can harm the liver, brain, and heart. Alcoholic drinks also contain calories, which matter if you are trying to lose weight. If you drink alcoholic beverages, have only a moderate amount—one drink a day for women; two drinks a day for men.

6. **Quitting Smoking**

   Smoking injures blood vessel walls and speeds up the process of hardening of the arteries. This applies even to filtered cigarettes. So although it does not cause high blood pressure, smoking is bad for anyone, especially those with high blood pressure. If you smoke, quit. If you don't smoke, don't start. Once you quit, your risk of having a heart attack is reduced after the first year, so you have a lot to gain by quitting.

Part II: High Blood Cholesterol: What You Need to Know

Your blood cholesterol level has a lot to do with your chances of getting heart disease. High blood cholesterol is one of the major risk factors for heart disease. A risk factor is a condition that increases your chance of getting a disease. In fact, the higher your blood cholesterol level, the greater your risk for developing heart disease or having a heart attack. Heart disease is the number one killer of women and men in the United States. Each year, more than a million Americans have heart attacks, and about a half million people die from heart disease.

☛ How Does Cholesterol Cause Heart Disease?

When there is too much cholesterol (a fat-like substance) in your blood, it builds up in the walls of your arteries. Over time, this buildup causes "hardening of the arteries" so that arteries become narrowed and blood flow to the heart is slowed down or blocked. The blood carries oxygen to the heart, and if enough blood and oxygen cannot reach your heart, you may suffer chest pain. If the blood supply to a portion of the heart is completely cut off by a blockage, the result is a heart attack.

High blood cholesterol itself does not cause symptoms, so many people are unaware that their cholesterol level is too high. It is important to find out what your cholesterol numbers are because lowering cholesterol levels that are too high lessens the risk for developing heart disease and reduces the chance of a heart attack or dying of heart disease, even if you already have it. Cholesterol lowering is important for everyone—younger, middle age, and older adults; women and men; and people with or without heart disease.

☛ What Do Your Cholesterol Numbers Mean?

Everyone age 20 and older should have their cholesterol measured at least once every five years. It is best to have a blood test called a "lipoprotein profile" to find out your cholesterol numbers. This blood test is done after a 9- to 12-hour fast and gives information about your:

» *Total cholesterol*

» *LDL (bad) cholesterol—the main source of cholesterol buildup and blockage in the arteries*

» *HDL (good) cholesterol—helps keep cholesterol from building up in the arteries*

» *Triglycerides—another form of fat in your blood*

If it is not possible to get a lipoprotein profile done, knowing your total cholesterol and HDL cholesterol can give you a general idea about your cholesterol levels. If your total cholesterol is 200 mg/dL* or more or if your HDL is less than 40 mg/dL, you will need to have a lipoprotein profile done. See how your cholesterol numbers compare to the tables below.

Total Cholesterol Level	Category
Less than 200 mg/dL	Desirable
200-239 mg/dL	Borderline high
240 mg/dL and above	High

*Cholesterol levels are measured in milligrams (mg) of cholesterol per deciliter (dL) of blood

LDL Cholesterol Level	Category
Less than 100 mg/dL	Optimal
100-129 mg/dL	Near optimal/above optimal

Part VII

130-159 mg/dL	Borderline high
160-189 mg/dL	High
190 mg/dL and above	Very high

HDL (good) cholesterol protects against heart disease, so for HDL, higher numbers are better. A level less than 40 mg/dL is low and is considered a major risk factor because it increases your risk for developing heart disease. HDL levels of 60 mg/dL or more help to lower your risk for heart disease.

Triglycerides can also raise heart disease risk. Some people with levels that are borderline high (150-199 mg/dL) or high (200 mg/dL or more) may need treatment.

☛ What Affects Cholesterol Levels?

A variety of things can affect cholesterol levels. These are things you can do something about:

» **Diet**—Saturated fat and cholesterol in the foods you eat raise your blood cholesterol level. Saturated fat is the main culprit, but cholesterol in foods also matters. Reducing the amount of saturated fat and cholesterol in your diet helps lower your blood cholesterol level.

» **Weight**—Being overweight is a risk factor for heart disease. It also tends to increase your cholesterol. Losing weight can help lower your LDL and total cholesterol levels, as well as raise your HDL and lower your triglyceride levels.

» **Physical Activity**—Not being physically active is a risk factor for heart disease. Regular physical activity can help lower LDL (bad) cholesterol and raise HDL (good) cholesterol levels. It also helps you lose weight. You should try to be physically active for 30 minutes on most, if not all, days.

Things you cannot do anything about also can affect cholesterol levels. These include:

» **Age and Gender**—As women and men get older, their cholesterol levels rise. Before the age of menopause, women have lower total cholesterol levels than men of the same age. After the age of menopause, women's LDL levels tend to rise.

» **Heredity**—Your genes partly determine how much cholesterol your body makes. High blood cholesterol can run in families.

☛ Lowering Cholesterol With Therapeutic Lifestyle Changes (TLC)

TLC is a set of things you can do to help lower your LDL cholesterol. The main parts of TLC are as follows:

» **The TLC Diet**—A low saturated fat, low cholesterol eating plan that calls for less than 7 percent of calories from saturated fat and less than 200 mg of dietary cholesterol per day, the TLC diet recommends only enough calories to maintain a desirable weight and avoid weight gain. If your LDL is not lowered enough by reducing your saturated fat and cholesterol intakes, the amount of soluble fiber in your diet can be increased. Certain food products that contain plant stanols or plant sterols (for example, cholesterol-lowering margarines) can also be added to the TLC diet to boost its LDL-lowering power.

» **Weight Management**—Losing weight if you are overweight can help lower LDL and is especially important for those with a cluster of risk factors that includes high triglyceride and/or low HDL levels and being overweight with a large waist measurement (more than 40 inches for men and more than 35 inches for women).

» **Physical Activity**—Regular physical activity (30 minutes on most, if not all, days) is recommended for everyone. It can help raise HDL and lower LDL and is especially important for those with high triglyceride and/or low HDL levels who are overweight with a large waist measurement.

Foods low in saturated fat include fat-free or 1 percent dairy products, lean meats, fish, skinless poultry, whole grain foods, and fruits and vegetables. Look for soft margarines (liquid or tub varieties) that are low in saturated fat and contain little or no trans fat (another type of dietary fat that can raise your cholesterol level). Limit foods high in cholesterol such as liver and other organ meats, egg yolks, and full-fat dairy products.

Good sources of soluble fiber include oats, certain fruits (such as oranges and pears) and vegetables (such as Brussels sprouts and carrots), and dried peas and beans.

Digging Deeper

National Heart, Lung, and Blood Institute: Guide to Lowering High Blood Pressure

http://www.nhlbi.nih.gov/hbp/

A useful guide to lowering high blood pressure is provided at this government health website. The article explains blood pressure, high blood pressure, detection, prevention, treatment, and issues for women.

National Heart, Lung, and Blood Institute: What is Cholesterol?

http://www.nhlbi.nih.gov/health/dci/Diseases/Hbc/HBC_WhatIs.html

The causes, symptoms, methods of diagnosis, and treatment of elevated cholesterol are all addressed at this National Institutes of Health website. A series of links will take you to additional resources and more clinical information on this important subject.

Part VIII

Diet and Nutrition

Chapter 37

Healthy Eating Recommendations From the FDA

U.S. Food and Drug Administration

Too Many Calories, Not Enough Nutrients

Most Americans consume too many calories and not enough nutrients, according to the latest revision to Dietary Guidelines for Americans. In January 2005, two federal agencies—the Department of Health and Human Services and the Department of Agriculture (USDA)—released the guidelines to help adults and children ages two and up live healthier lives.

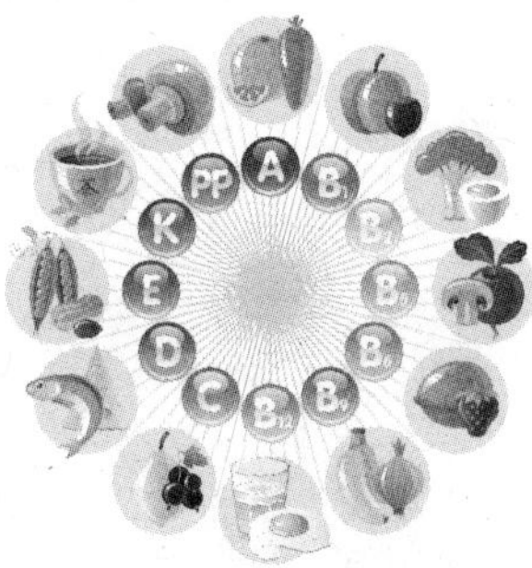

Currently, the typical American diet is low in fruits, vegetables, and whole grains and high in saturated fat, salt, and sugar. As a result, more Americans than ever are overweight, obese, and at increased risk for chronic diseases such as heart disease, high blood pressure, diabetes, and certain cancers.

Improving Eating Habits

Of course old habits are hard to break, and the notion of change can seem overwhelming. But with planning and a gradual approach it can be done, says Dee Sandquist, a spokeswoman for the American Dietetic Association (ADA) and manager of nutrition and diabetes at the Southwest Washington Medical Center in Vancouver,

Washington. "Some people can improve eating habits on their own, while others need a registered dietitian to guide them through the process," Sandquist says. You may need a dietitian if you are trying to lose weight or if you have a health condition such as osteoporosis, high blood pressure, high cholesterol, or diabetes. Sandquist says that many people she counsels have been used to eating a certain way and never thought about what they were actually putting into their bodies. "Someone may tell me they drink six cans of regular soda every day," she says. "When they find out there are about nine teaspoons of sugar in one can, it puts things in perspective. Then I work with the person to cut back to three cans a day, then to two, and so on, and to start replacing some of the soda with healthier options."

Others are eating a lot of food between mid-day and bedtime because they skip breakfast, Sandquist says. Another common scenario is when someone has grown up thinking that meat should be the focus of every meal. "We may start by having the person try eating two-thirds of the meat they would normally eat, and then decreasing the portion little by little," Sandquist says. Cutting portion size limits calories. So does eating lean cuts of meat and using lower-fat methods of preparation, such as broiling.

More Balance Can Be Satisfying

Sandquist says that when people strive for more balance in their diets, they tend to enjoy mixing up their food choices. "A lot of times, they've been eating the same things over and over. So when they start trying new foods, they find out what they've been missing."

Barbara Schneeman, Ph.D., director of the Food and Drug Administration's Office of Nutritional Products, Labeling, and Dietary Supplements, encourages consumers to make smart food choices from every food group. "The Nutrition Facts label is an important tool that gives guidance for making these choices," she says. The label shows how high or low a food is in various nutrients.

Know What You're Eating: Check the Label

Experts say that once you start using the label to compare products, you'll find there is flexibility in creating a balanced diet and enjoying a variety of foods in moderation. For example, you could eat a favorite food that's higher in fat for breakfast and have lower-fat foods for lunch and dinner. You could have a full-fat dip on a low-fat cracker. "What matters is how all the food works together," Sandquist says.

12-POINT ACTION PLAN

So what if you're feeling trapped by a diet full of fast-food burgers and cookies? You can work your way out slowly but surely. Here are tips to move your eating habits in the right direction.

1. Look at What You Eat Now

Write down what you eat for a few days to get a good picture of what you're taking in, suggests Cindy Moore, director of nutrition therapy at the Cleveland Clinic Foundation. "By looking at what you eat and how much you're eating, you can figure out what adjustments you need to make," she says.

2. Start With Small Changes

You don't have to go cold turkey. In the end, you want to achieve a long term healthy lifestyle. Small changes over time are the most likely to stick. "If you want to eat more vegetables, then try to add one more serving by sneaking it in," Moore says. "Add bits of broccoli to something you already eat like pizza or soup. If you need more whole grains, add barley, whole wheat pasta, or brown rice to your soup."

When you think about what you need to get more of, the other things tend to fall into place, Moore says. "If you have some baby carrots with lunch or add a banana to your cereal in the morning, you're going to feel full longer."You won't need a food that's high in sugar or fat an hour later, she adds.

Also, look for healthier versions of what you like to eat. If you like luncheon meat sandwiches, try a reduced-fat version. If you like the convenience of frozen dinners, look for those with lower sodium. If you love fast-food meals, try a salad as your side dish instead of french fries.

3. Use the Nutrition Facts Label

To make smart food choices quickly and easily, compare the Nutrition Facts labels on products. Look at the percent Daily Value (%DV) column. The general rule of thumb is that 5 percent or less of the Daily Value is considered low and 20 percent or more is high.

Keep saturated fat, trans fat, cholesterol, and sodium low, while keeping fiber, potassium, iron, calcium, and vitamins A and C high. Be sure to look at the serving size and the number of servings per package. The serving size affects calories, amounts of each nutrient, and the percentage of Daily Value.

4. Control Portion Sizes

Understanding the serving size on the Nutrition Facts label is important for controlling portions, Moore says. "Someone may have a large bottled drink, assuming it's one serving," she says. "But if you look at the label, it's actually two servings. And if you consume two servings of a product, you have to multiply all the numbers by two." When the servings go up, so do the calories, fat, sugar, and salt.

Moore also suggests dishing out a smaller amount on your plate or using smaller plates. "If you put more food in front of you, you'll eat it because it's there," she says.

5. Control Calories and Get the Most Nutrients

You want to stay within your daily calorie needs, especially if you're trying to lose weight, says Eric Hentges, Ph.D., director of the USDA Center for Nutrition Policy and Promotion. "But you also want to get the most nutrients out of the calories, which means picking nutritionally rich foods," he says. Children and adults should pay particular attention to getting adequate calcium, potassium, fiber, magnesium, and vitamins A, C, and E.

6. Know Your Fats

Fat provides flavor and makes you feel full. It also provides energy and essential fatty acids for healthy skin and helps the body absorb the fat-soluble vitamins A, D, E, and K. But fat also has nine calories per gram, compared to four calories per gram in carbohydrates and protein. If you eat too much fat every day, you may get more calories than your body needs, and too many calories can contribute to weight gain.

Too much saturated fat, trans fat, and cholesterol in the diet increases the risk of unhealthy blood cholesterol levels, which may increase the risk of heart disease. "Consumers should lower all three, not just one or the other," says Schneeman. Saturated fat is found mainly in foods from animals. Major sources of saturated fats are cheese, beef, and milk. Trans-fat results when manufacturers add hydrogen to vegetable oil to increase the food's shelf life and flavor. Trans fat can be found in vegetable shortenings, some margarines, crackers, cookies, and other snack foods. Cholesterol is a fat-like substance in foods from animal sources such as meat, poultry, egg yolks, milk, and milk products.

Most of your fats should come from polyunsaturated and monounsaturated fatty acids, such as those that occur in fish, nuts, soybean, corn, canola, olive, and other vegetable oils. This type of fat does not raise the risk of heart disease and may be beneficial when consumed in moderation.

7. Make Choices That Are Lean, Low-fat, or Fat-free

When buying meat, poultry, milk, or milk products, choose versions that are lean, low-fat, or fat-free. Choose lean meats like chicken without the skin and lean beef or pork with the fat trimmed off.

If you frequently drink whole milk, switch to 1 percent milk or skim milk.

Eat more fish, which is usually lower in saturated fat than meat. Bake, grill, and broil food instead of frying it because more fat is absorbed into the food when frying. You could also try more meatless entrees like veggie burgers and add flavor to food with low-fat beans instead of butter.

8. Focus on Fruit

Dietary Guidelines recommends two cups of fruit per day at the 2,000-calorie reference diet. Fruit intake and recommended amounts of other food groups vary at different calorie levels. An example of two cups of fruit includes: one small banana, one large orange, and one-fourth cup of dried apricots or peaches.

Ways to incorporate fruit in your diet include adding it to your cereal, eating it as a snack with low-fat yogurt or a low-fat dip, or making a fruit smoothie for dessert by mixing low-fat milk with fresh or frozen fruit such as strawberries or peaches. Also, your family is more likely to eat fruit if you put it out on the kitchen table.

9. Eat Your Veggies

Dietary Guidelines recommends two and one-half cups of vegetables per day if you eat 2,000 calories each day.

Tanner suggests adding vegetables to foods such as meatloaf, lasagna, omelettes, stir-fry dishes, and casseroles. Frozen chopped greens such as spinach, and peas, carrots, and corn are easy to add. Also, add dark leafy green lettuce to sandwiches. Get a variety of dark green vegetables such as broccoli, spinach, and greens; orange and deep yellow vegetables such as carrots, winter squash, and sweet potatoes; starchy vegetables like corn; legumes, such as dry beans, peas, chickpeas, pinto beans, kidney beans, and tofu; and other vegetables, such as tomatoes and onions.

10. Make Half Your Grains Whole

Like fruits and vegetables, whole grains are a good source of vitamins, minerals, and fiber. The Dietary Guidelines recommend at least three ounces of whole grains per day. One slice of bread, one cup of breakfast cereal, or one-half cup of cooked rice or pasta are each equivalent to about one ounce. Tanner suggests baked whole-grain corn tortilla chips or whole-grain cereal with low-fat milk as good snacks.

11. Lower Sodium and Increase Potassium

Higher salt intake is linked to higher blood pressure, which can raise the risk of stroke, heart disease, and kidney disease. Dietary Guidelines recommend that people consume less than 2,300 milligrams of sodium per day (approximately one teaspoon of salt).

Also, increase potassium-rich foods such as sweet potatoes, orange juice, bananas, spinach, winter squash, cantaloupe, and tomato puree. Potassium counteracts some of sodium's effect on blood pressure.

12. Limit Added Sugars

Dietary Guidelines recommend choosing and preparing food and beverages with little added sugars. Added sugars are sugars and syrups added to foods and beverages in processing or preparation, not the naturally occurring sugars in fruits or milk. Major sources of added sugars in the American diet include regular soft drinks, candy, cake, cookies, pies, and fruit drinks. In the ingredients list on food products, sugar may be listed as brown sugar, corn syrup, glucose, sucrose, honey, or molasses. Be sure to check the sugar in low-fat and fat-free products, which sometimes contain a lot of sugar, Tanner says.

Instead of drinking regular soda and sugary fruit drinks, try diet soda, low-fat or fat-free milk, water, flavored water, or 100 percent fruit juice.

For snacks and desserts, try fruit. "People are often pleasantly surprised that fruit is great for satisfying a sweet tooth," Tanner says. "And if ice cream is calling your name, don't have it in the freezer. Make it harder to get by having to go out for it. Then it can be an occasional treat."

Digging Deeper

Nutrition.gov

http://www.nutrition.gov/

Nutrition.gov is the nutritional information website of the federal government. It consists of daily nutrition news stories, educational tutorials, food content data, nutrition for different life stages, health and weight issues, dietary supplements, and food assistance programs.

Dietary Guidelines for Americans

http://www.health.gov/dietaryguidelines/

Visitors can learn a great deal about good diets at this webpage of the U.S. Department of Health and Human Services. Resources include a series of fact-filled books on recommended dietary guidelines, recommendations for exercise and improved nutrition, making good food choices, and resources for professionals.

SmallStep.gov

http://www.smallstep.gov/index.html

Learning about portion control is the subject of this website, with a section for teens and adults. It is part of a larger government initiative called HealthierUS.gov, which focuses on ways to improve health and fitness with exercise and improved nutrition.

U.S. Department of Agriculture: Food and Nutrition

http://www.usda.gov/wps/portal/!ut/p/_s.7_0_A/7_0_1OB?navtype=SU&navid=FOOD_NUTRITION

The Food and Nutrition Section of the U.S. Department of Agriculture offers detailed nutrient-content profiles of thousands of foods, questions and answers about meat and poultry, food preservation and home canning, child nutrition programs, the food pyramid, and food safety.

FDA: Food Safety and Applied Nutrition

http://www.cfsan.fda.gov/list.html

The Center for Food Safety and Applied Nutrition in the Food and Drug Administration is another excellent resource on diets, food content, and sound nutrition. There are regularly posted articles and alerts on food issues and recalls, infant formula, food allergens, and produce safety, and numerous other issues related to the food supply, food safety, and government regulations and programs.

Chapter 38

The Food Pyramid: New Tools for a Healthy Diet

Food and Nutrition Service
U.S. Department of Agriculture

Part I: Understanding and Using the Food Pyramid

The Food Guide Pyramid is one way for people to understand how to eat a healthy diet. Developed by the U.S. Department of Agriculture's Food and Nutrition Service, the pyramid consists of a rainbow of colored, vertical stripes, each corresponding to one of the five food groups, plus fats and oils. For a full-color version of the pyramid, visit www. *http://www.mypyramid.gov/*.

The five food groups are (1) grains, (2) vegetables, (3) fruits, (4) milk and dairy products, and (5) meat, beans, fish and nuts. There is also provision for intake of fats and oils.

To translate the colored food group stripes in the pyramid into more practical information, you can click on any color and get advice about which foods in the group are most highly recommended.

Part II: Online Tools for Monitoring Nutrition

- **MyPyramid Plan (www.mypyramid.gov)**

Based upon age, sex, weight, height, and customary level of physical activity, you can generate a program called "MyPyramid Plan" at this same website. The plan provides recommended amounts of each food group to include in your diet and recommendations for exercise.

- **MyPyramid Tracker (www.mypyramidtracker.gov)**

  Another tool at the site enables the user to follow his or her progress over time, utilizing MyPyramid Tracker.

Part III: Weight Control Information Network From the NIDDK

The National Institute for Diabetes and Digestive and Kidney Diseases (NIDDK) offers extensive resources on weight management and diet evaluation.

- **Recommendations**

  If you wish to lose weight and you want to find a weight-loss program to help you, look for a program that is based on regular physical activity and an eating plan that is balanced, healthy, and easy to follow. Weight-loss programs should encourage healthy behaviors that help you lose weight and that you can stick with every day. Safe and effective weight-loss programs should include:

- ✓ Healthy eating plans that reduce calories but do not forbid specific foods or food groups.
- ✓ Tips to increase moderate-intensity physical activity.
- ✓ Tips on healthy behavior changes that also keep your cultural needs in mind.
- ✓ Slow and steady weight loss. Depending on your starting weight, experts recommend losing weight at a rate of one-half to two pounds per week. Weight loss may be faster at the start of a program.
- ✓ Medical care if you are planning to lose weight by following a special formula diet, such as a very low-calorie diet.

✓ A plan to keep the weight off after you have lost it.

Digging Deeper

Center for Nutrition Policy and Promotion

http://www.cnpp.usda.gov/

The U.S. Department of Agriculture's Center for Nutrition Policy and Promotion posts frequent news stories on food and nutrition and includes extensive information on the food pyramid and how to use it to build a healthy diet. The Healthy Eating Index (HEI), which is a measure of diet quality, is a major topic at this site, along with information on food costs, expenditures on children, and data on the science of nutrition.

USDA Food, Nutrition and Consumer Services

http://www.fns.usda.gov/fncs/fncs.htm

USDA's Food, Nutrition, and Consumer Services ensures access to nutritious, healthful diets for all Americans. Through food assistance and nutrition education for consumers, FNCS encourages consumers to make healthful food choices. Today, rather than simply providing food, FNCS works to empower consumers with knowledge of the link between diet and health, providing dietary guidance based on research.

MyPyramid.gov

http://www.mypyramid.gov/

MyPyramid Plan offers you a personal eating plan with the foods and amounts that are right for you. Click on the MyPyramid Plan box to get started. MyPyramid Tracker offers a detailed assessment of your food intake and physical activity level. Click on the Tracker box for an in-depth look at your food and physical activity choices.

Choosing a Safe Weight-Loss Program

http://www.win.niddk.nih.gov/publications/choosing.htm#responsible

The National Institute of Diabetes and Digestive and Kidney Diseases (NIDDK) provides a link to the Weight Control Information Network and recommendations for safe weight-loss programs. The site focuses on the characteristics of safe weight-loss diets, the importance of professional guidance, program risks, diet costs, and typical results to expect.

Chapter 39

Reading and Understanding Food Labels

Office of Nutritional Products. Labeling, and Dietary Supplements, Food and Drug Administration

The Nutrition Facts Label: An Overview

The information in the main or top section (see #1-4 and #6 on the sample nutrition label below), can vary with each food product; it contains product-specific information (serving size, calories, and nutrient information).

Sample Label for Macaroni & Cheese

1.Start Here

Nutrition Facts

Serving Size 1 cup (228g)
Servings Per Container 2

2. Check Calories

Amount Per Serving

Calories 250
Calories from Fat 110

3. Limit these Nutrients

Quick Guide to %DV

% Daily Value *	
Total Fat 12g	18%
Saturated Fat 3g	15%
Trans Fat 3g	
Cholesterol 30mg	10%
Sodium 470mg	20%
Total Carbohydrate 31g	10%
Dietary Fiber 0g	0%
Sugars 5g	
Protein 5g	

4. Get Enough of These Nutrients

5% or Less is Low

Vitamin A	4%
Vitamin C	2%
Calcium	20%
Iron	4%

20% or More is High

5. Footnote

6. Quick Guide to %DV

* Percent Daily Values are based on a 2,000 calorie diet. Your Daily Values may be higher or lower depending on your calorie needs.

	Calories:	2,000	2,500
Total Fat	Less than	65g	80g
Sat Fat	Less than	20g	25g
Cholesterol	Less than	300mg	300mg
Sodium	Less than	2,400mg	2,400mg
Total Carbohydrate		300g	375g
Dietary Fiber		25g	30g

The bottom part (see note #6 on the sample label above) contains a footnote with Daily Values (DVs) for 2,000 and 2,500 calorie diets. This footnote provides recommended dietary information for important nutrients, including fats, sodium, and fiber. The footnote is found only on larger packages and does not change from product to product.

Note 1: Serving Size

The place to start when you look at the Nutrition Facts label is the serving size and the number of servings in the package. Serving sizes are standardized to make it easier to compare similar foods; they are provided in familiar units, such as cups or pieces, followed by the metric amount, e.g., the number of grams.

The size of the serving on the food package influences the number of calories and all the nutrient amounts listed on the top part of the label. Pay attention to the serving size, especially how many servings there are in the food package. Then ask yourself, "How many servings am I consuming?" (e.g., one-half serving, one serving, or more). In the sample label, one serving of macaroni and cheese equals one cup. If you ate the whole package, you would eat two cups. That doubles the calories and other nutrient numbers, including the %Daily Values as shown in the sample label.

Note 2: Calories (and Calories From Fat)

Calories provide a measure of how much energy you get from a serving of a particular food. Many Americans consume more calories than they need without meeting recommended intakes for a number of nutrients. The calorie section of the label can help you manage your weight (i.e., gain, lose, or maintain.) Remember: the number of servings you consume determines the number of calories you actually eat (your portion amount).

In the example, there are 250 calories in one serving of this macaroni and cheese. How many calories from fat are there in one serving? Answer: 110 calories, which means almost half the calories in a single serving come from fat. What if you ate the whole package? In that case, you would consume two servings, or 500 calories, and 220 would come from fat.

Notes 3 and 4: The Nutrients

Look at the top of the nutrient section in the sample label. It shows you some key nutrients that impact on your health and separates them into two main groups:

Part VIII

Note 3: Nutrients to Limit

The nutrients listed first are the ones Americans generally eat in adequate amounts, or even too much. They are identified as: Limit These Nutrients. Eating too much fat, saturated fat, trans fat, cholesterol, or sodium may increase your risk of certain chronic diseases, such as heart disease, high blood pressure, and some cancers.

Note 4: Nutrients You Need

Most Americans don't get enough dietary fiber, vitamin A, vitamin C, calcium, and iron in their diets. They are identified as: Get Enough of These Nutrients. Eating enough of these nutrients can improve your health and help reduce the risk of some diseases and conditions. For example, getting enough calcium may reduce the risk of osteoporosis, a condition that results in brittle bones as one ages. Eating a diet high in dietary fiber promotes healthy bowel function. Additionally, a diet rich in fruits, vegetables, and grain products that contain dietary fiber, particularly soluble fiber, and low in saturated fat and cholesterol may reduce the risk of heart disease.

Note 5: Understanding the Footnote

The Footnote in the lower part of the nutrition label, which tells you "%DVs are based on a 2,000 calorie diet." This statement must be on all food labels. But the remaining information in the full footnote may not be on the package if the size of the label is too small. When the full footnote does appear, it will always be the same. It doesn't change from product to product, because it shows recommended dietary advice for all Americans—it is not about a specific food product.

Look at the amounts circled in the footnote—these are the Daily Values (DV) for each nutrient listed and are based on the advice of public health experts. DVs are recommended levels of intakes. DVs in the footnote are based on a 2,000 or 2,500 calorie diet. Note how the DVs for some nutrients change, while others (for cholesterol and sodium) remain the same for both calorie amounts.

Note 6: Percent Daily Value (%DV)

The Percent Daily Values (%DVs) are based on the Daily Value recommendations for key nutrients, but only for a 2,000 calorie daily diet—not 2,500 calories. You, like most people, may not know how many calories you consume in a day. But you can still use the %DV as a frame of reference whether or not you consume more or less than

2,000 calories.

The %DV helps you determine if a serving of food is high or low in a nutrient. Note: a few nutrients, like trans fat, do not have a %DV--they will be discussed later.

Do you need to know how to calculate percentages to use the %DV? No, the label (the %DV) does the math for you. It helps you interpret the numbers (grams and milligrams) by putting them all on the same scale for the day (0-100%DV).

The %DV column doesn't add up vertically to 100%. Instead each nutrient is based on 100% of the daily requirements for that nutrient (for a 2,000 calorie diet). This way you can tell high from low and know which nutrients contribute a lot, or a little, to your daily recommended allowance (upper or lower).

Digging Deeper

FDA: How to Understand and Use the Nutrition Facts Label

http://www.cfsan.fda.gov/~dms/foodlab.html#see6

A somewhat more detailed discussion of the Nutrition Facts Label is included at this webpage, which presents the information in color for ease of identification, including additional graphics.

FDA: Food Labeling and Nutrition

http://www.cfsan.fda.gov/label.html

The FDA Office of Nutritional Products, Labeling, and Dietary Supplements provides additional resources on this topic, including an overview, electronic newsletter, and recent news bulletins. There are many additional Food Label Education Tools to access on the left margin of the website for further study.

Chapter 40

Shopping, Cooking and Meal Planning

National Agricultural Library
U.S. Department of Agriculture

The Power of Choice!

We have the power of choice to decide which foods to buy at the grocery store. Making the healthiest food choices when shopping and eating out is a key to consuming a well-balanced diet.

Guidelines for a Healthy You

Healthy food choices are important for good health and well-being. Eating well means eating a variety of nutrient-packed foods and beverages from the food groups of MyPyramid and staying within your calorie needs. This, combined with choosing foods low in saturated and trans fats, cholesterol, added sugars, and salt (sodium) will help to ensure that you are eating a healthy diet while helping to maintain a healthy weight. If you choose to drink alcoholic beverages, do so sensibly and in moderation.

Basic Healthy Shopping Skills

Keys for making your shopping the most healthful:

➤ Know Your Store!

Grocery stores have thousands of products, with most food items grouped together to make your decision making easier. Many grocery stores have sections where foods are shelved much like the food groups of MyPyramid.

The MyPyramid food groups put foods with similar nutritional value together. These groups are Fruits, Vegetables, Grains, Milk (calcium-rich foods), and Meat and Beans (protein-rich foods).

Where are these food groups located in your store?

Consult the following chart for information on the typical locations of foods in most supermarkets, as well as the "Best Choices" recommendations.

Food Group	Typical Store Location(s)	Best Choices
Fruits	Produce aisle Canned goods Freezer aisle Salad bar	Variety! Fresh, frozen, canned, and dried fruits
Vegetables	Produce aisle Canned goods Freezer aisle Salad bar Pasta, rice, and bean aisle(s)	Variety! Fresh, frozen, and canned (especially dark green and orange) Dry beans and peas
Grains	Bakery Bread aisle Pasta and rice aisle(s) Cereal aisle	Whole grains for at least half of choices
Milk, yogurt, and cheese (calcium-rich foods)	Dairy case Refrigerated aisle	Non-fat and low-fat milk, yogurt, low-fat and fat-free cheeses

Meat, beans, fish, poultry, eggs, soy, and nuts (protein-rich foods)	Deli Meat and poultry case Seafood counter Egg case Canned goods Salad bar	Lean meats, skinless poultry, fish, Legumes (dried beans and peas)and nuts

Don't forget that your local farmers' market is a great place for finding healthy foods. Find a farmers' market in your state by using the link in "Digging Deeper."

- Bring a List!

  And stick to it! Healthy decisions start at home. Planning ahead can improve your health while saving you time and money. Before shopping, decide which foods you need and the quantity that will last until your next shopping trip.

  Consider creating a shopping list based on the MyPyramid food groups to include a variety of healthy food choices. Think about your menu ideas when adding items to your list. Write your list so that you match the groups to the layout of your store.

- Use the Facts

  The Nutrition Facts that is! The Nutrition Facts panel on the food label is your guide to making healthy choices. Using the Nutrition Facts panel is important when shopping because it enables you to compare foods before you buy.

  What are the facts? When reading the Nutrition Facts panel consider this:

Keep these low	**Look for more of these**
Saturated fats Trans fats Cholesterol Sodium	Fiber Vitamins A, C, and E Calcium, potassium, magnesium, and iron

Use the %Daily Value (DV) column when possible: 5%DV or less is low, 20%DV or more is high.

☛ Learn to Cook

There are thousands of websites devoted to the subject of cooking. Here are three websites that focus on teaching the principles of cooking:

» Video Cooking Lessons from StartCooking.com
http://startcooking.com/
Short video segments have been created by the developer of this website to provide basic cooking lessons. For those learning to cook, this is a good place to start.

» Cooking 101 at AZCentral.com
http://www.azcentral.com/home/food/cooking101/
Moving up one level, Cooking 101 provides dozens of cooking lessons and recipes. Click on several of the lesson topics on the right margin to learn both basic and more advanced concepts.

» Learn to Cook from CheftoChef.com
http://recipes.chef2chef.net/learn-to-cook/
Chef to Chef is a more sophisticated site developed by a chef. The subjects are diverse, and many of the lessons deal with more advanced cooking concepts and techniques.

☛ Meal Planning

Good nutrition goes hand in hand with careful meal planning. Here are five excellent websites dealing with recipes and meal planning for all levels of cooking skill:

» FoodNetwork.com
http://www.foodnetwork.com/
The Food Network offers extensive resources on cooking and meal preparation, with recipes, articles, nutrition information, and access to past episodes presented on the Food Network television programs.

» MealsforYou.com
http://www.mealsforyou.com/
MealsforYou is a family meal planning website, with 8,000 recipes, 1,400 meal plans, tips and guides, and a database that produces a shopping list for any of the posted recipes.

» RecipeGoldmine.com
http://www.recipegoldmine.com/
Recipe Goldmine is the home of thousands of recipes from around the world, including a collection of restaurant and clone recipes. You can also find kitchen charts, a food dictionary, grilling tips and recipes from the BBQ Guru, and much more.

» Love to Know Recipes
http://recipes.lovetoknow.com/wiki/Main_Page
Well-organized by topics and meals, LovetoKnow offers an extensive recipe website for all levels of cooking knowledge and skill. Information is organized along the left margin for ease of use, and there are numerous photographs of appetizing recipes.

» AllRecipes.com
http://allrecipes.com/
AllRecipes, a recipe exchange, cooking tips, and featured meal ideas are all part of this 10-year-old website. Accompanied by attractively presented examples, this extensive site has a list of subjects along the left margin for quick access.

Digging Deeper

Farmers' Markets in Every State

http://apps.ams.usda.gov/FarmersMarkets/

Because fruits and vegetables offer so many nutritional benefits, the U.S. Department of Agriculture (USDA) has assembled a database of farmers' markets in cities and towns throughout the United States. This is a handy place to search for a market near you.

USDA: How to Buy

http://www.ams.usda.gov/howtobuy/

Advice on how to buy foods of all kinds is presented at this USDA website. Topics include points to consider, nutritional value, quality, and grades available.

Federal Citizen Information Center: Action List for Fruits and Vegetables

http://www.pueblo.gsa.gov/cic_text/food/guideeat/fruitveg.html

The dietary benefits of fruits and vegetables are explained at this USDA website. Advice on incorporating fruits and vegetables in meals, numerous tips, and nutritional information are all part of this presentation.

Federal Citizen Information Center: Action List for Whole Grains

http://www.pueblo.gsa.gov/cic_text/food/guideeat/grains.html

Because of the nutritional benefits of whole grains, the USDA offers a site highlighting this group of foods. Nutritional benefits are explained, and the site contains ideas on how to include whole grains in meal planning.

National Institute of Child Health and Human Development: Milk Matters

http://www.nichd.nih.gov/milk/prob/calcium_sources.cfm

Geared especially to families with young children, Milk Matters highlights the nutritional benefits of milk and milk products, and includes extensive information on lactose intolerance and how to overcome its effects.

Nutrition.gov: Shopping, Cooking, and Meal Planning

http://www.nutrition.gov/nal_display/index.php?info_center=11&tax_level=1

Nutritional content of different classes of foods, official USDA dietary guidelines, nutrition at different life stages, weight management, dietary supplements, and food assistance programs are all covered here, along with advice on food shopping, cooking, and meal planning.

Chapter 41

Obesity in America: A National Health Problem

Centers for Disease Control and Prevention

Introduction

Since the mid-1970s, the prevalence of overweight and obesity has increased sharply for both adults and children. Data from two surveys conducted by the National Health and Nutrition Examination Survey (NHANES) show that among adults aged 20–74 years the prevalence of obesity increased from 15.0 percent (in the 1976–1980 survey) to 32.9 percent (in the 2003–2004 survey).

The two surveys also show increases in overweight among children and teens. For children aged 2–5 years, the prevalence of overweight increased from 5.0 percent to 13.9 percent; for those aged 6–11 years, prevalence increased from 6.5 percent to 18.8 percent; and for those aged 12–19 years, prevalence increased from 5.0 percent to 17.4 percent.

These increasing rates raise concern because of their implications for Americans' health. Being overweight or obese increases the risk of many diseases and health conditions, including the following:

1. Hypertension
2. Dyslipidemia (for example, high total cholesterol or high levels of triglycerides)
3. Type 2 diabetes
4. Coronary heart disease
5. Stroke
6. Gallbladder disease
7. Osteoarthritis
8. Sleep apnea and respiratory problems
9. Some cancers (endometrial, breast, and colon)

Although one of the national health objectives for the year 2010 is to reduce the prevalence of obesity among adults to less than 15 percent, current data indicate that the situation is worsening, rather than improving. This site provides a variety of information designed to help people understand this serious health issue and the efforts being made to address it.

Defining Overweight and Obesity

Overweight and obesity are both labels for ranges of weight that are greater than what is generally considered healthy for a given height. The terms also identify ranges of weight that have been shown to increase the likelihood of certain diseases and other health problems.

Definitions for Adults

For adults, overweight and obesity ranges are determined by using weight and height to calculate a number called the "body mass index" (BMI). BMI is used because, for most people, it correlates with their amount of body fat.

An adult who has a BMI between 25 and 29.9 is considered overweight.
An adult who has a BMI of 30 or higher is considered obese.

See the following table for an example.

Height	Weight Range	BMI	Considered
5' 9"	124 lbs. or less	Below 18.5	Underweight
	125 lbs. to 168 lbs.	18.5 to 24.9	Healthy weight
	169 lbs. to 202 lbs.	25.0 to 29.9	Overweight
	203 lbs. or more	30 or higher	Obese

It is important to remember that although BMI correlates with the amount of body fat, BMI does not directly measure body fat. As a result, some people, such as athletes, may have a BMI that identifies them as overweight even though they do not have excess body fat. For more information about BMI, visit Body Mass Index.

Other methods of estimating body fat and body fat distribution include measurements of skinfold thickness and waist circumference, calculation of waist-to-hip circumference ratios, and techniques such as ultrasound, computed tomography, and magnetic resonance imaging (MRI).

Definitions for Children and Teens

For children and teens, BMI ranges above a normal weight have different labels (at risk of overweight and overweight). Additionally, BMI ranges for children and teens are defined so that they take into account normal differences in body fat between boys and girls and differences in body fat at various ages. For more information about BMI for children and teens (also called BMI-for-age), visit BMI for Children and Teens.

Assessing Health Risks Associated With Being Overweight and Obese

BMI is just one indicator of potential health risks associated with being overweight or obese. For assessing someone's likelihood of developing overweight- or obesity-related diseases, the National Heart, Lung, and Blood Institute guidelines recommend looking at two other predictors:

The individual's waist circumference (because abdominal fat is a predictor of risk for obesity-related diseases).

Other risk factors the individual has for diseases and conditions associated with obesity (for example, high blood pressure or physical inactivity).

Digging Deeper

U.S. Surgeon General's Call to Action

http://www.surgeongeneral.gov/topics/obesity/

Overweight and obesity in America are major public health problems. The Surgeon General of the United States has developed a "Call to Action" to address these health conditions in his Vision of the Future. There are links to explain the nature and extent of this problem today, the health consequences, ways of addressing the problem, and special advice for teens and adolescents.

State-Based Programs to Prevent Obesity and Other Chronic Diseases

http://www.cdc.gov/nccdphp/dnpa/obesity/state_programs/index.htm

State programs to address and prevent obesity as well as other chronic conditions can be accessed through the link to Funded States. Twenty-eight states currently have special programs funded by the federal government.

Part IX

Exercise and Physical Fitness

Chapter 42

The Many Benefits of Physical Activity

Centers for Disease Control and Prevention

"It's easier to maintain your health than regain it," said world-renowned physician and expert on fitness and health, Dr. Kenneth H. Cooper.

Consider the following 2004 figures from the National Center for Health Statistics:

Percent of adults 18–24 engaged in regular leisure time physical activity	36.6%
Percent of the same group who are inactive.	30.1%

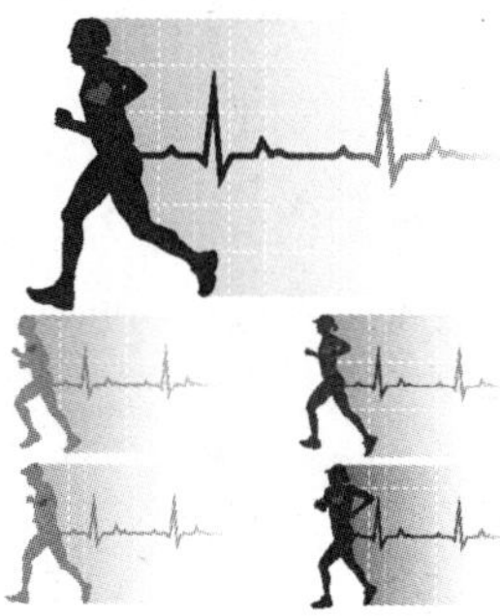

Physical activity can bring you many health benefits. People who enjoy participating in moderate or vigorous physical activity on a regular basis benefit by lowering their risk of developing coronary heart disease, stroke, non-insulin-dependent (type 2) diabetes mellitus, high blood pressure, and colon cancer by 30–50 percent (according to the U.S. Department of Health and Human Services, 1996). Additionally, active people have lower premature death rates than people who are the least active.

Having Fun and Staying Healthy

Regular physical activity can improve health and reduce the risk of premature death in the following ways:

1. Reduces the risk of developing coronary heart disease (CHD) and the risk of dying from CHD
2. Reduces the risk of stroke
3. Reduces the risk of having a second heart attack in people who have already had one heart attack
4. Lowers both total blood cholesterol and triglycerides and increases high-density lipoproteins (HDL or "good" cholesterol)
5. Lowers the risk of developing high blood pressure
6. Helps reduce blood pressure in people who already have hypertension
7. Lowers the risk of developing non-insulin-dependent (type 2) diabetes mellitus
8. Reduces the risk of developing colon cancer
9. Helps people achieve and maintain a healthy body weight
10. Reduces feelings of depression and anxiety
11. Promotes psychological well-being and reduces feelings of stress
12. Helps build and maintain healthy bones, muscles, and joints
13. Helps older adults become stronger and better able to move about without falling or becoming excessively fatigued

Can a Lack of Physical Activity Hurt Your Health?

Evidence shows that those who are not physically active are not helping their health, and may be hurting it. The closer we look at the health risks associated with a lack of physical activity, the more convincing it is that Americans who are not yet regularly physically active should become active.

Physical Activity and Weight Management

An increase in physical activity is an important part of your weight management program. Most weight loss occurs because of decreased caloric intake. Sustained physical activity is most helpful in the prevention of weight regain. In addition, exercise has a benefit of reducing the risks of cardiovascular disease and diabetes, beyond that produced by weight reduction alone. Start exercising slowly, and gradually increase the intensity. Trying too hard at first can lead to injury.

Examples of moderate amounts of physical activity	
Common Chores	**Sport Activities**
Washing and waxing a car for 45–60 minutes	Playing volleyball for 45–60 minutes
Washing windows or floors for 45–60 minutes	Playing touch football for 45 minutes
Gardening for 30–45 minutes	Walking 1.75 miles in 35 minutes (20 min/mile)
Wheeling self in wheelchair 30–40 minutes	Basketball (shooting baskets) 30 minutes
Pushing a stroller 1.5 miles in 30 minutes	Bicycling 5 miles in 30 minutes
Raking leaves for 30 minutes	Dancing fast (social) for 30 minutes
Walking 2 miles in 30 minutes (15 min/mile)	Water aerobics for 30 minutes
Shoveling snow for 15 minutes	Swimming laps for 20 minutes
Stairwalking for 15 minutes	Basketball (playing game) for 15–20 minutes
	Bicycling 4 miles in 15 minutes
	Jumping rope for 15 minutes
	Running 1.5 miles in 15 min. (10 min/mile)

Your exercise can be done all at one time, or intermittently throughout the day. Initial activities may be walking or swimming at a slow pace. You can start out by walking 30 minutes for three days a week, building to 45 minutes of more intense walking at least five days a week. With this regimen, you can burn 100 to 200 calories more each day. All adults should set a long term goal to accumulate at least 30 minutes or more of moderate physical activity on most, and preferably all, days of the week. This regimen can be adapted to other forms of physical activity, but walking is particularly attractive because of its safety and accessibility. Also, try to increase "every day" activity, such as taking the stairs instead of the elevator. Reducing sedentary time is a good strategy to increase activity by undertaking frequent, less strenuous activities. With time, you may be able to engage in more strenuous activities. Competitive sports, such as tennis and volleyball, can provide an enjoyable form of exercise for many, but care must be taken to avoid injury.

Activity Progression

For the beginner, the activity level can begin at very light intensity and would include an increase in standing activities, special chores like room painting, pushing a wheelchair, yard work, ironing, cooking, and playing a musical instrument.

The next level would be light activity, such as slow walking of 24 minutes/mile, garage work, carpentry, house cleaning, child care, golf, sailing, and recreational table tennis.

The next level would be moderate activity such as walking 15 minute/mile, weeding and hoeing a garden, carrying a load, cycling, skiing, tennis, and dancing.

High activity would include walking 10 minutes/mile or walking with load uphill, tree felling, heavy manual digging, basketball, climbing, or soccer/kick ball.

You may also want to try:

- flexibility exercise to attain full range of joint motion
- strength or resistance exercise
- aerobic conditioning

Digging Deeper

President's Council on Physical Fitness and Sports

http://www.fitness.gov/

Fitness.gov is the health, physical activity, fitness, and sports information website of the President's Council on Physical Fitness and Sports. You can find out about the council and its work, view its publications, and link to the resources of other government agencies, as well as to health and fitness organizations. To find out how you can start a physical activity program today and stay active and fit for life while earning presidential awards, visit the free, interactive physical activity and fitness website at www.presidentschallenge.org.

National Institutes of Health: Exercise and Physical Fitness

http://health.nih.gov/result.asp/245

All aspects of exercise and physical fitness are addressed at the website of the National Institutes of Health, organized by body system focus. Available resources are related to exercise and heart health, bone health, digestive health, obesity, and other topics. The link to the Body Mass Index Table from the National Heart Institute is worth visiting, because it applies to individuals of all ages.

National Association for Health and Fitness

http://www.physicalfitness.org/

The National Association for Health and Fitness (NAHF) is a non-profit organization that exists to improve the quality of life for individuals in the United States through the promotion of physical fitness, sports, and healthy lifestyles. NAHF accomplishes this work by fostering and supporting governor's and state councils and coalitions that promote and encourage regular physical activity. There are extensive resources at this site, including news postings, information on health observances related to fitness, links to individual state councils (at the bottom of the website), and links to numerous other programs and organizations, also located at the bottom of this site.

Chapter 43

The Components of Physical Fitness

Centers for Disease Control and Prevention

What does it mean to be "physically fit?"

According to the U.S. Department of Health and Human Services (USDHHS), physical fitness is defined as "a set of attributes that people have or achieve that relates to the ability to perform physical activity" (USDHHS, 1996). In other words, it is more than being able to run a long distance or lift a lot of weight at the gym. Being fit is not defined only by what kind of activity you do, how long you do it, or at what level of intensity. While these are important measures of fitness, they only address single area.

Overall fitness is made up of five main components:

1. Cardiorespiratory endurance
2. Muscular strength
3. Muscular endurance
4. Body composition
5. Flexibility

In order to assess your level of fitness, look at all five components together.

What is "cardiorespiratory endurance (cardiorespiratory fitness)?"

Cardiorespiratory endurance is the ability of the body's circulatory and respiratory systems to supply fuel during sustained physical activity (USDHHS, 1996, as adapted from Corbin and Lindsey, 1994). To improve your cardiorespiratory endurance, try activities that keep your heart rate elevated at a safe level for a sustained length of time, such as walking, swimming, or bicycling. The activity you choose does not have to be strenuous to improve your cardiorespiratory endurance. Start slowly with an activity you enjoy, and gradually work up to a more intense pace.

What is "muscular strength?"

Muscular strength is the ability of the muscle to exert force during an activity (USDHHS, 1996, as adapted from Wilmore and Costill, 1994). The key to making your muscles stronger is working them against resistance from either weights or gravity. If you want to gain muscle strength, try exercises such as lifting weights or climbing stairs rapidly.

What is "muscular endurance?"

Muscular endurance is the ability of the muscle to continue to perform without fatigue (USDHHS, 1996, as adapted from Wilmore and Costill, 1994). To improve your muscle endurance, try cardiorespiratory activities such as walking, jogging, bicycling, or dancing.

What is "body composition?"

Body composition refers to the relative amount of muscle, fat, bone, and other vital parts of the body (USDHHS, 1996, as adapted from Corbin and Lindsey, 1994). A person's total body weight (what you see on the bathroom scale) may not change over time. But the bathroom scale does not assess how much of that body weight is fat and how much is lean mass (muscle, bone, tendons, and ligaments). Body composition is important to consider for health and managing your weight!

What is "flexibility?"

Flexibility is the range of motion around a joint (USDHHS, 1996, as adapted from Wilmore and Costill, 1994). Good flexibility in the joints can help prevent injuries through all stages of life. If you want to improve your flexibility, try activities that lengthen the muscles, such as swimming or a basic stretching program.

DIGGING DEEPER

CDC: Measuring Physical Activity Intensity

http://www.cdc.gov/nccdphp/dnpa/physical/measuring/index.htm

Various tests to measure the intensity of different physical activities are presented at this website of the Centers for Disease Control and Prevention. On the left margin one finds links about getting started with a physical program, incorporating physical activity into daily life, fitness terms, and other resources.

American Heart Association: Body Composition Tests

http://www.americanheart.org/presenter.jhtml?identifier=4489

Tests to measure body composition can be found at the website of the American Heart Association, as well as information on the Body Mass Index (BMI) which includes a chart of different heights and weights, recommended BMI levels, and high risk levels.

Mayo Clinic: Aerobic Physical Exercise

http://www.mayoclinic.com/health/aerobic-exercise/EP00002

The benefits of 30 minutes of aerobic physical exercise are discussed at this web page of the Mayo Clinic, including a lengthy list of health benefits. There are also a series of useful links to related information on this topic.

Chapter 44

Getting Started: Recommendations for Adult Exercise Programs

Centers for Disease Control and Prevention

Physical activity does not need to be hard to provide some benefit. Participating in moderate-intensity physical activity is a vital component of a healthy lifestyle for people of all ages and abilities. There is no demographic or social group in America that could not benefit from becoming more active. The following table provides recommendations on how to increase your physical activity based on your current activity level. Check it out to see where you are and how you can challenge yourself.

If...	**Then...**
You do not currently engage in regular physical activity,	you should begin by incorporating a few minutes of physical activity into each day, gradually building up to 30 minutes or more of moderate activities.
You are now active, but at less than the recommended levels,	you should strive to adopt more consistent activity: -moderate physical activity for 30 minutes or more on five or more days of the week, or -vigorous physical activity for 20 minutes or more on three or more days of the week.

You currently engage in moderate-intensity activities for at least 30 minutes on give or more days of the week,	you may achieve even greater health benefits by increasing the time spent on or the intensity of those activities.
You currently regularly engage in vigorous-intensity activities 20 minutes or more on three or more days of the week,	you should continue to do so.

**Scientific evidence to date supports the statements above.*

What is "moderate-intensity physical activity?"

Moderate-intensity physical activity refers to any activity that burns 3.5–7 calories per minute (kcal/min) (Ainsworth et al., 2000). These levels are equal to the effort a healthy individual might burn while walking briskly, mowing the lawn, dancing, swimming for recreation, or bicycling.

What is "vigorous-intensity physical activity?"

Vigorous-intensity physical activity refers to any activity that burns more than 7 calories per minute (kcal/min) (Ainsworth et al., 2000). These levels are equal to the effort a healthy individual might burn while jogging, engaging in heavy yard work, participating in high-impact aerobic dancing, swimming continuous laps, or bicycling uphill.

- ☛ On average, regularly participating in one or more moderate-intensity or vigorous-intensity activities is required to burn a minimum of 150 calories of energy per day, seven days per week, or total of 1,000 calories/week (Jones et al., 1998).
- ☛ The time needed to burn 150 calories of energy in a day depends on the intensity of the activities chosen. For example, if someone selects moderate-intensity activities, the time required to meet the minimum

recommendation would be generally 30 minutes per day. The more vigorous the activities chosen, the less time needed (22 minutes or less) to burn the minimum of 150 calories during the day.

Number of Minutes of Activity Required to Burn 150 calories

Activity	Minutes
Stair walking	15
Shoveling snow	15
Running 1/2 mile (10 minutes/mile)	5
Jumping rope	15
Bicycling 4 miles	15
Playing basketball	15–20
Participating in wheelchair basketball	20
Swimming laps	20
Engaging in water aerobics	30
Walking 2 miles (15 min/mile)	30
Raking leaves	30
Pushing a stroller 1 1/2 miles	30
Dancing fast (social)	30
Bicycling 5 miles	30
Shooting baskets	30
Walking 1 3/4 miles (20 minutes/mile)	35
Wheeling self in wheelchair	30–40
Gardening (standing)	30–45
Playing touch football	30–45
Playing volleyball	45
Washing windows or floors	45–60
Washing and waxing a car or boat	45–60

For examples of activities that are considered "moderate-intensity" and "vigorous-intensity," check out "Digging Deeper," below.

Digging Deeper

Physical Activities Defined by Level of Intensity

http://www.cdc.gov/nccdphp/dnpa/physical/pdf/PA_Intensity_table_2_1.pdf

This page defines moderate and vigorous physical activity, and gives many examples of each type. Activities include sports as well as everyday activities such as cleaning, gardening, and washing a car.

HealthierUS.gov

http://www.healthierus.gov/exercise.html

Exercise fundamentals and programs are presented at this federal government website, which focuses on the importance of active exercise as a regular daily habit. There are links to getting started, establishing a program, keeping track, and learning fitness fundamentals.

Part X

Health and Healthcare

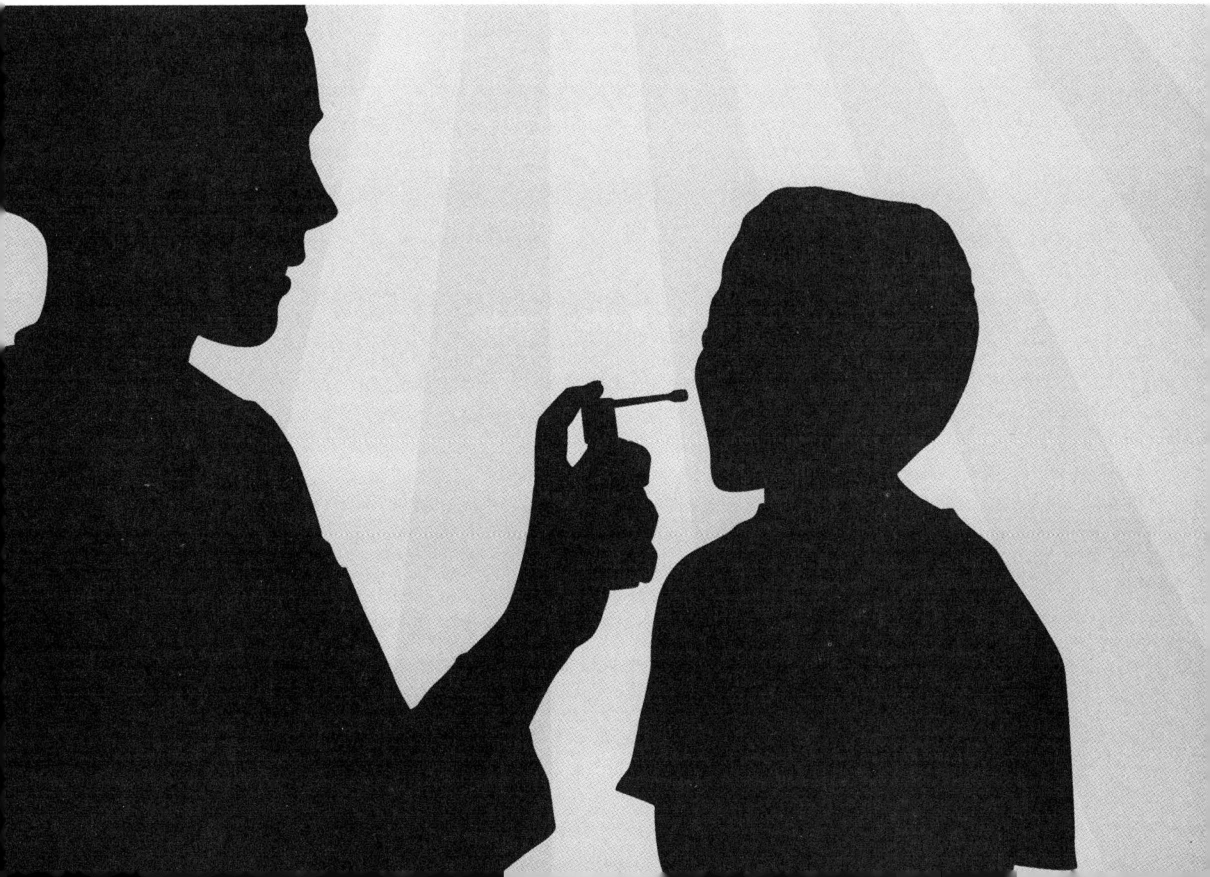

Chapter 45

Staying Healthy: How to Take Charge of Your Health

U.S. Agency For Healthcare And Research Quality

Introduction

You may ask yourself, "How do I begin to improve my health habits?" A good way to start is to set small goals instead of large ones that you won't be able to meet. For example, instead of setting a goal of losing 15 pounds in the next year, set some smaller goals for eating better and being more active. You may decide to trade your morning doughnut for a bowl of cereal or start taking the stairs instead of the elevator at work.

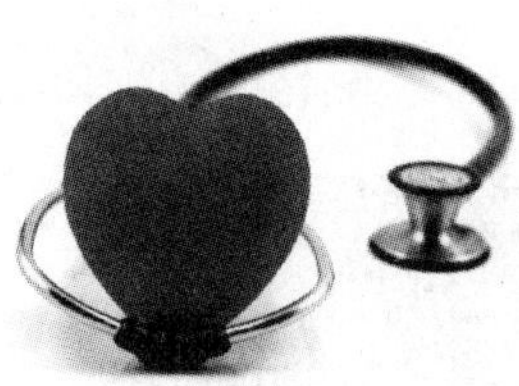

Below are a series of recommendations that apply to everyone, young and old:

I. Reducing Your Risk for Heart Disease

Overall, you can reduce your risk of heart disease if you:

- Maintain a healthy weight, by eating right and staying physically active
- Quit smoking
- Control your blood pressure and cholesterol levels
- If you have diabetes, control your disease

II. Watching Your Weight

Being overweight increases your risk for heart disease, diabetes, and high blood pressure. Your doctor can tell you what you should weigh for your height. To stay at a healthy weight, you need to balance the number of calories you eat with the number you burn off during your activities. You can get to your healthy weight and stay there by doing two things: eating right and being physically active.

III. Eating Right

Eating the right foods in the right amounts can help you live a longer, healthier life. Many illnesses and conditions—such as heart disease, obesity, high blood pressure, and type 2 diabetes—can be prevented or controlled by eating right. A healthy diet also provides the vitamins and minerals you need. It's never too late to start eating right. Here are some helpful tips:

Part X

1. Eat a variety of foods, including:
   - Fruits and vegetables
   - Proteins, such as meat, eggs, and dried beans
   - Dairy products, such as milk, yogurt, and cheese
   - Grains, especially whole grains, and legumes
   - Foods with unsaturated fats, which do not raise cholesterol levels. These include vegetable oils, fish, avocados, and many varieties of nuts.

2. Limit calories and saturated fat. Foods high in saturated fats are high in calories, so they can cause weight gain. They also increase your cholesterol levels. Try to limit:

- High-fat dairy products such as ice cream, butter, cheese, cream, and whole milk.
- Meats high in fat.
- Palm and coconut oils and lard.
- Portion sizes. Don't choose "super" or other oversized portions. Be aware of how much you eat.

IV. Keeping Active

Physical activity can help prevent heart disease, obesity, high blood pressure, type 2 diabetes, osteoporosis (thinning bones), and mental health problems such as depression. Physical activity helps you feel better overall.

- What to Do

  All kinds of physical activity will help you stay healthy, whether it is moderate or vigorous. It's a good idea to aim for at least moderate activity— such as brisk walking, raking leaves, house cleaning, or playing with children—for 20 to 30 minutes most days of the week. Generally, the more active you are, the healthier you will become.

- How to Get Started and Keep at It

  If you have not been active, start slowly. Choose something that fits into your daily life. Choose an activity you like, or try a new one. Activities such as dancing, swimming, or biking can be fun.

- Ask a Friend to Exercise with You, or Join a Group.

  Make time in your day for physical activity. If the weather is bad, try an exercise show on TV, watch an exercise tape, walk in the mall, or work around the house.

➤ V. Skin cancer is often preventable.

You can lower your risk for skin cancer by:

» Limiting the amount of time you spend in the sun, especially between the hours of 10:00 a.m. and 3:00 p.m.

» Using sunscreen and protective clothing—such as broad-brimmed hats and long-sleeved shirts—when you are in the sun. (But don't stay out in the sun longer.)

➤ VI. Preventing Injury

Following basic safety rules can prevent many serious injuries. Here are two checklists to follow to help keep you and your family safe.

To help protect yourself at home:

» Use smoke detectors. Remember to check the batteries every month and change them every year.

» Lock up guns and ammunition and store them separately.

» Keep hallways and stairwells well lit.

» Remove or repair things that someone could trip on, such as loose rugs, electrical cords, and toys.

To help protect yourself away from home:

» Wear seat belts.

» Never drive after drinking alcohol.

» Wear a safety helmet while riding a motorcycle or bicycle.

» Follow workplace safety rules.

➤ VII. Taking Medicines Correctly

Always be sure you know everything about a medicine before you take it. This information will help you get the full benefits from your medicine. It will also help you avoid taking too much or too little of a medicine. Taking medicine in the wrong way can make you worse instead of better.

VIII. Making Smart Choices About Sexual and Reproductive Health

Sexually transmitted diseases, such as HIV infection, herpes, and hepatitis B, are passed easily from one person to another during sex. Sexually transmitted diseases may cause serious health problems, and many STDs can harm a pregnancy and the health of the baby. If you have sex, you may be at risk for a sexually transmitted disease. Your risk is increased if:

- You or your partner has or has had other sexual partners.
- You do not always use condoms consistently and correctly.
- Your partner has a sexually transmitted disease.
- You use injection drugs.
- You live in an area where a particular sexually transmitted disease is common.

If you are at increased risk for sexually transmitted diseases, talk to your doctor about whether you should be tested. This is especially important because some diseases, such as chlamydia, may have no symptoms. Serious health problems may develop before you realize you have a disease. You can greatly lower your risk for sexually transmitted diseases by using a male condom every time you have sex.

IX. Planning Your Family

If you have sex and are not ready to have a child, you and your partner may want to use some form of birth control. Many birth control methods are available for men and women, each with advantages and disadvantages. The condom, however, is the only birth control method that protects against most STDs, including HIV/AIDS. Whichever birth control method you choose, remember that for it to work, you must use it all the time and use it correctly.

X. For Women: Folic Acid During Childbearing Years

If you are a woman who can become pregnant, you should take at least 400 micrograms (or 0.4 mg) of folic acid, or folate, every day. If you have enough folic acid in your body when you become pregnant, this vitamin can lower the risk for birth defects of your baby's brain or spine. You need to be taking the vitamin before you become pregnant because by the time you know you are pregnant, birth defects may already have formed in your child.

XI. Overcoming Depression

Everybody feels "down" or "blue" sometimes. But if these feelings are very strong or last for most of the day nearly every day for two weeks or longer, they may be due to a medical illness called depression. The good news is that depression can be treated. You do not have to face this problem without help. Here are some warning signs of depression.

Changes in the way you feel:

- You feel sad, hopeless, or guilty most of the time.
- You feel tired or lack energy.
- You have thoughts of suicide or death.

Changes in sleeping and eating habits:

- You sleep either too much or too little.
- Your appetite has changed. You have gained or lost weight.

Changes in daily living:

- You have lost interest and pleasure in daily activities.

» You have problems making decisions or thinking clearly.

If you have had most of these symptoms for at least two weeks, you may be suffering from depression. Talk to your doctor about whether you are depressed and what you should do about it. The sooner you get treatment for depression, the sooner you will begin to feel better. The longer you wait, the harder depression is to treat. Depression usually is treated with counseling, medicine, or both. Medicines are not habit forming and work for people with all levels of depression. Treatment works gradually over several weeks. If you do not start to feel better after this time, tell your doctor. It may take some time to find what works best for you.

➤ XII. Getting Help for Smoking and Alcohol or Drug Abuse

» Smoking

More than 430,000 Americans die each year from smoking. Smoking causes illnesses such as cancer, heart and lung disease, stroke, and problems with pregnancy. When you quit, you lower your chances of getting sick from smoking. Quitting is hard. Most people try several times before they quit for good.

» Alcohol or Drug Abuse

Abusing alcohol or drugs can cause serious medical and personal problems. Alcohol and drug abuse can lead to accidents, depression, and problems with friends, family, and work. Drug use can cause heart and breathing problems. Alcohol abuse can cause liver disease, heart problems, and several kinds of cancer.

➤ XIII. Other Recommendations for Good Health

In addition to the above recommendations, health experts recommend the following:

» Learn about and control your cholesterol level.

» Find out if you have high blood pressure and how to control it.

» For women, get regular Pap smears and learn how to check for breast cancer.

» Get regular dental checkups and practice good oral hygiene.

Digging Deeper

Centers for Disease Control: Healthy Living Resources

http://www.cdc.gov/HealthyLiving/

Resources and recommendations for healthy living are provided at this webpage from the U.S. Centers for Disease Control and Prevention (CDC), including antibiotic resistance, bone health, physical activity, reproductive health, and vaccines and immunizations. Other topics on the site address nutrition, statistics, and behavioral risk factors.

Understanding Drug Abuse and Addiction

http://www.nida.nih.gov/Infofacts/understand.html

The National Institute on Drug Abuse provides extensive information on the major drugs of abuse, the biology of addiction, drug abuse and AIDS/HIV, and links to information on treatment and prevention.

National Institute on Alcohol Abuse and Alcoholism

http://www.niaaa.nih.gov/

Alcohol abuse is a major topic relating to people of all ages, and the National Institute on Alcohol Abuse and Alcoholism provides consumer and clinical information, alerts and news briefs, and special resources on underage drinking. In addition, there are important articles on alcohol and pregnancy and alcohol and family history.

CDC: Sexually Transmitted Diseases

http://www.cdc.gov/std/

The Centers for Disease Control and Prevention offers this informative website on the nature and serious risks associated with all the major sexually transmitted diseases, including risk factors, identification, prevalence, and treatment.

Chapter 46

How to Choose a Doctor or Hospital

Joint Commission on Accreditation
Federal Citizen Information Center

Part I: Choosing a Health Professional: Recommended Search Criteria

When searching for a doctor, dentist, or other healthcare professional:

1. Find out whether they are licensed in your state. A state or local occupational and professional licensing board will be able to give you this information

2. Research whether they are board certified in the appropriate specialty. You can find this information on the websites of the American Medical Association and the American Board of Medical Specialties, listed in "Digging Deeper," below.

3. Ask how often they have done the procedure you need and their success rate. You may be able to find some of this information on the internet. For example, the Centers for Disease Control and Prevention report the success rates and number of procedures performed by fertility clinics. Some states collect and post data on the success of heart-bypass surgery.

4. Check whether there have been any complaints or disciplinary actions taken by visiting *www.docboard.org* which is listed in "Digging Deeper." There are also pay-for-use sites with similar information, such as *www.Docinfo.org*,

maintained by the Federation of State Medical Boards.

Part II: Selecting a Hospital

You may not always have the opportunity to choose the hospital from which you receive care, especially in an emergency. However, when you or a loved one has a planned admission to the hospital, obtaining some important information first can help make your hospital experience a positive one.

The following recommendations are provided by the Joint Commission, an independent, not-for-profit organization that evaluates and accredits more than 15,000 health care organizations and programs in the United States:

- ✓ Begin by asking your doctor about the advantages or special characteristics of each hospital where he or she practices. Your doctor can help you select the hospital that is best for you. You should also verify which hospitals are accepted by your insurance, HMO or PPO plan. Then ask the following questions to help you determine which hospital meets your needs.
- ✓ Is the hospital conveniently located? Can you and your family get there easily for scheduled as well as emergency medical care?
- ✓ Is the hospital accredited by a nationally recognized accrediting body, such as the Joint Commission? Joint Commission accreditation means the organization voluntarily sought accreditation and met national health and safety standards. The Joint Commission provides on-site surveys to review the hospital's medical and nursing care, physical condition, life safety program, special care units, pharmaceutical services, infection control procedures, and a number of other areas affecting patient care.
- ✓ Does the hospital have a written description of its services and fees? What resources does the hospital provide to help you find financial assistance if you need it?
- ✓ Is the hospital clean? Visit the hospital and look around. Ask to see the waiting rooms and patient rooms.

- ✓ Do the services and specialties provided by the hospital meet your specific medical needs? Do you have a medical condition requiring specialized attention? Your medical history and current medical condition may affect the type of hospital you choose.
- ✓ Do you know the hospital's success record in carrying out the specific medical procedure you need? What is the training of the doctor who will perform the procedure? Ask how often the particular procedure is done.
- ✓ Does the hospital explain the patient's rights and responsibilities? Ask to see a copy of the hospital's patient rights and responsibilities information.
- ✓ Do you know who is responsible for maintaining your personal care plan? How are the caregivers kept informed about your specific care needs? Can you or your family be kept up to date on your medical care?
- ✓ Does the hospital have social workers? Ask what services the social workers provide. Social workers usually help patients and their families find emotional, social, clinical, physical, and financial support services.

Part III: Filing a Complaint Against a Physician

If you have a complaint about the medical services you received from a physician, you may file a complaint with your state medical board. The Federation of State Medical Boards, listed in "Digging Deeper," offers a complete online directory of state medical boards. You can also call **817-868-4000** to get the phone number for your state medical board.

Digging Deeper

Joint Commission on Accreditation

http://www.jointcommission.org/

An independent, not-for-profit organization, the Joint Commission accredits and certifies more than 15,000 health care organizations and programs in the United States. Extensive resources about the organization and its services are provided at this website.

American Medical Association (AMA)

http://www.ama-assn.org/

http://www.ama-assn.org/

The AMA is the largest medical advocacy organization for physicians, with extensive resources on 650,000 physicians offered through DoctorFinder, accessible by the public, as well as professional resources and physician management tools and databases.

American Board of Medical Specialties (ABMS)

http://www.abms.org/

The ABMS can be of assistance in determining whether a particular physician is certified in a given specialty or can help you find physicians with specific certifications. For consumers, the site explains the importance of certification and how a physician gains this standing in a particular field.

Federation of State Medical Boards

http://www.fsmb.org

Through the website of the Federation of State Medical Boards, a visitor can check the credentials of a particular physician and/or obtain information from a medical board in a particular state. Under "Medical Services," one can access a directory of medical boards through the United States.

Docboard.org

http://www.docboard.org

DocBoard and its search engine called DocFinder provide access to a database of physicians in the United States, organized by state, in order to check their licensing credentials.

American Dental Association: Find a Dentist

http://www.ada.org/public/directory/index.asp

The American Dental Association is, according to their website, the "world's largest and oldest national dental asssociation." Look for a member dentist by specialty or location, or search for a specific dentist by name.

Chapter 47

Using Urgent Care Clinics and Hospital Emergency Rooms

Urgent Care Association of America
American College of Emergency Physicians

Many young people do not have regular physicians or have not visited a doctor in many years. Nevertheless, medical needs arise all the time, from accidents or injuries or from a sudden flu or bad cold. The question then becomes: "Where should I go for medical care?"

This chapter examines the roles of both hospital emergency rooms and the newer urgent care clinics which are being opened in towns and cities all across the country.

When should I go to an Emergency Department?

According to the American College of Emergency Physicians, more than 300,000 Americans, on average, are treated in our nation's emergency departments every day, and patients are treated for a wide variety of medical conditions.

How do you decide when a medical condition rises to the level of a medical "emergency?" The American College of Emergency Physicians (ACEP) offers the following list of warning signs that indicate a medical emergency:

- **Difficulty breathing, shortness of breath**

- **Chest or upper abdominal pain or pressure**
- **Fainting, sudden dizziness, weakness**
- **Changes in vision**
- **Confusion or changes in mental status**
- **Any sudden or severe pain**
- **Uncontrolled bleeding**
- **Severe or persistent vomiting or diarrhea**
- **Coughing or vomiting blood**
- **Suicidal feelings**
- **Difficulty speaking**
- **Shortness of breath**
- **Unusual abdominal pain**

Children have unique medical problems and may display different symptoms than adults. Symptoms that are serious for a child may not be as serious for an adult. Children may also be unable to communicate their condition, which means an adult will have to interpret the behavior. Always get immediate medical attention if you think your child is having a medical emergency.

"If you or a loved one think you need emergency care, come to the emergency department and have a doctor examine you," says Dr. Frederick Blum, president of American College of Emergency Physicians (ACEP). "If you think the medical condition is life-threatening or the person's condition will worsen on the way to the hospital, then you need to call 9-1-1 and have your local emergency medical services provider come to you."

Emergency departments see patients based on the severity of their illnesses or injuries, not on a first-come, first serve basis. With that in mind, ACEP offers the following tips to patients when they come to an emergency department in order to get the best possible care as quickly as possible:

1. **Bring a list of medications and allergies.**

   What's the name of the medication you are taking? How often do you take it and for how long? A list of allergies is important, especially if there are many of them. Be sure to include medications, foods, insects, or any other product that may cause an allergic reaction.

2. **Bring a medical history form with you.**

   ACEP has medical history forms available on its website, as listed in "Digging Deeper" below.

3. **Know your immunizations.**

   This will likely be a long list for children, mainly tetanus, flu, and hepatitis B for adults.

4. **Remain calm.**

   Obviously it is difficult to remain composed if you've been badly injured, but a calm attitude can help increase communication with the doctors and nurses who are caring for you.

"Communication is important when you arrive at an emergency department," according to Dr. Blum. "I want to know as much about the patient, as quickly as I can, so the proper treatment can begin. There can be long waits in the emergency department as doctors and nurses tend to those with the most severe conditions, but by all means tell us if you are in pain or there is any change in your condition while you're at the hospital."

What is urgent care?

According to the Urgent Care Association of America, urgent care is defined as the delivery of ambulatory medical care outside of a hospital emergency department on an unscheduled basis. Urgent care centers treat many of the same problems that can be seen in a primary care physician's office.

What are some of the advantages of urgent care?

- They do not require an appointment and operate on a "walk-in" basis.
- They offer extended hours in evenings and on weekends.
- They are especially appropriate for non-emergency needs, such as treatment for minor injuries or common illnesses.
- They may offer savings over the cost of emergency visits.
- They complement primary care, since they function as overflow valves for the public, when timely appointments to a primary care physician office are not available or after regular office hours when patients needing immediate attention would otherwise be diverted to a hospital emergency department.

What should you bring to an urgent care center?

Because you will not be known by the physicians at a local urgent care center, try to bring the same information (listed above) that you should bring to the emergency room of a hospital. The more information you provide, especially about allergies to medications and the names of all the drugs you are taking, the safer your experience will be.

Digging Deeper

American College of Emergency Physicians

http://www.acep.org/

The American College of Emergency Physicians (ACEP) is the largest emergency medicine association in the world. Founded in 1968, it represents more than 25,000 emergency medicine specialists and serves as the leading advocate for emergency physicians, their patients, and the public.

Urgent Care Association of America

http://www.ucaoa.org/

UCAOA represents the many urgent care centers that provide appropriate and timely alternatives to the more costly and inconvenient hospital emergency departments. True emergencies require hospital emergency services, but urgent care centers meet the need for convenient access for minor injuries and illnesses.

Urgent Care Centers by State

http://www.ucaoa.org/buyers/ucaoa_orgs.php

This link provides listings of the urgent care centers in each state that are members of the Urgent Care Association of America. There could be other similar facilities which are not members, and which are listed in the Yellow Pages. Be sure that the facility you intend to us is accredited, and ask to see the credentials of the physician on duty.

Chapter 48

Where to Find Reliable Health Information

National Institutes of Health

Introduction

There are thousands of health-related websites on the internet, but most of them are private or commercial in nature, making it difficult to be assured of their reliability. For this reason, we have provided a listing of some of the most comprehensive government, educational, and non-profit health and medical resources for consumers.

I. Finding Health Information

In general, good sources of health information include the following:

- Sites that end in ".gov," sponsored by the federal government, like the U.S. Department of Health and Human Services *(www.hhs.gov)*, the FDA *(www.fda.gov)*, the National Institutes of Health *(www.nih.gov)*, the Centers for Disease Control and Prevention *(www.cdc.gov)*, and the National Library of Medicine *(www.nlm.nih.gov)*.
- ".edu" sites, which are run by universities or medical schools, such as Johns Hopkins University School of Medicine and the University of California at Berkeley Hospital health system, as well as other health

care facility sites, like the Mayo Clinic and the Cleveland Clinic.

- ".org" sites maintained by not-for-profit groups whose focus is research and teaching the public about specific diseases or conditions, such as the American Diabetes Association, the American Cancer Society, and the American Heart Association.
- Medical and scientific journals, such as The New England Journal of Medicine and the Journal of the American Medical Association, although these aren't written for consumers and could be hard to understand.

II. Noteworthy Federal Government Health Information Sources

- Healthfinder from the U.S. Department of Health and Human Services
  http://www.healthfinder.gov
  Healthfinder.gov is an award-winning federal website for consumers, developed by the U.S. Department of Health and Human Services together with other federal agencies. Since 1997, *www.healthfinder.gov* has been recognized as a key resource for finding the best government and non-profit health and human services information on the internet. Healthfinder.gov links to carefully selected information and websites from over 1,500 health-related organizations.
- Medlineplus: Health Information from the National Library of Medicine
  http://www.nlm.nih.gov/medlineplus/
  Medlineplus is a service of the National Library of Medicine and is rich in health and medical resources on every possible topic. The site boasts "750 topics on conditions, diseases and wellness," along with a section on prescription drugs, a medical encyclopedia, medical dictionary, current news articles, and interactive tutorials.
- Health and Safety Topics from the Centers for Disease Control and Prevention
  http://www.cdc.gov
  The Centers for Disease Control and Prevention, an agency of the federal government, offers a comprehensive site on diseases and condi-

tions, emergency preparedness and response, environmental health, life stages and populations, healthy living, injury violence and safety, travelers' health, and workplace safety and health.

- National Institutes of Health (NIH)
  http://health.nih.gov/
  The mission of the National Institutes of Health, an umbrella federal agency, is science in pursuit of fundamental knowledge about the nature and behavior of living systems and the application of that knowledge to extend healthy life and reduce the burdens of illness and disability. It provides especially useful resources classified by body system, such as the brain and nervous system, the digestive system, the circulatory system, and the urinary system. Excellent links will send a visitor to a section on environmental health, food and nutrition, substance abuse, or wellness and lifestyle. Another section covers medical procedures and therapies, as well as symptoms and their meanings.

- Food and Drug Administration (FDA)
  http://www.fda.gov
  The federal agency that oversees all drugs, food additives, and animal health products is the FDA. Here a visitor can learn more about specific drugs, dietary supplements, animal feeds and drugs, and vaccines. News is constantly updated on the latest drugs, drug recalls, public health alerts, and food contamination.

III. Noteworthy Consumer Educational Sources Offering Health Information

- Familydoctor.org from the American Academy of Family Physicians
  http://www.familydoctor.org
  The American Academy of Family Physicians offers an extensive health and medical database for the public. Chief among the features is an A to Z section on hundreds of medical conditions, along with resources geared to particular age and gender groups.

Part X

- Online Edition of The Merck Manual of Diagnosis and Therapy
  http://www.merck.com/mmhe/index.html
  For those seeking more extensive insights into medical conditions and treatments, there is always the online edition of the Merck Manual, considered by many to be the "bible" of the latest medical information on every major disorder.

IV. Noteworthy Medical Institution Resources

- MayoClinic.com: Tools for Healthier Lives
  http://www.mayoclinic.com/
  Most major medical institutions provide some information for patients. However, there are several that are especially well known. The Mayo Clinic offers one of these nationally recognized websites. A visitor can look up diseases, symptoms, first aid procedures, preventive health information, and general disease management recommendations for the most common medical conditions.

- Harvard Medical School's InteliHealth
  http://www.intelihealth.com
  With medical information provided or approved by Harvard Medical School, InteliHealth is one of the most popular general information hubs for the public. As with other sites, there is an extensive alphabetical section on diseases and conditions, another section on healthy lifestyles and preventive health, resources by age and gender, changing medical news, and interactive tools. Special articles are posted on the latest new developments in medical treatment, such as transplants without drugs and surgery for diabetes in obese patients.

Digging Deeper

Health.gov

http://www.health.gov/

Health.gov is a portal to the websites of a number of multi-agency health initiatives and activities of the U.S. Department of Health and Human Services (HHS) and other federal departments and agencies. There is a link to dozens of federal health information centers and clearinghouses, major national health observance dates and events, toll-free numbers for health information on numerous topics, and health news links.

U.S. Department of Health & Human Services (HHS)

http://www.hhs.gov/

HHS is the federal government's principal agency for protecting the health of all Americans and providing essential human services, especially for those who are least able to help themselves. Links at the site take you to further information on such topics as aging, disasters and emergencies, diseases and medical conditions, grants, policies, and numerous other resources.

Centers for Disease Control and Prevention (CDC)

http://www.cdc.gov/

The CDC offers major databases on diseases and conditions, emergency preparedness, environmental health, life-stage health, injuries, violence and safety, travelers' health, and workplace safety. There are also links to health statistics, health news, and other health and research tools.

National Institute of Mental Health (NIMH)

http://www.nimh.nih.gov/

NIMH supports innovative science that will profoundly transform the diagnosis, treatment, and prevention of mental disorders, paving the way for a cure. There is an extensive A to Z topical mental health index covering disease diagnosis and treatment, as well as mental health news, clinical trials for new mental health drugs, and research activities of the agency.

National Women's Health Information Center

http://www.4women.gov/

The mission of this important center is to "provide leadership to promote health equity for women and girls through sex/gender-specific approaches." Falling under the Office of Women's Health, the center's approach involves the development of innovative programs, educating health professionals, and motivating behavior change in consumers through the dissemination of health information. As a result of this focus, there are excellent resources on all aspects of this topic, including data and statistics, health conditions, health campaigns, funding, and research.

Occupational Safety and Health Administration (OSHA)

http://www.osha.gov/

Every aspect of workplace safety and health is covered at this OSHA site, including compliance assistance, laws and regulations, and enforcement. There are numerous links to current news topics and articles, state programs on workplace safety and health, and other related resources.

Health Resources and Services Administration (HRSA)

http://www.hrsa.gov/

Professional health resources, healthcare systems, HIV/AIDS, maternal and child health, primary healthcare, and rural health are the major topical links at the website of the HRSA. Health news articles are posted and updated, including information on health service delivery, and health system concerns.

Chapter 49

What You Should Know About Your Employer Health Plan

Employee Benefits Security Administration
U.S. Department of Labor

ERISA: Governing Your Health Benefit Plan

The Employee Retirement Income Security Act (ERISA) governs approximately 2.5 million health benefit plans sponsored by private sector employers nationwide. These plans provide a wide range of medical, surgical, hospital, and other health care benefits to some 134 million Americans.

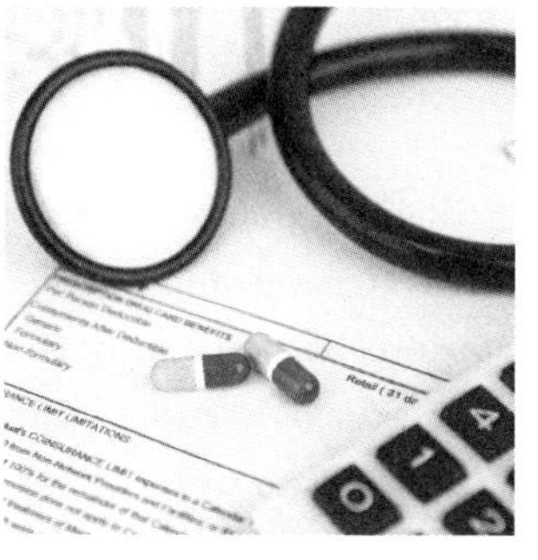

What is in My Plan? Obtaining a Summary Plan Description (SPD)

Under ERISA, workers and their families are entitled to receive a Summary Plan Description (SPD). The SPD is the primary document that gives information about the plan, what benefits are available under the plan, the rights of participant and beneficiaries under the plan, and how the plan works.

Among other information, the plan summary must describe the following:

1. Cost-sharing provisions, including premiums, deductibles, and coinsurance and co-payment amounts for which the participant or beneficiary will be responsible.

2. Annual or lifetime caps or other limits on benefits under the plan.

3. The extent to which preventive services are covered under the plan.

4. Whether, and under what circumstances, existing and new drugs are covered under the plan.

5. Whether, and under what circumstances, coverage is provided for medical tests, devices, and procedures.

6. Provisions governing the use of network providers, the composition of provider networks, and whether, and under what circumstances, coverage is provided for out-of-network services.

7. Conditions or limits on the selection of primary care providers or providers of specialty medical care.

8. Conditions or limits applicable to obtaining emergency medical care.

9. Provisions requiring pre-authorizations or utilization review as a condition to obtaining a benefit or service under the plan.

The plan summary must also explain how plan benefits may be obtained and the process for appealing denied benefits. ERISA also requires that Summary Plan Descriptions be updated periodically. It requires disclosure of any material reduction in covered services or benefits to participants and beneficiaries generally within 60 days of the adoption of the change through either a revised Summary Plan Description or a Summary of Material Modification (SMM). Material changes that do not result in a reduction in covered services or benefits must be disclosed through an SMM or revised SPD not later than 210 days after the end of the plan year in which the change was adopted.

The department's claims procedure regulation describes your right to get an answer from your health plan regarding your health benefit claim. The regulation protects you—providing for a timely response by describing the time frames for a decision, providing for a fair process by describing the standards for a decision, and providing for meaningful disclosure by describing the notice and disclosure that you are entitled to receive from your plan. Look to your Summary Plan Description for information on your health plan's claims procedure.

What is COBRA?

The Consolidated Omnibus Budget Reconciliation Act (COBRA) gives workers and their families who lose their health benefits the right to choose to continue group health benefits provided by their group health plan for limited periods of time under certain circumstances, such as voluntary or involuntary job loss, reduction in the hours worked, transition between jobs, death, divorce, and other life events. Qualified individuals may be required to pay the entire premium for coverage up to 102 percent of the premium cost.

COBRA generally requires that group health plans sponsored by employers with 20 or more employees in the prior year offer employees and their families the opportunity for a temporary extension of health coverage (called continuation coverage) in certain instances where coverage under the plan would otherwise end.

Digging Deeper

Consumer Health Plan Information

http://www.dol.gov/ebsa/consumer_info_health.html

The Employee Benefits Security Administration (EBSA) provides health benefits education focusing on life and work events and the benefit decisions they impact, as well as information on the federal health benefits laws related to employment-based group health plans to help employees and their families make informed decisions. The website provides information on getting the most out of your health plan, along with information on how to access the transitional benefits program called COBRA, which provides coverage between jobs.

Questions and Answers About Health Insurance: A Consumer Guide

http://www.ahrq.gov/consumer/insuranceqa/

This consumer guide describes the different types of health insurance plans available today, including network based plans, non-network based coverage, and individually directed plans. There is also a glossary of health plan terminology.

America's Health Insurance Plans (AHIP)

http://www.ahip.org/

AHIP is the national association that represents the nearly 1,300 member companies that provide health insurance coverage to more than 200 million Americans. The member companies offer medical expense insurance, long term care insurance, disability income insurance, dental insurance, supplemental insurance, stop-loss insurance, and reinsurance to consumers, employers, and public purchasers. There are several consumer guides and a link to health insurance plans listed alphabetically and offered by the member companies.

FAQS About COBRA Continuation Health Coverage

http://www.dol.gov/ebsa/faqs/faq_consumer_cobra.html

A more detailed description of continuation of coverage benefits that are often available to workers between jobs is provided at this website from the Employee Benefits Security Administration. It explains eligibility, coverage, duration, and beneficiaries.

Chapter 50

Privacy and Your Health Information

Office for Civil Rights
U.S. Department of Health and Human Services

What are my general privacy rights?

Most of us feel that our health and medical information is private and should be protected, and we want to know who has this information. A federal law called the Health Insurance Portability and Accountability Act of 1996 (HIPAA) was expanded in 2000 to include patient medical privacy provisions. Those new provisions give you two important types of protections:

1. It gives you rights over your health information, and
2. It sets rules and limits on who can look at and receive your health information.

Who must follow this law?

1. Most doctors, nurses, pharmacies, hospitals, clinics, nursing homes, and many other health care providers.
2. Health insurance companies, HMOs, most employer group health plans.

3. Certain government programs that pay for health care, such as Medicare and Medicaid

What information is protected?

1. Information your doctors, nurses, and other health care providers put in your medical record.
2. Conversations your doctor has about your care or treatment with nurses and others.
3. Information about you in your health insurer's computer system.
4. Billing information about you at your clinic.
5. Most other health information about you held by those who must follow this law.

What are my specific rights under this law?

Providers and health insurers who are required to follow this law must comply with your right to:

1. Ask to see and receive a copy of your health records.
2. Have corrections added to your health information.
3. Receive a notice that tells you how your health information may be used and shared.
4. Decide if you want to give your permission before your health information can be used or shared for certain purposes, such as for marketing.
5. Get a report on when and why your health information was shared for certain purposes.

What actions can I take?

If you believe your rights are being denied or your health information isn't being protected, you can:

1. File a complaint with your provider or health insurer.
2. File a complaint with the federal government.

You should get to know these important rights, which help you protect your health information. You can ask your provider or health insurer questions about your rights. You also can learn more about your rights, including how to file a complaint, from the website at *www.hhs.gov/ocr/hipaa/*.

Digging Deeper

The Health Insurance Portability and Accountability Act (HIPAA)
http://www.hhs.gov/ocr/hipaa/

The Health Insurance Portability and Accountability Act (HIPAA) established the national standards for medical privacy of personal health information. This website offers information on all aspects of HIPAA and its provisions on this subject, including consumer fact sheets.

The Patient Safety and Quality Improvement Act of 2005 (PSQIA)
http://www.hhs.gov/ocr/psqia/

Patient confidentiality was expanded in 2005 with the passage of the Patient Safety and Quality Improvement Act of 2005 (PSQIA). This act establishes a voluntary reporting system designed to enhance the data available to assess and resolve patient safety and health care quality issues. To encourage the reporting and analysis of medical errors within health care systems, PSQIA provides federal privilege and confidentiality protections for patient safety work product. Patient safety work product includes patient, provider, and reporter identifying information that is collected, created, or used for patient safety activities.

Part XI

Housing

Chapter 51

All About Renting

Federal Citizen Information Center

Apartment and House Leases

A lease is an agreement that outlines the obligations of the owner and the tenants of a house or apartment. It is a legally binding document that courts will generally uphold in legal proceedings, so it is important for you to know the exact terms of the lease agreement before you sign it. The lease should state every agreement that you believe exists between you and the landlord. Some things to look for in a lease:

- ✓ Watch for clauses that allow the landlord to change the terms of the lease after it is signed.
- ✓ Note requirements/responsibilities of the tenants to do routine repairs such as lawn maintenance, cleaning, or notification of repairs.
- ✓ Be on guard for restrictions that would prevent you from living normally or comfortably in the home.
- ✓ Be aware of the term of the lease and any important dates, such as when the rent is due or garbage is picked up.

- ✓ Change or remove anything that is not clearly understood or agreeable.
- ✓ All landlord responsibilities should be clearly stated.
- ✓ Always get a copy of the signed lease to keep in your records; any clause or terms in the agreement affects ALL parties who sign.

Non-Discrimination Under the Fair Housing Act

Tenants who lease or rent property are protected against discrimination by the Fair Housing Act. If you think your rights have been violated, you may write a letter or telephone the Housing and Urban Development (HUD) office nearest you. You have one year after the alleged violation to file a complaint with HUD, but you should file as soon as possible.

State Tenant Rights, Laws, and Protections

Each state has its own tenant rights, laws, and protections. For a state-by-state directory, visit *www.hud.gov/local*.

Public Housing and Housing Assistance

You can search for available public housing at *www.hud.gov*. The agency offers several housing assistance programs for tenants and landlords.

Ten Tips for Renters

1. The best way to win over a prospective landlord is to be prepared by bringing with you a completed rental application; written references from previous landlords, employers, friends and colleagues; and a current copy of your credit report.
2. Carefully review all the important conditions of the lease before you sign.
3. To avoid disputes or misunderstandings with your landlord, get everything in

writing.

4. Ask about your privacy rights before you sign the lease.
5. Know your rights to live in a habitable rental unit, and don't give them up.
6. Keep communication open with your landlord.
7. Purchase renter's insurance to cover your valuables.
8. Make sure the security deposit refund procedures are spelled out in your lease or rental agreement.
9. Learn whether your building and neighborhood are safe and what you can expect your landlord to do about it if they aren't.
10. Know when to fight an eviction notice and when to move. Unless you have the law and provable facts on your side, fighting an eviction notice is usually shortsighted.

Digging Deeper

U.S. Department of Housing and Urban Development (HUD)

http://www.hud.gov/

Resources about housing can be found at the website of the U.S. Department of Housing and Urban Development. There are sections on buying, owning, selling, renting, and financing. Foreclosure is also an importance topic, since homes offered by lenders after foreclosure can often be purchased attractively. A link to "Consumer Information" offers a series of useful articles that point out pitfalls, scams, and problems that should be avoided.

Rental Housing Information by State

http://www.hud.gov/local/

HUD maintains offices throughout the country. These links take the visitor to the HUD office in each state, with resources similar to those offered at the national home page.

USA.gov: Homes and Housing

http://www.usa.gov/Citizen/Topics/Family_Homes.shtml

If you own a home or are contemplating purchasing one, this webpage offers a series of consumer articles on such subjects as buying a home, foreclosure, moving, mortgages, flood insurance, renting, and property insurance.

Chapter 52

Protecting Your Home With Renters Insurance

Insurance Information Institute

What Does Renters Insurance Cover?

Renters insurance provides financial protection against the loss or destruction of your possessions when you rent a house or apartment. While your landlord may be sympathetic to a burglary you have experienced or a fire caused by your iron, destruction or loss of your possessions is not usually covered by your landlord's insurance. Because, in most cases, renters insurance covers only the value of your belongings, not the physical building, the premium is relatively inexpensive.

Renters insurance covers your possessions against losses from fire or smoke, lightning, vandalism, theft, explosion, windstorm, and water damage (not including floods). Like homeowners insurance, renters insurance also covers your responsibility to other people injured at your home or elsewhere by you, a family member, or your pet and pays legal defense costs if you are taken to court.

Renters insurance covers your additional living expenses if you are unable to live in your apartment because of a fire or other covered peril. Most policies will reimburse you the difference between your additional living expenses and your normal living expenses but still may set limits as to the amount they will pay.

Types of Renters Insurance

There are two types of renters insurance policies you may purchase:

1. Actual Cash Value—pays to replace your possessions minus a deduction for depreciation up to the limit of your policy; and
2. Replacement Cost—pays the actual cost of replacing your possessions (no deduction for depreciation) up to the limit of your policy.

How Much Coverage Do I Need?

Add up the cost of everything you would want to replace if it were damaged or stolen. This could also serve as the basis for an inventory that will make filing a claim easier. For an inventory, also record model numbers and dates and places of purchase. Take photographs or make a video of these items and place a copy of the inventory in safe place away form your home.

Adding a "Floater" for Special Items

With either policy, you may want to consider purchasing a floater. A standard renters policy offers only limited coverage for items such as jewelry, silver, furs, etc. If you own property that exceeds these limits, it is recommended that you supplement your policy with a floater. A floater is a separate policy that provides additional insurance for your valuables and covers them for perils not included in your policy, such as accidental loss.

Amending Policy Coverage

If you are getting married or divorced, call you insurance agent. You may need to change the names on the policy. If you make a major purchase, such as a diamond engagement ring, you may need to increase your coverage limits.

How Do I File a Claim?

As soon as you become aware of a loss, note the date, time of day, and list of goods stolen or damaged. In case of a theft, call the police as soon as possible. Then, contact your insurance company or agent to report the loss and get the appropriate claim form. Written and documented reports of losses are especially important when theft is involved.

Digging Deeper

More Information on Renters Insurance

http://www.iii.org/media/publications/brochures/rentersins/

The Insurance Information Institute covers additional topics about renter policies at this website, such as deductibles, policy discounts, and policy exclusions. There is also a series of useful questions and answers that help address further issues.

Chapter 53

Buying Vs. Renting: What Should I Know?

Ginnie Mae (Government National Motrgage Association)
Starting Out!® Research Group

Although most young people rent or share apartments after graduating from high school or college, it is useful to understand some of the advantages and disadvantages of renting vs. buying in order to make future plans.

Why People Rent

- **Flexibility**

Renting provides the greatest amount of flexibility, which is extremely important when you are starting out. Because people change jobs quite frequently today, a new job may require a move to another city or state on fairly short notice. According to the Bureau of Labor Statistics in the U.S. Department of Labor, the average person born in the later years of the baby boom held 10.5 jobs from age 18 to age 40. Nearly three-fifths of these jobs were held from ages 18 to 25, suggesting that young people change jobs every year or two.

- **Cost**

Renting is usually cheaper in the short run, because it does not require more than the ability to pay the monthly costs of rent and utilities and post a deposit, expenses that can be shared among several people, if necessary.

Maintenance-Free Living

Many people choose to rent because they prefer the maintenance-free living of an apartment or other rental unit. The repairs are normally the responsibility of the landlord.

Renting vs. Buying: Understand the Differences

The chart below, prepared by the Government National Mortgage Association (GNMA) called "Ginnie Mae," sets forth some of the advantages and limitations of each form of housing.

The issues associated with renting or buying change over a lifetime as people go through different stages. Here are some statistics to consider:

- The average age of a first-time buyer has risen by 26 percent during the past 30 years, increasing from 27 in 1977 to 34 today, according to mortgage lender GE Money Home Lending.
- In December 2007, the average house price was $307,500, according to the Federal Housing Finance Board.

A Comparison of Renting vs. Buying:

	Advantages	Considerations
Buy	Property builds equity	Responsible for maintenance
	Sense of community, stability, and security	Responsible for property taxes
	Free to change decor and landscaping	Possibility of foreclosure and loss of equity

	Not dependent on landlord to maintain property	Less mobility than renting
Rent	Little or no responsibility for maintenance	No tax benefits
	Easier to move	No equity is built up
		No control over rent increases
		Possibility of eviction

The Advantages of Renting When You're Starting Out

For most young people, renting is the preferred avenue of home occupancy for a considerable period of time, because it affords the opportunity for flexibility in employment location. According to the Bureau of Labor Statistics, "individuals held an average of 10.5 jobs from ages 18 to 40, with the majority of the jobs being held before age 31." For many, this translates into a new job every 12 to 18 months.

Generally speaking, a year-to-year lease is the most flexible and advantageous arrangement to consider when establishing a new career. Renting is also the more realistic alternative from a cost point of view, since the purchase of a home requires a significant down payment.

Digging Deeper

Apartments.com: Why Rent?

http://living.apartments.com/apartment-basics/why-rent

An interesting article called "Why Rent?" is presented at this website that is generally devoted to apartment living. Consider whether the advantages of renting are important to you. Many people, regardless of wealth, prefer the overall flexibility of renting, especially if they travel a great deal and cannot deal with maintenance and security issues.

GinnieMae.gov: Buy vs. Rent Calculator

http://www.ginniemae.gov/rent_vs_buy/rent_vs_buy_calc.asp?Section=YPTH

Just fill in the blanks in this online calculator, and you will see whether your finances would be better or worse if you purchased a home instead of renting. In some cases, such as in very low interest mortgage climates, purchasing becomes increasingly feasible.

Chapter 54

The American Dream of Home Ownership

Federal Home Loan Mortgage Corporation

Buying a home is the largest purchase most people will ever make. Homeownership has great benefits, but also comes with certain responsibilities.

Are you ready for homeownership?

Look at your current situation and determine if:

- ✓ You have a steady, reliable source of income and a steady employment history for at least two years.
- ✓ You have a credit history.
- ✓ Your total debt is manageable and you can afford to take on the costs associated with homeownership.
- ✓ You have money saved for a down payment and closing costs or you have access to other sources of funds, such as an employment bonus, tax refund, or a gift from a relative.
- ✓ Your future plans might affect your ability to manage the costs of homeownership.
- ✓ You need to make lifestyle changes to reduce expenses.

- ✓ Your future plans might include a wedding or college education for yourself or your children.

And remember, the mortgage is not the only expense you need to consider. Homeownership comes with other potential budget items such as repairs, maintenance, taxes, landscaping, etc.

Once you fully understand your current situation, your future plans, and the big picture in terms of homeownership, it's important to look at the pros and cons of homeownership to make the best decision for you and your family.

Why Own?

There are many great reasons to consider owning a home:

- **You'll have a place that is yours!**

  You'll own it, have a place to raise your children, and become a part of your community. You can pass your home down to your children and their children, creating security for generations to come.

- **You may pay less to own a home than you would to rent—and it's yours at the end!**

  Homeownership can reduce the federal income taxes you pay. You can deduct the interest on your home mortgage and the property taxes you pay on your home on the tax returns you file each year. These tax savings partially reduce, or offset somewhat, the actual cost of owning your home.

- **Your monthly payments won't ever go up if you choose a fixed-rate mortgage!**

  If you choose a mortgage with a fixed interest rate (one that stays the same for the life of the loan, say 30 years), you'll pay the same mortgage payment each month for the entire 30 years of the loan (if your taxes go up, your escrow will go up—increasing your monthly payment).

☛ **You'll build a good nest egg!**

Owning a home and building equity is the single greatest source of financial security and independence for the majority of people who've taken this step.

What Are the Risks?

Overall, homeownership is a good investment for most people, but there are risks. If you understand the benefits and risks of homeownership, you can make the best decision about when to buy a home.

So what are the risks of homeownership?

- Monthly housing expenses can increase.
- You become your own landlord.
- You may need to sell your house due to life circumstances.
- Property values can depreciate.
- Downsizing quickly may be difficult.

Nine Steps to Buying a House

Once you have decided to purchase a house, you will need to following these steps:

Part XI

1. Figure out how much you can afford.

   What you can afford depends on your income, credit rating, current monthly expenses, down payment and the interest rate. The calculators available in "Digging Deeper" can help, but it is best to visit a lender to find out for sure.

2. Know your rights.

   This may be the largest and most important loan you get during your lifetime. You should be aware of certain rights before you enter into any loan agreement.

   - You have the RIGHT to shop for the best loan for you and compare the charges of different mortgage brokers and lenders.
   - You have the RIGHT to be informed about the total cost of your loan, including the interest rate, points, and other fees.
   - You have the RIGHT to ask for a Good Faith Estimate of all loan and settlement charges before you agree to the loan and pay any fees.
   - You have the RIGHT to ask your mortgage broker to explain exactly what the broker will do for you and how much the broker is getting paid by you and the lender for your loan.
   - You have the RIGHT to ask questions about charges and loan terms that you do not understand.
   - You have the RIGHT to a credit decision that is not based on your race, color, religion, national origin, sex, marital status, age, or whether any income is from public assistance.
   - You have the RIGHT to know the reason if your loan is turned down.

3. Shop for a loan.

   Obtain information from several lenders and compare interest rates, points charged, down payments, the need for private mortgage insurance, and closing fees.

4. Learn about home buying programs.

   Look into HUD home buying programs in your state. There are usually special first-time home buyer mortgage programs. Visit the link under "Digging Deeper."

5. Shop for a home.

   Look at real estate listings in your area, talk with real estate brokers, and consider less common sources, such as foreclosed homes, which are sometimes listed as bank-owned homes. Always consider homes offered for sale directly by owners; you may be able to negotiate a better price because there is no real estate commission cost for the seller.

6. Make an offer.

   Be sure to use a real estate lawyer to help you evaluate the contract and assist you at the closing. Also discuss the process with your real estate agent or with more experienced family members or friends. Decide what you are comfortable offering. Always make your offer contingent on a home inspection and on receipt of a satisfactory mortgage commitment. If the seller counters your offer, you may need to negotiate until you both agree to the terms of the sale.

7. Get a home inspection.

   An inspection will tell you about the condition of the home and can help you avoid buying a home that needs major repairs. If the inspector finds problems, you can ask the seller to address them as a condition of your purchase. Be prepared to walk away from the purchase if the inspection is unsatisfactory. You should also do your own investigation of the house and neighborhood.

8. Shop for homeowners insurance.

   Homeowners insurance is a requirement of any purchase. It will protect you and the lender against loss and ensure that you have repair or replacement funds if there is a fire or other major casualty.

9. Sign papers.

   You're finally ready to go to "settlement" or "closing." You should read everything carefully before you sign. Ask your lawyer questions. Be sure you understand all of your obligations after the purchase.

Digging Deeper

GinnieMae.gov: Your Path to Home Ownership

http://www.ginniemae.gov/ypth/index.asp?Section=YPTH

Useful calculators are available to compare renting vs. buying, the affordability of a home, and mortgage costs. Other links explore the many other aspects of homeownership.

HUD: Buying a Home

http://www.hud.gov/buying/index.cfm

The Federal Department of Housing and Urban Development offers extensive links about buying or selling a home, mortgage financing, special loan programs for new homebuyers, educational videos, a mortgage glossary, and much more.

ConsumerAction.gov: Shopping for a Mortgage

http://www.consumeraction.gov/caw_housing_mortgages.shtml

Practical advice about shopping for a mortgage is offered at this consumer page of the Federal Consumer Action website, along with links about moving, mortgage counseling, foreclosure, and other related topics.

HUD: Local Home-Buying Programs in Each State

http://www.hud.gov/buying/localbuying.cfm

The Department of Housing and Urban Development provides links to each state for information about local home-buying programs. Programs may vary from state to state.

Part XII

Your Consumer Role

Chapter 55

Learning To Be a Smart Consumer

Federal Trade Commission
Starting Out!® Research Group

Handling Large and Small Purchases

The Federal Trade Commission's Bureau of Consumer Protection provides extensive resources pertaining to different types of purchases and what to know about each.

Visit *http://www.ftc.gov/bcp/consumer.shtm* to learn how to handle transactions in each of the following areas, and what to pay attention to:

- ✓ Automobiles
- ✓ Credit and Loans
- ✓ Education, Scholarships, and Job Placement
- ✓ Identity Theft, Privacy, and Security
- ✓ Shopping for Products and Services
- ✓ Fair Packaging and Labeling Act
- ✓ Computers and the Internet
- ✓ Diet, Health, and Fitness
- ✓ Energy and the Environment
- ✓ Investment and Business Opportunities
- ✓ Telemarketing and Telephone Services

Today's packaging provides extensive information on the content or ingredients of the product, weights, and, if necessary, warnings for use. Learn to check unit pricing as you compare similar products by weight, as well as dating of the contents if freshness is relevant, such as in the purchase of dairy products. For food products, learn to check product ingredients, including the inclusion of preservatives and other additives.

Merchant Policies

When you purchase an item in a store or on the Internet, learn whether it can be returned if you find it does not meet your needs. Ask for the "return policy" which will indicate your right to return merchandise, and over what period of time. Be sure to ask whether you would be entitled to a refund or a store credit. Such policies are especially important for high-priced items or items for which you pay cash.

Warranty vs. Guarantee: What is the Difference?

Normally a warranty is an agreement to repair or replace an item that does not work or perform properly within a specified period of time according to the manufacturer's claims. A warranty therefore might last 30 days, three months, or longer, and may only ensure that a repair is made, not that a replacement is offered. It may give the seller the option to repair or replace the item.

A guarantee, on the other hand, is a formal assurance, without time limit, that a product conforms to certain specific qualitative standards. For example, a work of art that is guaranteed to be authentic is an assurance against receiving a fake, and such a guarantee is a standing assurance, without time limit, unless the seller limits the period of time for evaluation and final acceptance. If the guaranteed item does not conform to the product description, it can be returned.

Coupons and Loss Leaders

Coupons in newspapers or available on the Internet for every type of product can help you save money on everyday food products or on very expensive purchases, such as for computers, appliances, and entertainment systems. Often items listed in a weekly newspaper can be loss leaders, saving you larger amounts than usual, because these discounted items help bring customers into a store. It is even possible to purchase any type of coupon on eBay *(www.ebay.com)* just by entering the name of the type of coupon in the search bar.

Seasonal Timing and Internet Comparison Shopping

All of us know that there are sales, especially at certain times of the year. If you are planning a major purchase, consider waiting for a major sale, or asking your retailer when the next sale is scheduled.

Spring and summer merchandise is usually available during clearance sales in June and July, while fall and winter merchandise usually goes on sale in January.

Shopping on the Internet for name-brand merchandise can also save money, and you may not have to worry about timing. There are many comparative-price search engines you can use, such as *Nextag.com* and *Bizrate.com*. In addition, you can visit clearance merchandise websites such as *Overstock.com* and *SmartBargains.com*.

Wholesale Merchandise Clubs

Outlets such as BJ's Wholesale Club *(www.bjs.com)*, Costco *(www.costco.com)*, and Sam's Club *(www.samsclub.com)* provide merchandise at prices that are frequently well below retail establishments. Less widely located chains, such as DirectBuy *(www.directbuy.com)* are especially designed to offer savings on renovation and household decorating items, such as carpets, fixtures, flooring, and appliances, although the types of merchandise available cover all categories.

Digging Deeper

Federal Trade Commission: Consumer Information

http://www.ftc.gov/bcp/consumer.shtm

Consumers are protected by numerous laws that regulate the commercial marketplace. The Federal Trade Commission is the central government agency charged with protecting consumers through the Bureau of Consumer Protection. This website offers links and advice regarding purchases of automobiles and computers, obtaining credit and loans, diet and fitness products and services, educational expenditures, energy products, identity theft, investments and business opportunities, franchises, telemarketing services, and numerous other types of consumer transactions and services.

Consumer Federation of America (CFA)

http://www.consumerfed.org

The Consumer Federation of America is a non-profit advocacy organization that provides consumers with a "well-reasoned and articulate voice" in decisions that affect their lives. Day in and day out, CFA's professional staff gathers facts, analyzes issues, and disseminates information to the public, policymakers, and the rest of the consumer movement.

National Consumers League (NCL)

http://www.nclnet.org

According to its website, the mission of the National Consumer League is to "protect and promote social and economic justice for consumers and workers in the United States and abroad. The National Consumers League is a private, non-profit advocacy group representing consumers on marketplace and workplace issues." It is the nation's oldest consumer organization. NCL provides government, businesses, and other organizations with the consumer's perspective on concerns including child labor, privacy, food safety, and medication information.

Consumer Reports

http://www.consumerreports.org/cro/index.htm

Although it requires an online subscription, Consumer Reports is an independent organization that evaluates products and services for consumers. It provides comparisons of products, along with its own quality and effectiveness ratings.

Chapter 56

Consumer Fraud: Don't Be a Victim

Federal Trade Commission
Federal Citizen Information Center
General Services Administration

As a savvy consumer, you should always be on the alert for shady deals and scams. To protect your money and avoid being a victim of fraud, keep these things in mind:

- **A deal that sounds too good to be true usually is!**

  Offers that often fall into this category are promises to fix your credit problems, low-interest credit cards, deals that let you skip credit card payments, business/job opportunities, risk-free investments, and free travel.

- **Extended warranties and service contracts are rarely worth what you pay for them.**

- **There is no universal three-day cooling-off period.**

  Don't be misled into thinking that you have an automatic three days to cancel a purchase. Only a few types of contracts give you a right to cancel.

- **Think twice before sharing personal information.**

- **Beware of payday and tax refund loans.**

  Interest rates on these loans are usually excessive. Even a high-interest cash advance on a credit card could be a better option.

- **Not all plastic cards offer the same protections.**

  Your liability for the unauthorized use of a gift card and debit/ATM card may be much higher than the $50 maximum on your credit card.

- **Real estate agents usually represent the seller—not the buyer.**

  When buying, consider hiring an agent or lawyer who represents you. Some states have buyer agents, however.

- **Home improvement and auto repairs are the subject of frequent complaints.**

  Second opinions are especially important when you are dealing with a repair service you do not know, or if you are facing a costly repair or renovation.

- **Don't buy under stress.**

  Research suggests senior citizens, people in crisis (e.g., coping with a death or debt), college students, small business owners, minorities, and immigrants are especially at risk of being victimized. Avoid making big-ticket purchases during times of duress.

- **Work-at-home ads usually don't pay off.**

  Be especially wary of ads that promise huge annual salaries; they often require expensive upfront fees with no guarantee of income. You risk losing your money and wasting a lot of time and energy.

Digging Deeper

Federal Trade Commission, Bureau of Consumer Protection

http://www.ftc.gov/bcp/index.shtml

The Federal Trade Commission is the nation's consumer protection agency. The FTC's Bureau of Consumer Protection works for the consumer to prevent fraud, deception, and unfair business practices in the marketplace. The bureau enhances consumer confidence by enforcing federal laws that protect consumers and empowers consumers with free information to help them exercise their rights and spot and avoid fraud and deception. The bureau also provides assistance to consumers who wish to file a consumer fraud complaint.

Consumer.gov: Consumer Information from the Federal Government

http://www.consumer.gov/yourmoney.htm

Directed at improving consumer decision making, this federal website offers resources on food, product safety, health, home and community, money, transportation, children, careers, and education. Within each category there are numerous articles and resources to guide consumers.

Fraud.org: The National Consumer League's Fraud Center

http://www.fraud.org/

Created to stop consumer fraud of all kinds, the Fraud Center offers answers to commonly asked questions about fraud, with special resources on telemarketing fraud, internet fraud, and common scams.

eCommerce.gov: Cross-Border Fraud

http://www.econsumer.gov/

Focused on fraud arising from transactions with venders in other countries, this multi-lingual federal government website provides information on reporting and resolving such frauds. In addition, the site offers online shopping tips and information on consumer protection in the countries that participate in this international fraud protection program.

Chapter 57

Consumer Rights and How They Are Protected

Federal Deposit Insurance Corporation
Federal Trade Commission

Fortunately, U.S. consumers are protected by many strong laws that govern how transactions are handled, how merchants must conduct themselves, how consumers are protected against fraud, and how violators will be held accountable for their actions. The following discussion examines the major federal consumer protection agencies and their state counterparts, followed by resources on federal laws for consumer protection.

Federal Consumer Protection Agencies

- Federal Trade Commission (FTC)
- Consumer Product Safety Commission (CPSC)
- Federal Deposit Insurance Corporation (FDIC)
- Securities and Exchange Commission (SEC)
- Department of Agriculture, Food Safety and Inspection Service
- Food and Drug Administration (FDA)

State Consumer Protection Agencies

City, county, and state consumer offices offer a variety of important services. They might mediate complaints, conduct investigations, prosecute offenders of consumer laws, license and regulate professional service providers, provide educational materials, and advocate for consumer rights. To save time, call before sending a written complaint. Ask if the office handles the type of complaint you have and if complaint forms are provided. Visit the link under "Digging Deeper" to access this information.

Federal Consumer Protection Laws

Consumers' financial rights are protected by federal and state laws and regulations covering all services offered by financial institutions. Many similar laws exist within each state and can be found in the "Digging Deeper" section.

- **1. Adjustable-Rate Mortgage Loans:** Adjustable-rate mortgage loans are covered by regulations that require, at a minimum, disclosure of the circumstances under which the rate may increase, any limitations on the increase, the effects of an increase, and an example of the payment terms that would result from an increase.

- **2. Consumer Leasing Act:** The Consumer Leasing Act requires disclosure of information that helps consumers compare the cost and terms of various leases and the cost and terms of buying on credit versus cash. The act does not apply to real estate leases or to leases of four months or less.

- **3. Electronic Fund Transfer Act:** The Electronic Fund Transfer Act provides consumer protection for all transactions using a debit card or electronic means to debit or credit an account. It also limits a consumer's liability for unauthorized electronic fund transfers.

- **4. Equal Credit Opportunity Act:** The Equal Credit Opportunity Act prohibits discrimination against an applicant for credit because of age, sex, marital status, religion, race, color, national origin, or receipt of public assistance. It also prohibits discrimination because of a good faith exercise of any rights under the federal consumer credit laws. If a consumer has been denied credit, the law requires notification of the denial in writing. The consumer may request, within 60 days, that the reason for denial be provided in writing.

- **5. Expedited Funds Availability Act:** The Expedited Funds Availability Act requires all banks, savings and loan associations, savings banks, and credit unions to make funds deposited into checking, share draft and NOW accounts available according to specified time schedules and to disclose their funds availability policies to their customers. The law does not require an institution to delay the customer's use of deposited funds but instead limits how long any delay may last. The regulation also establishes rules designed to speed the return of unpaid checks.

- **6. Fair Credit and Charge Card Disclosure Act:** The Fair Credit and Charge Card Disclosure Act requires new disclosures on credit and charge cards, whether issued by financial institutions, retail stores, or private companies. Information such as annual percentage rates, annual fees, and grace periods must be provided in tabular form, along with applications and pre-approved solicitations for cards. The regulations also require card issuers that impose an annual fee to provide disclosures before annual renewal. Card issuers that offer credit insurance must inform customers of any increase in rate or substantial decrease in coverage should the issuer decide to change insurance providers.

- **7. Fair Credit Billing Act:** The Fair Credit Billing Act establishes procedures for the prompt correction of errors on open-end credit accounts. It also protects a consumer's credit rating while the consumer is settling a dispute.

- **8. Fair Credit Reporting Act:** The Fair Credit Reporting Act establishes procedures for correcting mistakes on a consumer's credit record and requires that a record only be provided for legitimate business needs. It also requires that the record be kept confidential. A credit record may be retained for seven years for judgments, liens, suits, and other adverse information except for bankruptcies, which may be retained for 10 years. If a consumer has been denied credit, a cost-free credit report may be requested from a consumer reporting agency within 30 days of denial.

- **9. Fair Debt Collection Practices Act:** The Fair Debt Collection Practices Act is designed to eliminate abusive, deceptive, and unfair debt collection practices. It applies to third party debt collectors or those who use a name other than their own in collecting consumer debts. Very few commercial banks, savings banks, savings and loan associations, or credit unions are covered by this act, because they usually collect only their own debts. Complaints concerning debt collection practices should generally be filed with the Federal Trade Commission.

- **10. Fair Housing Act:** The Fair Housing Act prohibits discrimination on the basis of race, color, sex, religion, handicap, familial status, or national origin in the financing, sale, or rental of housing.

- **11. The Federal Trade Commission Act:** The Federal Trade Commission Act requires federal financial regulatory agencies to maintain a consumer affairs division to assist in resolving consumer complaints against institutions they supervise. This assistance is given to help get necessary information to consumers about problems they are having in order to address complaints concerning acts or practices that may be unfair or deceptive.

- **12. Home Equity Loan Consumer Protection Act:** The Home Equity Loan Consumer Protection Act requires lenders to disclose terms, rates, and conditions (annual percentage rates, miscellaneous charges, payment terms, and information about variable rate features) for home equity lines of credit with the applications and before the first transaction under the home equity plan. If the disclosed terms change, the consumer can refuse to open the plan and is entitled to a refund of fees paid in connection with the application. The act also limits the circumstances under which creditors may terminate or change the terms of a home equity plan after it is opened.

- **13. National Flood Insurance Act:** National Flood Insurance is available to any property holder whose local community participates in the national program by adopting and enforcing flood plain management. Federally regulated lenders are required to compel borrowers to purchase flood insurance in certain designated areas. Lenders also must disclose to borrowers if their structure is located in a flood hazard area.

- **14. Real Estate Settlement Procedures Act:** The Real Estate Settlement Procedures Act requires that a consumer be given advance information about the services and costs involved in the closing or settlement of a residential mortgage transaction. It also limits the amount that can be collected for mortgage escrow.

- **15. Rights to Financial Privacy Act:** The Right to Financial Privacy Act provides that customers of financial institutions have a right to expect that their financial activities will have a reasonable amount of privacy from federal government scrutiny. The act establishes specific procedures and exemptions concerning the release of the financial records of customers and imposes limitations on and requirements of financial institutions prior to the release of such information to the federal government.

- **16. Truth in Lending Act:** The Truth in Lending Act requires disclosure of the "finance charge" and the "annual percentage rate"—and certain other costs and terms of credit—so that a consumer can compare the prices of credit from different sources. It also limits liability on lost or stolen credit cards.

Digging Deeper

Federal Reserve: Consumer Handbook to Credit Protection Laws

http://www.federalreserve.gov/pubs/consumerhdbk/

The Federal Reserve offers an excellent website covering credit protection laws, with information on each statute. These laws cover every aspect of credit protection, as well as financial privacy, real estate transactions, credit card use, electronic funds transfer, leasing, and other credit-related transactions.

USA.gov: Consumer Guides and Protection

http://www.usa.gov/Citizen/Topics/Consumer_Safety.shtml

Dozens of consumer information guides are provided at this government website dealing with such subjects as air travel, automobile safety, cable television, food and drugs, identity theft, internet transactions, mail security, meat and poultry safety, and numerous other interesting topics.

Consumer Action Website: Where and How to File Complaints

http://www.consumeraction.gov/

You can obtain a current copy of the federal government's Consumer Action Handbook or learn how to file a consumer complaint at this website. Additional resources include articles on the most common consumer frauds, as well as information directed at specific audiences, such as military service personnel, the disabled, and teachers.

State Consumer Protection Laws

http://www.consumeraction.gov/caw_state_resources.shtml

Links to the consumer protection agencies in each state are provided at this federal government site, as well as links to state banking authorities, insurance regulatory offices, securities regulators, and state utility agencies.

Part XIII

All About Insurance

Chapter 58

The ABC's of Auto Insurance

With Permission From: The Insurance Information Institute

What is auto insurance?

Auto insurance protects you against financial loss if you have an accident. It is a contract between you and the insurance company. You agree to pay the premium and the insurance company agrees to pay your losses as defined in your policy.

Auto insurance provides property, liability, and medical coverage. Property coverage pays for damage to or theft of your car. Liability coverage pays for your legal responsibility to others for bodily injury or property damage. Medical coverage pays for the cost of treating injuries, rehabilitation, and sometimes lost wages and funeral expenses.

An auto insurance policy is comprised of six different kinds of coverage. Most states require you to buy some, but not all, of these coverages. If you're financing a car, your lender may also have requirements.

Most auto policies are for six months to a year. Your insurance company should notify you by mail when it's time to renew the policy and to pay your premium.

What is covered by a basic auto policy?

Your auto policy may include six coverages. Each coverage is priced separately.

- **Bodily Injury Liability**

  This coverage applies to injuries that you, the designated driver or policy-holder, cause to someone else. You and family members listed on the policy are also covered when driving someone else's car with their permission.

  It's very important to have enough liability insurance because if you are involved in a serious accident, you may be sued for a large sum of money. Definitely consider buying more than the state-required minimum to protect assets such as your home and savings.

- **Medical Payments or Personal Injury Protection (PIP)**

  This coverage pays for the treatment of injuries to the driver and passengers of the policyholder's car. At its broadest, PIP can cover medical payments, lost wages, and the cost of replacing services normally performed by someone injured in an auto accident. It may also cover funeral costs.

- **Property Damage Liability**

  This coverage pays for damage you (or someone driving the car with your permission) may cause to someone else's property. Usually, this means damage to someone else's car, but it also includes damage to lamp posts, telephone poles, fences, buildings, or other structures your car hit.

- **Collision**

  This coverage pays for damage to your car resulting from a collision with another car or object or as a result of flipping over. It also covers damage caused by potholes. Collision coverage is generally sold with a deductible of $250 to $1,000—the higher your deductible, the lower your premium. Even if you are at fault for the accident, your collision coverage will reimburse you for the costs of repairing your car, minus the deductible. If you're not at fault, your insurance company may try to recover the amount they paid you from the other driver's insurance company. If they are successful, you'll also be reimbursed for the deductible.

☛ Comprehensive

This coverage reimburses you for loss due to theft or damage caused by something other than a collision with another car or object, such as fire, falling objects, missiles, explosion, earthquake, windstorm, hail, flood, vandalism, riot, or contact with animals such as birds or deer.

Comprehensive insurance is usually sold with a $100 to $300 deductible, though you may want to opt for a higher deductible as a way of lowering your premium.

Comprehensive insurance will also reimburse you if your windshield is cracked or shattered. Some companies offer glass coverage with or without a deductible.

States do not require that you purchase collision or comprehensive coverage, but if you have a car loan, your lender may insist you carry it until your loan is paid off.

☛ Uninsured and Underinsured Motorist Coverage

This coverage will reimburse you, a member of your family, or a designated driver if one of you is hit by an uninsured or hit-and-run driver.

Underinsured motorist coverage comes into play when an at-fault driver has insufficient insurance to pay for your total loss. This coverage will also protect you if you are hit as a pedestrian.

Can I drive legally without insurance?

NO! Almost every state requires you to have auto liability insurance. All states also have financial responsibility laws. This means that even in a state that does not require liability insurance, you need to have sufficient assets to pay claims if you cause an accident. If you don't have enough assets, you must purchase at least the state minimum amount of insurance. But insurance exists to protect your assets. Trying to see how little you can get by with can be very shortsighted and dangerous.

If you've financed your car, your lender may require comprehensive and collision insurance as part of the loan agreement.

☛ What if I lease a car?

If you lease a car, you still need to buy your own auto insurance policy. The auto dealer or bank that is financing the car will require you to buy collision and comprehensive coverage. You'll need to buy these coverages in addition to the others that may be mandatory in your state, such as auto liability insurance.

Collision covers the damage to the car from an accident with another automobile or object.

Comprehensive covers a loss that is caused by something other than a collision with another car or object, such as a fire or theft or collision with a deer.

The leasing company may also require "gap" insurance. This refers to the fact that if you have an accident and your leased car is damaged beyond repair, or "totaled," there's likely to be a difference between the amount that you still owe the auto dealer and the check you'll get from your insurance company. That's because the insurance company's check is based on the car's actual cash value which takes into account depreciation. The difference between the two amounts is known as the "gap."

On a leased car, the cost of gap insurance is generally rolled into the lease payments. You don't actually buy a gap policy. Generally, the auto dealer buys a master policy from an insurance company to cover all the cars it leases and charges you for a "gap waiver." This means that if your leased car is totaled, you won't have to pay the dealer the gap amount. Check with the auto dealer when leasing your car.

If you have an auto loan rather than a lease, you may want to buy gap insurance to protect yourself from having to come up with the gap amount if your car is totaled before you've finished paying for it. Ask your insurance agent about gap insurance or search the internet. Gap insurance may not be available in some states.

☛ Do I need insurance to rent a car?

When renting a car, you need insurance. If you have adequate insurance on your own car, including collision and comprehensive, this may be enough.

Before you rent a car:

- ✓ Contact your insurance company. Find out how much coverage you have on your own car. In most cases, the coverage and deductibles you have on your personal auto policy would apply to a rental car, providing it's used for pleasure and not business. If you don't have comprehensive and collision coverage on your own car, you will not be covered if your rental car is stolen or if it is damaged in an accident.

- ✓ Call your credit card company. Levels of coverage vary. Find out what insurance your card provides, particularly if you rent a car in a different country. Israel, for example, is almost never covered.

If you don't have auto insurance, you have two choices: you can buy coverage at the car rental counter or you can purchase a non-owner auto liability insurance policy.

Digging Deeper

Insurance Information Institute: Auto Insurance

http://www.iii.org/individuals/auto/

The Auto Insurance Section of the Insurance Information Institute (I.I.I.) is located on this webpage. Located in New York City, the Insurance Information Institute seeks to improve public understanding of insurance—what it does and how it works. It offers explanatory resources on all major forms of insurance.

American Automobile Association (AAA)

http://www.aaa.com

As the pre-eminent consumer advocacy and service organization in the automobile industry, the AAA not only provides maps and emergency road assistance, but also assists individuals with many types of travel and lodging, automobile buying, leasing, renting, and repair, as well as financial and insurance needs.

Chapter 59

The Basics of Health Insurance

With Permission From: The Insurance Information Institute

What kinds of health insurance are there?

There are essentially two kinds of heath insurance: Fee-for-Service and Managed Care. Although these plans differ, they both cover an array of medical, surgical, and hospital expenses. Most cover prescription drugs and some also offer dental coverage.

1. Fee-for-Service

These plans generally assume that the medical professional will be paid a fee for each service provided to the patient. Patients are seen by a doctor of their choice and the claim is filed by either the medical provider or the patient.

2. Managed Care

More than half of all Americans have some kind of managed-care plan. Various plans work differently and can include: health maintenance organizations (HM0s), preferred provider organizations (PPOs), and point-of-service (POS) plans. These plans provide comprehensive health services to their members and offer financial incentives to patients who use the providers in the plan.

How do I pick a health plan?

If your employer gives you a choice of plans or you need to purchase your own coverage, it is crucial that you understand your health insurance choices and pick the insurance that is best for you and your family.

Here are some questions you should ask yourself when choosing a health insurance plan:

- ✓ How affordable is the cost of care?
- ✓ What is the monthly premium I will have to pay?
- ✓ Should I try to insure most of my medical expenses or just the large ones?
- ✓ What deductibles will I have to pay out-of-pocket before insurance starts to reimburse me?
- ✓ After I've met my deductible, what percentage of my medical expenses are reimbursed?
- ✓ How much less am I reimbursed if I use doctors outside the insurance company's network?
- ✓ Does the insurance plan cover the services I am likely to use?
- ✓ Are the doctors, hospitals, laboratories, and other medical providers that I use in the insurance company's network?
- ✓ If I want to use a doctor outside the network, will the plan permit it?
- ✓ How easily can I change primary-care physicians if I want to?
- ✓ Do I need to get permission before I see a medical specialist?
- ✓ If I have a pre-existing medical condition, will the plan cover it?

- ✓ If I have a chronic condition such as asthma, cancer, AIDS, or alcoholism, how will the plan treat it?
- ✓ Are the prescription medicines that I use covered by the plan?
- ✓ Does the plan cover the costs of pregnancy and childbirth?

Can I buy an individual policy?

Yes. If you are unemployed, self-employed, or decide to return to school, you may want to buy an individual health insurance policy. Here are a number of options that you may consider:

- ✓ Ask your insurance company if you can convert its group policy to an individual policy. You will pay a higher rate than you did before, and your benefits may be limited, but the terms will still probably be better than if you buy your own policy.
- ✓ If you are married, see if your spouse's employer will add you to its group plan.
- ✓ Try to join a group health plan through a trade association, alumni group, or professional association that may offer reasonable rates. If you are over age 50, you can join the American Association of Retired Persons (AARP), which offers an extensive plan. Even some credit card companies offer health insurance coverage.
- ✓ As a last resort, you can buy an individual policy. The rates will be high and coverage limited, but it is important that you will be protected against financial catastrophe if you or your family are hit with a major illness or injury. If you are self-employed, most of the health insurance premium will be tax deductible.
- ✓ To find the best policy, contact a health insurance agent or broker who will help you find the contract that gives you the most for your money.
- ✓ If I change jobs or become unemployed, can I bring my coverage with me?

✓ If you switch employers, you have the right to carry your group health insurance coverage with you to a new job for up to 18 months under the Consolidated Omnibus Budget Reconciliation Act (COBRA).

✓ You must pay the full premium, but at group rates that are far cheaper than the individual rates you would pay for similar coverage. Health insurance under COBRA is available for up to 18 months if you leave a company or become unemployed or self-employed.

Digging Deeper

Insurance Information Institute: Health Insurance

http://www.iii.org/individuals/health/

The mission of the Insurance Information Institute (I.I.I.) is to improve public understanding of insurance—what it does and how it works. The above article is reproduced with permission from the I.I.I. site.

Americas Health Insurance Plans (AHIP)

http://www.ahip.org/

AHIP is the national association representing nearly 1,300 member companies that provide health insurance coverage to more than 200 million Americans. Its member companies offer medical expense insurance, long-term care insurance, disability income insurance, dental insurance, supplemental insurance, stop-loss insurance, and reinsurance to consumers, employers, and public purchasers. The organization's goal is to provide a unified voice for the health care financing industry, to expand access to high quality, cost effective health care to all Americans, and to ensure Americans' financial security through robust insurance markets, product flexibility and innovation, and an abundance of consumer choices.

Life and Health Insurance Foundation for Education (LIFE)

http://www.life-line.org/

The Life and Health Insurance Foundation for Education (LIFE) is a non-profit advocacy organization dedicated to addressing the public's growing need for information and education about life, health, disability, and long term care insurance. LIFE also seeks to remind people of the important role agents perform in helping families, businesses, and individuals find the insurance products that best fit their needs.

Chapter 60

All About Life Insurance

With Permission From: The Insurance Information Institute

Why should I buy life insurance?

Many financial experts consider life insurance to be the cornerstone of sound financial planning. It can be an important tool in the following situations:

1. **Replace income for dependents**

   If people depend on your income, life insurance can replace that income for them if you die. The most commonly recognized example of this is parents who have young children. However, it can also apply to couples when the survivor would be financially stricken by the income lost through the death of a partner, and to dependent adults, such as parents, siblings, or adult children who continue to rely on you financially. Insurance to replace your income can be especially useful if the government- or employer-sponsored benefits of your surviving spouse or domestic partner will be reduced after your death.

2. **Pay final expenses**

   Life insurance can pay your funeral and burial costs, probate and other estate administration costs, debts and medical expenses not covered by health insurance.

3. **Create an inheritance for your heirs**

   Even if you have no other assets to pass to your heirs, you can create an inheritance by buying a life insurance policy and naming them as beneficiaries.

4. **Pay federal "death" taxes and state "death" taxes**

   Life insurance benefits can pay estate taxes so that your heirs will not have to liquidate other assets or take a smaller inheritance. Changes in the federal "death" tax rules between now and January 1, 2011, will likely lessen the impact of this tax on some people, but some states are offsetting those federal decreases with increases in their state-level "death" taxes.

5. **Make significant charitable contributions**

   By making a charity the beneficiary of your life insurance, you can make a much larger contribution than if you donated the cash equivalent of the policy's premiums.

6. **Create a source of savings**

   Some types of life insurance create a cash value that, if not paid out as a death benefit, can be borrowed or withdrawn on the owner's request. Since most people make paying their life insurance policy premiums a high priority, buying a cash-value type policy can create a kind of "forced" savings plan. Furthermore, the interest credited is tax deferred (and tax exempt if the money is paid as a death claim).

How much life insurance do I need?

In most cases, if you have no dependents and have enough money to pay your final expenses, you don't need any life insurance.

If you want to create an inheritance or make a charitable contribution, buy enough life insurance to achieve those goals.

If you have dependents, buy enough life insurance so that, when combined with other sources of income, insurance will replace the income you now generate for them, plus enough to offset any additional expenses they will incur to replace services you provide. For a simple example, if you do your own taxes, the survivors might have to hire a professional tax preparer. Also, your family might need extra money to make some changes after you die. For example, they may want to relocate, or your spouse may need to go back to school to be in a better position to help support the family.

You should also plan to replace "hidden income" that would be lost at death. Hidden income is income that you receive through your employment but that isn't part of your gross wages. It includes things like your employer's subsidy of your health insurance premium, the matching contribution to your 401(k) plan, and many other "perks," large and small. This is an often overlooked insurance need: the cost of replacing just your health insurance and retirement contributions could be the equivalent of $2,000 per month or more.

Of course, you should also plan for expenses that arise at death. These include funeral costs, taxes, and administrative costs associated with "winding up" an estate and passing property to heirs. At a minimum, plan for $15,000.

What are the principal types of life insurance?

There are two major types of life insurance—term and whole life. Whole life is sometimes called permanent life insurance, and it encompasses several subcategories, including traditional whole life, universal life, variable life, and variable universal life. In 2003, about 6.4 million individual life insurance policies bought were term and about 7.1 million were whole life.

Life insurance products for groups are different from life insurance sold to individuals. The information below focuses on life insurance sold to individuals.

1. **Term Insurance**

   Term Insurance is the simplest form of life insurance. It pays only if death occurs during the term of the policy, which is usually from one to 30 years. Most term policies have no other benefit provisions.

There are two basic types of term life insurance policies—level term and decreasing term. Level term means that the death benefit stays the same throughout the duration of the policy. Decreasing term means that the death benefit drops, usually in one-year increments, over the course of the policy's term. In 2003, virtually all (97 percent) of the term life insurance bought was level term.

2. **Whole Life/Permanent Insurance**

   Whole life or permanent insurance pays a death benefit whenever you die—even if you live to 100! There are three major types of whole life or permanent life insurance—traditional whole life, universal life, and variable universal life, and there are variations within each type.

How is life insurance sold?

You can buy life insurance either as an "individual" or as part of a "group" plan.

☛ Individual Policy

When you buy an individual policy, you choose the company, the plan, and the benefits and features that are right for you and your family. You might be able to buy the policy from the same agent or company representative who sells you property and liability insurance for your home, auto, or business. And although you won't qualify for any discounts by buying your life insurance and other insurance from the same representative, working with a single advisor for all your insurance needs can make your financial life simpler.

☛ Group Policy

You might have life insurance automatically through your employer; many large companies provide this. Your employer also might offer you the chance to buy additional life insurance under a group policy. And you might be eligible to buy life insurance under a group policy from a union or trade association or other group you belong to (such as a college alumni association or an automobile club).

☛ Credit Life Insurance

Credit cards and lending institutions may offer life insurance to pay off your outstanding loans in the event of your death. This is generally made available in two ways:

- » As part of the loan at no extra charge. In this case the cost of the life insurance is borne by the lender and is included in its interest rate or other finance charges. If you have this type of credit life insurance, you don't need separate life insurance to pay off that loan if you die.
- » As an option at an extra charge. In this case, you should usually reject the optional coverage, provided that you have some other life insurance (group or individual) that can be designated to pay off the loan if you die. If you're under age 50 and you don't have other insurance that could pay off this loan, consider buying individual life insurance for this purpose as the rates will probably be better. At 50 or over (or younger with health issues), if you have no other life insurance for this purpose, the optional credit life insurance is likely to be cheaper than individual life insurance.

What is a beneficiary?

A beneficiary is the person or entity you name in a life insurance policy to receive the death benefit. You can name: one person, two or more people, the trustee of a trust you've set up, a charity, or your estate. If you don't name a beneficiary, the death benefit will be paid to your estate.

Digging Deeper

Insurance Information Institute: Life Insurance

http://www.iii.org/individuals/life/

The Insurance Information Institute (I.I.I.) provides detailed information on all aspects of life insurance at this section of its site. The mission of the Insurance Information Institute is to improve public understanding of insurance—what it does and how it works.

Life and Health Insurance Foundation for Education

http://www.life-line.org

The Life and Health Insurance Foundation for Education (LIFE) is a non-profit advocacy organization dedicated to addressing the public's growing need for information and education about life, health, disability, and long term care insurance. LIFE also seeks to remind people of the important role agents perform in helping families, businesses, and individuals find the insurance product that best fits their needs.

Chapter 61

Other Common Types of Insurance

With Permission From: The Insurance Information Institute

What is homeowners insurance?

Homeowners insurance provides financial protection against disasters. A standard policy insures the home itself and the things you keep in it.

Homeowners insurance is a package policy. This means that it covers both damage to your property and your liability or legal responsibility for any injuries and property damage you or members of your family cause to other people. This includes damage caused by household pets.

Damage caused by most disasters is covered, but there are exceptions. The most significant are damage caused by floods, earthquakes, and poor maintenance.

What is renters insurance?

Renters insurance provides financial protection against the loss or destruction of your possessions when you rent a house or apartment. While your landlord may be sympathetic to a burglary you have experienced or a fire caused by your iron, destruction or loss of your possessions is not usually covered by your landlord's insurance. Because in most cases, renters insurance covers only the value of your belongings, not the physical building, the premium is relatively inexpensive.

Disability Insurance

Disability insurance pays an insured person an income when that person is unable to work because of an accident or illness.

Long Term Care Insurance

Because of old age, mental or physical illness, or injury, some people find themselves in need of help with eating, bathing, dressing, toileting or continence, and/or transferring (e.g., getting out of a chair or out of bed). These six actions are called Activities of Daily Living, sometimes referred to as ADLs. In general, if you can't do two or more of these activities, or if you have a cognitive impairment, you are said to need "long term care." There are numerous types of long term care insurance.

Other Specialized Types of Insurance

There is a type of insurance for every possible purpose, providing coverage for boats and personal watercraft, travel accidents and loss of luggage, motorcycle use, coverage of household help, coverage for identity theft, and even wedding insurance.

Digging Deeper

Insurance Information Institute
http://www.iii.org

The mission of the Insurance Information Institute (I.I.I.) is to improve public understanding of insurance—what it does and how it works. The site offers details on numerous types of insurance for consumer and business users. This website also has links to every type of insurance company, as well as to state insurance regulatory agencies and educational institutions in the insurance industry.

Part XIV

Money, Banking, and Credit

Chapter 62

Learning to Budget and Save: A 6-Step Plan

The Federal Reserve Bank of Chicago

As a consumer, you face many choices on how to manage your money. Knowing how to manage money can help you make smart choices. Your money will work harder for you. You'll be more likely to avoid traps that can undermine your ability to attain your financial goals. You'll be in a better position to pay off debt and build savings.

Being smart about money can help you buy a house, finance higher education, or start a retirement fund. A money management game plan can help you get started and stay with it until you achieve the goals you set for yourself.

Step 1: Establish goals. Where do you want to be?

Without goals, it's difficult to accomplish anything. When you think about your future and what you want to achieve, it's helpful to establish a time frame:

- Short term: such as paying off credit card debt, saving for a vacation, or buying new clothes
- Intermediate: such as saving to buy a car

- Long term: such as saving for education or for retirement.

  Estimate the cost of each goal and the date you want to achieve it. Then figure out how much you need to save each month. Try to set realistic goals and saving requirements.

Step 2: Create a budget. Determine your current situation. Where are you today?

Now that you've figured out your financial goals, you are ready to create a budget that will help you attain them.

- Monthly fixed expenses

  Start with monthly fixed expenses such as regular savings, housing, groceries, utilities, and car payments.

- Monthly variable expenses

  Once you have noted all your fixed expenses, write down your expenses that vary each month such as clothing, vacations, gifts, and personal spending money.

- List your monthly income

  Now that you have figured out your expenses, write down your monthly income after all taxes and deductions.

- Now compare expenses to income

  One of the advantages of comparing expenses to income is that it provides a quick reality check. If you are spending more than you're bringing home every month in income, you have a deficit. If you're spending less than you're bringing home, you have a surplus. In either case, it's time to step back and consider some options.

- If you have a deficit, ask yourself:

  - Can I spend less on some of my variable expenses?

  - How much interest am I paying with credit card and other loans?

  - Where did my money go?

- If you have a surplus, ask yourself:
  - Am I saving enough to meet my goals? Are my spending estimates accurate?
  - Have I included all my fixed and variable expenses?

Step 3: Save your way to a more secure future.

An estimated 75 percent of families will experience a major financial setback in any given 10-year period. So it's smart to be prepared for financial thunderstorms. Save early, save often.

A consistent, long term savings program can help you achieve your goals. It also can help you build a financial safety net. Experts recommend that you save from three to six months worth of living expenses for emergencies.

Step 4: Conserve—spend sensibly; pay wisely.

Experts recommend paying with cash whenever possible. This helps you spend less than you otherwise might have spent if you had charged the purchase. You'll also avoid credit card interest charges and check-cashing fees.

Step 5: Act—implement your plan/assess/adjust.

Once you have set goals, estimated your fixed and variable expenses, and identified monthly savings targets, it's time to put your plan to work.

Give it some time. Then see how you're doing. Were you able to meet your savings goals? If so, stick with it. If not, look at your variable expenses for opportunity areas to cut back spending and increase savings.

Evaluate your plan every three months and make adjustments as needed. If you're not saving enough to meet your monthly goals, you may need to spend less.

Step 6: Select a financial institution.

Creating a safety net is easier if you work with a good financial institution, such as a credit union, a bank, or a thrift.

Interview employees at several locations. Look for people who are willing and able to answer your questions. Be ready to talk about the services and the advice you need.

For example, if it's important to you to conduct transactions face-to-face rather than through Automatic Teller Machines (ATM), ask if the financial institution charges for the services of a person at the counter. If you prefer to use ATMs, make sure they're readily accessible and don't charge transaction fees.

Once you select a financial institution, consider opening a checking account if you don't have one. A checking account can save you fees you may now be paying for cashing your paycheck and paying your bills.

Saving is the key to successful financial plans. Use payroll deductions or automatic transfers to checking, savings, or money market accounts. It's easier to save if you never see the money.

Use budget plans for paying utilities if they're available. Use cash for purchases rather than charging if you can.

Enter each check you write in a check register. Balance the account every month. If you use a debit card, enter those amounts in your check register.

Digging Deeper

Federal Reserve Tips for Saving Money

http://www.federalreserve.gov/consumerinfo/savingsresources.htm

The Federal Reserve provides links to a number of articles containing information on saving money.

Mymoney.gov

http://www.mymoney.gov

The U.S. Financial Literacy and Education Commission has established an excellent website covering numerous important monetary topics, such as budgeting and taxes, credit, financial planning, home ownership, educational costs, financial scams, retirement, saving and investment, and starting a business.

Online Budget Calculator

http://www.ed.gov/offices/OSFAP/DirectLoan/BudgetCalc/budget.html

A simple online budget calculator, with clear instructions, is offered by the Student Financial Aid website from the federal Department of Education. To use this tool, be sure your browser is JavaScript-compatible.

Chapter 63

Learn to Balance Your Checkbook

Federal Reserve System

Balancing your checkbook every month is a tedious but necessary process to avoid overdrafts, expensive fees, or even closure of your account.

Your Monthly Bank Statement

Your checking account statement is issued at the same time each month and is normally available both by mail and online. The statement will include all the transactions for the previous month. The types of transactions you will see in your statement will be checks cleared, deposits added, ATM withdrawals, debit card transactions, any automatic monthly debits for memberships or other services which you have pre-authorized, and banking fees.

Steps to Balance Your Checkbook

Using this statement and your checkbook register, use the following steps to balance your checkbook.

1. Compare all of the items listed on your statement to those listed in your checkbook register. Place a checkmark next to each item in your register. Add any deposits and subtract any withdrawals you'd forgotten so that your

checkbook register has a listing of all transactions.

2. On a sheet of paper write down the ending balance from your statement.
3. Then, under the ending balance, write the amount of all deposits made after the ending date of the statement. (There would be no checkmarks in the register next to these deposits.)
4. Add the deposit amounts to the ending balance from Step 2.
5. Make a list of all of the checks and the check amounts and other transactions that are still outstanding. (There would be no checkmarks next to these, either.)
6. Subtract the amount of the checks that are still outstanding from the balance in Step 4.

The ending amount should match the balance you have written in your checkbook register. Keep in mind that your bank balance includes all checks you have written, even if they have not yet cleared, while the bank's balance only reflects cleared items.

Trouble-Shooting

If you find that you are not in balance try some of the following tips:

- ✓ Check your math—Make sure that each time you wrote down a transaction in your checkbook register, you subtracted correctly.
- ✓ Verify check amounts—Compare the dollar amount of the checks you wrote down in your register to the check amounts on the statement to make sure that all checks cleared for the correct amount.
- ✓ Verify deposit amounts—Compare the dollar amount of the deposits you wrote down in your register to the deposit amounts on the statement to make sure that all deposits were entered for the correct amount.

Keeping Your Account Balanced

Every time you write a check, use the ATM, or use your debit card, you should record the transaction in your checkbook register. That way, you will always be sure of your account balance. It also makes balancing easier if you enter each transaction in your checkbook register as it occurs. This process is known as keeping a running balance.

Controlling Bank Charges

- Bank Fees and Charges

  Your bank may charge your checking account a monthly service fee, a fee to move money between different accounts, a fee for using ATM machines outside your bank system, or a fee if you don't maintain a certain balance. If you overdraw your account, you will be charged a considerable amount for each overdrawn check. Depending upon your credit, the bank may or may not pay these overdrawn checks. Avoiding overdrafts is the most important reason for keeping your account balanced, for this practice will damage your credit rating.

- Comparing Bank Fees

  It is always worth comparing the fees charged by different neighborhood banks in order to keep your banking costs as low as possible. Also, if you are a student, you may be entitled to a lower-cost account.

- Speak Up; Ask to Waive Charges

  When you do receive an unexpected charge on your account, call your bank and ask if it can be waived. Always ask how such charges can be avoided in the future.

Digging Deeper

Federal Reserve: Protecting Your Checking Account

http://www.federalreserve.gov/pubs/checkingaccount/

This consumer advisory from the Federal Reserve offers five tips on protecting your checking account. Along with cautions not to give out account numbers and the importance of avoiding bank overdrafts, this site also offers links to federal consumer protection laws.

Federal Reserve: Electronic Check Conversion

http://www.federalreserve.gov/pubs/checkconv/default.htm

It is now possible for a retailer to convert a paper check into an immediate electronic debit. This website explains this new procedure and how the transaction appears on your bank statement.

Federal Reserve: Consumer Guide to Check 21

http://www.federalreserve.gov/pubs/check21/consumer_guide.htm

A federal law, known as Check 21, makes it easier for banks to electronically transfer check images instead of physically transfer paper checks. This guide explains your rights under Check 21 as they relate to substitute checks. Substitute checks are special paper copies of the front and back of your original checks that are created to replace the original check.

Federal Reserve: Protecting Yourself Against Overdraft Fees

http://www.federalreserve.gov/pubs/bounce/default.htm

A consumer advisory webpage at the Federal Reserve offers advice about how to protect yourself against bank overdraft fees. Banks, savings and loans, and credit unions may provide various overdraft services that may be less expensive that paying regular overdraft fees. This site explains each alternative.

Chapter 64

Banking Basics: Savings, Checking and ATM Cards

Consumer Action Website
Federal Citizen Information Center

When it comes to finding a safe place to put your money, there are a lot of options. Savings accounts, checking accounts, certificates of deposit, and money market accounts are popular choices. Each has different rules and benefits that fit different needs. When choosing the one that is right for you, consider the following:

Part I: General Account Guidelines

- **Minimum deposit requirements.** Some accounts can only be set up with a minimum dollar amount. If your account goes below the minimum, no interest is paid, or you are charged extra fees.

- **Limits on withdrawals.** Can you take money out whenever you want? Are there any penalties for doing so?

- **Interest.** How much (if anything) is paid and when: daily, monthly, quarterly, yearly? To compare rates offered locally to those from financial institutions around the nation, visit www.bankrate.com.

- **Deposit insurance.** Look for a sign that says your money is protected by the Federal Deposit Insurance Corporation. Credit union accounts have similar protection from the National Credit Union Administration.

- **Convenience.** How easy is it to put money in and take it out? Are there tellers or ATM machines close to where you work and live? Or would you receive most of your service via the telephone or internet? Can you make direct deposits and other electronic transfers?

Part II: Checking Accounts

If you are considering a checking account or another type of account with check-writing privileges, add these items to your list of things to think about:

1. **Number of checks.** Is there a maximum number of checks you can write per month? If you write more, what is the charge?
2. **Account and check fees.** Is there a monthly fee for the account or a charge for each check you write? Some accounts only charge a fee if you write more than a certain number of checks each month.
3. **Holds on checks.** Is there a "hold" or waiting period before you can access the money you deposit in your account? There may be a longer hold period for out-of-state checks.
4. **Overdrafts.** If you write a check for more money than you have in your account, what happens? You may be able to link your checking account to a savings account to protect yourself. There could also be high fees for "bounced" checks (from you or written to you). Bounced checks can blemish your credit record, so it's better to be covered.
5. **Check 21.** The new Check Clearing for the 21st Century Act (often referred to as Check 21) allows banks to clear checks electronically, which results in funds being credited or debited more quickly than in the past. Quicker clearing also means less time to stop payment on a check.

Part III: Savings Accounts

There are a variety of types of savings accounts available from banks and credit unions. Here are the principal examples:

- **Basic Personal Savings Account**

  This is the account that we most often consider when we open a new savings account. It is perfect for the beginning saver because it generally requires a smaller amount to open an account. The minimum deposit will vary between financial institutions, but it usually ranges from $25 to $200. The interest rate is generally lower on this type of account, but the restrictions for taking money out of the account are usually less severe. There will most likely be a fee if your balance falls below a certain amount, but this amount is usually related to the minimum deposit requirement. For instance, if the minimum opening deposit is $200, then you will incur a fee if your balance falls below $200 at any time. This will vary between financial institutions, so be certain to check the associated fees with your bank.

- **Special Personal Savings Account**

  Financial institutions like to have a special savings account for individuals wanting to place a larger sum of money into an account. This type of account will have a larger opening deposit requirement. The interest rate will be higher than a basic savings account, and the restrictions for taking money out of the account may be more specific. There is often no monthly service fee associated with this type of account.

- **Money Market Account**

  A Money Market Account combines saving and checking features. There may be a minimum balance requirement to earn interest and a possible limitation on the number of checks you can write in a single month.

- **Certificate of Deposit (CD)**

  CDs work much like a savings account in that you have to put a certain opening deposit amount into your account (or CD). In order to receive the stated interest rate, you will have to leave the CD undisturbed for a specified period of time, such as six months or one year. If you need access to the money in a CD, you will usually have to pay a penalty fee to cash it in, or you may lose the interest from the prior quarter. Each bank establishes its own rules.

Part IV: ATM Debit Cards

With a debit card and personal identification number (PIN), you can use an automated teller machine (ATM) to withdraw cash, make deposits, or transfer funds between accounts. Some ATMs charge a fee if you are not a member of the ATM network or are making a transaction at a remote location.

Retail purchases can also be made with a debit card. You enter your PIN or sign for the purchase. Some banks charge customers a fee for debit card purchases made with a PIN. Although a debit card looks like a credit card, the money for the purchase is transferred immediately from your bank account to the store's account. In addition, when you use a debit card, federal law does not give you the right to stop payment. You must resolve the problem with the seller.

If you suspect your debit card has been lost or stolen, immediately call the card issuer. Many companies have toll-free numbers and 24-hour service to deal with such emergencies.

Chapter 65

How to Establish, Use, and Protect Your Credit

Prepared by the Federal Reserve Bank of San Francisco

Good credit is valuable. Having the ability to borrow funds allows us to buy things we would otherwise have to save for years to afford: homes, cars, a college education. Credit is an important financial tool, but it can also be dangerous, leading people into debt far beyond their ability to repay. That is why learning how to use credit wisely is one of the most valuable financial skills anyone can learn.

What Lenders Look For

Before creditors lend money, they need to be assured that the funds will be repaid. In other words, is the prospective borrower creditworthy? To find out, they ask for various types of information, as explained below.

Income and Expenses

Lenders will look at what you earn and your regular expenses, such as rent, utilities, food, and other ongoing items. The amount left tells them whether you can afford to take on additional debt.

Assets

Do you have assets that can serve as collateral? Lenders will look for things like bank accounts, insurance, and valuable items such as a house, if you own one.

- **Credit History**

  How do you manage debt? If you have credit cards or have borrowed money before, you have a history that shows prospective lenders whether you are creditworthy by revealing details about the amount of debt you already have, how many credit cards you have, and whether you make payments on time.

  It's easy to qualify for credit if you have a good credit history, but what if you have never used credit before? This is a common problem for people who've just started working, those who work in the home, people who always pay in cash, and those who do not have assets or accounts in their own names. For them, the first step is to establish a credit history.

How to Establish Credit

Begin by opening individual savings and checking accounts in your name. Over time, your deposits, withdrawals, and transfers will demonstrate that you can handle money responsibly.

Applying for a loan is another option, but be aware that this method of establishing a credit history will cost, since loans require the payment of interest.

You could take out a bank loan secured by the funds you have on deposit or by items you own, such as a car. You could also ask a friend or relative who has good credit to cosign a loan, which means that he or she shares liability for the loan with you.

You could also apply for department store and gasoline credit cards, which generally are easier to obtain than major credit cards. Before you apply for any credit, however, make sure you understand the terms. For example, how long is the grace period or the time you have to pay the current balance in full before finance charges are added? Is there an annual fee or other fees associated with the credit? If you believe that you will carry a balance, you need to know how finance charges are calculated.

Patience is important in this process. It takes time to establish credit and build a record of consistency in making payments to demonstrate your creditworthiness. And it is much better to go slowly and develop a strong credit record than to apply for too many credit cards or a loan that is larger than you can handle.

Start slowly, be cautious, keep track of your overall debt, and pay on time. Most importantly, remember that credit actually represents real money and has to be repaid with interest.

Protecting Credit

Once you have obtained credit, it is necessary to protect it. This means being careful with your credit, debit, and ATM cards, as well as your account and personal identification numbers (PINs).

Carry only the cards you expect to use, and keep the others in a safe place. Maintain a list of account and telephone numbers of the companies that issued your cards. Then, if the cards are lost or stolen, you can notify the companies quickly. If your notification is received before the cards are used, you have no legal responsibility for the bills; if it is received after the cards are used, your legal responsibility is $50 for each card.

Be cautious about giving anyone your account numbers, especially over the telephone when someone calls you. Save sales receipts to compare with your bill, and when you discard documents with account numbers on them, be certain that the numbers can't be read.

If you disagree with an item on a bill, you are responsible for notifying the creditor in writing within 60 days of receiving the bill. You should include your name, account number, the item you believe is in error, and the reasons why.

Common Reasons for Denying Credit

Among the most common reasons people are turned down when they apply for credit are:

- Too little time in current job or at current residence.
- Too much outstanding debt.
- Unreasonable purpose for requesting credit.
- Co-signer cannot take on additional debt liability.
- Errors on applicant's credit report.
- Strict creditor's standards.

In general, creditworthiness must be determined on the basis of criteria that relate to your ability and willingness to repay debt. You cannot be denied credit based on your sex, marital status, race, religion, national origin, age, or dependence on income from public assistance.

If you are denied credit, the creditor must provide you with a written statement of the action and your rights, as well as the reason for denial or how to request the reason. For information on the laws applying to credit, see "Your Credit Rights," a Federal Reserve Bank of San Francisco brochure.

Improving Poor Credit

If you have fallen behind in your payments, begin immediately to repair your credit record. Here's how:

1. Face up to the problem. Recognize that you are overextended, and contact your creditors to see if they will set up a new payment schedule that you can maintain. In any case, don't ignore your bills.

2. Immediately stop purchasing with credit. Take your credit cards out of your wallet. Store them in a spot that is hard to reach, or even cut them up.

3. Consider consolidating debts. You may find it easier to make a single payment rather than several. You might also get a lower interest rate that will make it easier to keep up with payments. Remember that debt consolidation is not a cure-all. You have to learn to control your spending to avoid future debt.

4. Contact a credit counseling organization. You can obtain referrals for organizations in your area through the National Foundation for Consumer Credit, 800–388–2227.

5. Don't expect miracles. Don't believe companies that promise to fix a poor credit rating quickly and painlessly for a fee. As long as it is accurate and timely, negative information cannot be removed from your credit record. The only way to improve a credit record is to let time pass and establish a record of on-time payment.

Digging Deeper

Getting Credit

http://www.ftc.gov/gettingcredit/

The Federal Trade Commission (FTC) offers this useful online consumer guide to establishing, maintaining, improving, and protecting credit. There are also links to other related resources on identity theft, credit scams, credit fraud, and limitations on sharing your private financial data.

Credit and Your Consumer Rights

http://www.ftc.gov/bcp/edu/pubs/consumer/credit/cre01.shtm

There are extensive federal consumer protection laws in place that deal with credit reports, credit applications, debt collection, and solving credit problems. This website from the FTC reviews these topics.

Credit Reporting

http://www.ftc.gov/bcp/menus/consumer/credit/rights.shtm

Accessing a free copy of a credit report can be confusing, but this website explains how to obtain reports from the reporting agencies once per year without charge.

Credit Bureaus and Credit Scoring

http://www.consumeraction.gov/caw_credit_reports_scores.shtml

For those seeking to understand more about credit reports and credit scoring, this website gives the names and contact information for the three major credit reporting agencies, along with an explanation about credit scoring.

Free Annual Credit Report

https://www.annualcreditreport.com/cra/index.jsp

To obtain a free copy of your credit reports each year, visit this website, which was created by the three major credit reporting agencies.

Credit Tips

http://www.consumeraction.gov/caw_credit_general_tips.shtml

The Equal Credit Opportunity Act protects consumers who seek credit from banks and other lending institutions. This web resource offers tips on how to shop for credit and what to look out for as you compare offers.

Chapter 66

What You Should Know About Credit Cards

Federal Citizen Information Center

Chances are you've received "pre-approved" credit card offers in the mail. Examine the fine print carefully before you accept any offer for a credit or charge card. Here is what you should know about credit cards.

Part I: The Mechanics of Credit Cards

- The Annual Percentage Rate (APR). If the interest rate is variable, how is it determined and when can it change?
- The periodic rate. This is the interest rate used to figure the finance charge on your balance each billing period.
- The annual fee. While some cards have no annual fee, others expect you to pay an amount each year for being a cardholder.
- The grace period. This is the number of days you have to pay your bill before finance charges start. Without this period, you may have to pay interest from the date you use your card or when the purchase is posted to your account.
- The finance charges. Most lenders calculate finance charges using an average daily account balance, which is the average of what you owed each day in the billing cycle. Look for offers that use an adjusted balance, which subtracts your monthly payment from your beginning balance. This method usually has

the lowest finance charges. Stay away from offers that use the previous balance in calculating what you owe; this method has the highest finance charge. Also, don't forget to check if there is a minimum finance charge.

- Other fees. Ask about special fees when you get a cash advance, make a late payment, or go over your credit limit. Some companies charge a monthly fee regardless of whether you use your card.

Part II: Protections and Disclosures

The Fair Credit and Charge Card Disclosure Act requires credit and charge card issuers to include this information on credit applications. The Federal Trade Commission offers a wide range of free publications on credit and consumer rights at *www.ftc.gov*. The Federal Reserve Board provides a free brochure on choosing a credit card and a guide to credit protection laws at www.federalreserve.gov.

Part III: Comparing Cards

Visit these useful websites about credit cards:

- ✓ Bank Rate *(http://www.bankrate.com)* provides free credit card tips and information.
- ✓ Consumer Action *(www.consumer-action.org)* has a site that features credit card surveys of interest rates, fees and other terms from dozens of credit cards, as well as free brochures and guides on choosing and using credit cards.
- ✓ Card Web *(www.cardweb.com)* lists credit cards and offers e-mail newsletters, frequently asked questions and online credit card calculators.
- ✓ Card Ratings *(www.cardratings.com)* lists and reviews credit cards and offers tips and credit card calculators.

Part IV: Lost and Stolen Credit Cards

Immediately call the card issuer when you suspect a credit or charge card has been lost or stolen. Many companies have toll-free numbers and 24-hour service to deal with such emergencies.

By federal law, once you report the loss or theft of a card, you have no further responsibility for unauthorized charges. In any event, your maximum liability under federal law is $50 per card.

Part V: Complaints

To complain about a problem with your credit card company, call the company first and try to resolve the problem. If you fail to resolve the issue, ask for the name, address, and phone number of its regulatory agency.

If the word national appears in the name or the letters N.A. appear after the name, the Office of the Comptroller oversees its operations.

To complain about a credit bureau, department store or other FDIC-insured financial institution, write to the Consumer Response Center. You may also file a complaint online at *www.ftc.gov.*

Digging Deeper

FTC: Choosing and Using Credit Cards

http://www.ftc.gov/bcp/edu/pubs/consumer/credit/cre05.shtm

Credit card terms and methods of computing balances can significantly affect the costs associated with a particular credit card. This webpage from the FTC offers an explanation of card issuer practices, as well as information on disputing charges. Cardholders are also entitled to various rights, which are described here.

Federal Reserve Board: Choosing a Credit Card

http://www.federalreserve.gov/Pubs/shop/

The Federal Reserve publishes this online consumer pamphlet to help individuals compare credit cards and make selections. It also focuses on the costs of credit obtained from a credit card if payments are not made within the grace period.

Credit Cards: 8 Dirty Secrets

http://money.cnn.com/2002/03/12/pf/banking/q_creditcard/

CNN's Money website published this useful article to help consumers avoid extra credit card charges. Because credit card interest rates and late payment fees are very high, it is well worth the effort to handle credit cards extremely carefully.

Chapter 67

Beware of Identity Theft

Federal Citizen Information Center

You can reduce the chance a con artist can go on a spending spree with your money or steal your identify by taking the following precautions and corrective actions.

Part I: Precautions

- ✓ Give your Social Security number only when absolutely necessary. Ask to use other types of identifiers when possible. If your state uses your SSN as your driver's license number, ask to substitute another number.
- ✓ Sign credit/debit cards when they arrive. It's harder for thieves to forge your signature.
- ✓ Carry only the cards you need. Extra cards increase your risk and your hassle if your wallet is stolen.
- ✓ Keep your PIN numbers secret. Never write a PIN on a credit/debit card or on a slip of paper kept with your card.
- ✓ Avoid obvious passwords. Avoid easy-to-find names and numbers such as your birthday or phone number.
- ✓ Store personal information in a safe place at home and at work.

- ✓ Don't give card numbers to strangers. Confirm whether a person represents a company by calling the phone number on your account statement or in the telephone book.
- ✓ Watch out for "shoulder surfers." Use your free hand to shield the keypad when using pay phones and ATMs.
- ✓ Beware of blank spaces. Draw a line through blank spaces on credit slips. Never sign a blank slip.
- ✓ Keep your receipts. Ask for carbons and incorrect charge slips as well.
- ✓ Destroy documents with account information. Stop thieves from finding information in the trash by tearing up or shredding receipts, credit offers, account statements, expired cards, etc.
- ✓ Protect your mail. Ask your local post office to put your mail on hold when you are traveling and can't pick it up.
- ✓ Make life difficult for hackers. Install firewalls and virus-detection software on your home computers. If you have a high-speed internet connection, unplug the computer's cable or phone line when you aren't using it.
- ✓ Keep a record of your cards and accounts. List numbers, expiration dates, and contact information in case there is a problem.
- ✓ Pay attention to your billing cycles. A missing bill could mean a thief has taken over your account.
- ✓ Promptly compare receipts with account statements. Watch for unauthorized transactions. Shred receipts after verifying the charge on your monthly statement.
- ✓ Check your credit report once a year. Check it more frequently if you suspect someone has obtained your account information.

Part II: Identity Theft Problems and Actions to Take

1. Notify the Credit Card Company. Despite these precautions, problems can still occur. If a card is missing or you suspect another problem, notify the company immediately.

2. File a Police Report. If you become an ID theft victim, file a report with your local police. Keep a copy of the police report, which will make it easier to prove your case to creditors and retailers.

3. Contact the Credit-Reporting Bureaus. Ask them to flag your account with a fraud alert, which asks merchants not to grant new credit without your approval.

4. Use an ID Theft Reporting Affidavit. To simplify the lengthy credit-repair process, the FTC now offers an ID Theft Affidavit you can use to report the crime to most of the parties involved. Request a copy of the form by calling toll-free 1–877–ID–THEFT or visiting *www.ftc.gov/IDTheft*. All three credit bureaus and many major creditors have agreed to accept the affidavit. You
can also file complaint with the FTC at *www.ftc.gov*.

5. Use the Identity Theft Resource Center. When dealing with ID theft, you can also get advice from the Identify Theft Resource Center at *www.idtheftcenter.org*.

Digging Deeper

IDTheft.gov

http://www.idtheft.gov

Because identity theft has become such a huge national problem, President Bush established a special task force and strategic plan, both of which are described at this federal government website.

Identity Theft Resource Center

http://www.idtheftcenter.org

The mission of the Identity Theft Resource Center is to provide victim assistance at no charge to consumers throughout the United States, as well as to educate consumers, corporations, government agencies, and other organizations on best practices for fraud and identity theft detection, reduction, and mitigation.

FTC: Fighting Back Against Identity Theft

http://www.ftc.gov/bcp/edu/microsites/idtheft

This website, provided by the Federal Trade Commission, is a one-stop national resource to learn about the crime of identity theft. It provides detailed information to help you deter, detect, and defend against identity theft. On this site, consumers can learn how to avoid identity theft—and learn what to do if their identity is stolen. Businesses can learn how to help their customers deal with identity theft, as well as how to prevent problems in the first place. Law enforcement agencies can access resources and learn how to help victims of identity theft.

Part XV

Savings and Investing

Chapter 68

Basic Principles of Saving and Investing

Securities and Exchange Commission (SEC)

Saving and Investing are complex topics. There are many thousands of websites, as well as hundreds of government and non-profit resources on these important topics. This section introduces the basic principles of saving and investing and offers more extensive information in the "Digging Deeper" section.

Part I: Why Save and Invest?

Many people experience financial hard times when they get older because they never got the facts on saving and investing.

The best way to achieve financial success is to plan for it. Maybe you'd like to:

...buy a car when you graduate from high school or college;
...have money set aside for special occasions or emergencies;
...buy a house someday; or
...live comfortably in retirement.

Once you decide what you're saving for—and when you'd like to have it—you can decide how you should save and invest.

The best time to learn about money is when you're young and still in school. Starting a saving program when you are young lets you take advantage of the magic of compound interest, which refers to the earning of "interest on interest" as your capital grows over time. (Editor's note: There are rules of thumb that tell you how much you will have, before taxes, at different times in the future based upon the rate of interest you are earning. For example, if you are earning 5%, your money will double approximately every 14 years. See the "Digging Deeper" section for resources on compound interest.)

Part II: How Can I Save and Invest?

Many people get into the habit of saving or investing by following this advice: "Pay yourself first." Many people find it easier to pay themselves first if they allow their bank to automatically remove money from their paycheck and deposit it into a savings or investment account. Other people pay themselves first by having money automatically deposited into an employer-sponsored retirement savings account, such as a 401(k).

There are many different ways to save and invest, including:

- **Savings Accounts:** If you save your money in a savings account, the bank or credit union will pay you interest, and you can easily get your money whenever you want it. At most banks, your savings account will be insured by the Federal Deposit Insurance Corporation (FDIC).
- **Insured Bank Money Market Accounts:** These accounts tend to offer higher interest rates than savings accounts and often give you check-writing privileges. Like savings accounts many money market accounts will be insured by the FDIC. Note that bank money market accounts are not the same as money market mutual funds, which are not insured by the FDIC.
- **Certificates of Deposit:** You can earn an even higher interest if you put your money in a certificate of deposit, or CD, which is also protected by the FDIC. When you buy a CD, you promise that you're going to

keep your money in the bank for a certain amount of time.

- **Stocks:** Have you ever thought that you'd like to own part of a famous restaurant or the company that makes the shoes on your feet? That's what happens when you buy stock in a company—you become one of the owners. Your share of the company depends on how many shares of the company's stock you own.

- **Bonds:** Many companies borrow money so they can become even bigger and more successful. One way they borrow money is by selling bonds. When you buy a bond, you're lending your money to the company so it can grow. The company promises to pay you interest and to return your money on a date in the future.

- **Mutual Funds:** Stocks and bonds can be purchased individually, or you can buy them bybuying shares of a mutual fund. A mutual fund is a pool of money run by a professional or group of professionals who have experience in picking investments. After researching many companies, these professionals select the stocks or bonds of companies and put them into a fund. Investors can buy shares of the fund, and their shares rise or fall in value as the values of the stocks and bonds in the fund rise and fall.

Part III: Risk and Return

Every saving or investing product has its advantages and disadvantages. Differences include how fast you can get your money when you need it, how fast your money will grow, and how safe your money will be. For example,

- **Savings Accounts, Insured Money Market Accounts, and CDs:** With these products, your money tends to be very safe because it's federally insured, and you can easily get to your money if you need it for any reason. But there's a tradeoff for security and ready availability. Your money earns a low interest rate compared with investments. In other words, it gets a low return.

- **Stocks:** Over the past 60 years, the investment that has provided the highest average rate of return has been stocks. But there are no guarantees of profits when you buy stock, which makes stock one of the most risky investments. If the company doesn't do well or falls out of favor with investors, your stock can fall in price, and you could lose your money.

  You can make money from stock in two ways. First, the price of the-stock can rise if the company does well and other investors want to buy the company's stock. If a stock rises from $10 to $12, the $2 increase is called a capital gain or appreciation. Second, a company sometimes pays out a part of its profits to stock holders—that's called a dividend. Sometimes a company will decide not to pay out dividends, choosing instead to keep its profits and use them to expand the business, build new factories, design better products, or hire more workers.

  One of the riskiest investments you can make is buying stock in a new company. New companies go out of business more frequently than companies that have been in business for decades or longer. If you buy stock in a small, new company, you could lose it all. Or the company could turn out to be a success. You'll have to do your homework and learn as much as you can about the company before you invest. And only invest money that you can afford to lose.

- **Bonds:** The company's "promise to repay" your principal generally makes bonds less risky than stocks. But bonds can be risky. To assess how risky a bond is you can check the bond's credit rating. Unlike stockholders, bond holders know how much money they will make, unless the company goes out of business. If the company goes out of business or declares bankruptcy, bondholders may lose money. But if there is any money left in the company, they will get it before stockholders. Bonds generally provide higher returns (with higher risk) than savings accounts, but lower returns (with lower risk) than stocks.

- **Mutual Funds:** Mutual fund risk is determined by the stocks and bonds in the fund. No mutual fund can guarantee its returns, and no mutual fund is risk-free.

☛ **Conclusion:** Always remember: the greater the potential return, the greater the risk. Risk is scary because no one wants to lose money, but there's also such a thing as "too safe." We all know that prices go up. That's called inflation. For example, a loaf of bread that costs a dollar today could cost two dollars 10 years from now. If your money doesn't grow as fast as inflation does, that's like losing money, because while a dollar buys a whole loaf of bread today, in 10 years it might only buy half a loaf.

Part IV: What Is "Diversification"?

One of the most important ways to lessen the risks of investing is to diversify your investments. It's common sense: don't put all your eggs in one basket. If you buy a mixture of different types of stocks, bonds, or mutual funds, your savings will not be wiped out if one of your investments fails. Since no one can accurately predict how our economy or one company will do, diversification helps you to protect your savings. If you had just one investment and it went down in value, then you would lose money. But if you had ten different investments and one went down in value, you could still come out ahead.

Part V: Credit Management

Many adults—and plenty of students—have wallets filled with credit cards, some of which they've "maxed out" (meaning they've spent up to their credit limit). Credit cards can make it seem easy to buy expensive things when you don't have the cash in your pocket—or in the bank. But credit cards aren't free money.

Most credit cards charge high interest rates—as much as 18 percent or more—if you don't pay off your balance in full each month. If you owe money on your credit cards, the wisest thing you can do is pay off the balance in full as quickly as possible. Few investments will give you the high returns you'll need to keep pace with an 18 percent interest charge. That's why you're better off reducing your credit card debt.

Once you've paid off your credit cards, you can budget your money and begin to save and invest. Here are some tips for avoiding credit card debt:

- ✓ **Put Away the Plastic:** Don't use a credit card unless your debt is at a manageable level and you know you'll have the money to pay the bill when it arrives.
- ✓ **Know What You Owe:** It's easy to forget how much you've charged on your credit card. Every time you use a credit card, write down how much you spent and figure out how much you'll have to pay that month. If you know you won't be able to pay your balance in full, try to figure out how much you can pay each month and how long it will take to pay the balance in full.
- ✓ **Pay Off the Card with the Highest Rate:** If you've got unpaid balances on several credit cards, you should first pay down the card that charges the highest rate. Pay as much as you can toward that debt each month until your balance is once again zero, while still paying the minimum on your other cards.

Part VI: Achieving Financial Security

- ✓ **Make a Plan:** The key to financial security is to have a "financial plan." That means you should set financial goals and start saving or investing to reach those goals. While that may sound hard, it doesn't have to be. You'll first need to figure out where you're starting from—for example, how much you owe, how much money have you saved already, how much money you will get from your job or your parents. Next, you should set goals. Do you want a car? A college education? New clothes? Once you know what you want, when you want it, and how much it costs, you can figure out how much you need to save each week or month or year.
- ✓ **Keep Trade-Offs and "Opportunity Cost" in Mind:** Unless you're lucky enough to have an unlimited amount of money, you'll have to choose

how you spend your money. That means you'll have to make trade-offs and consider the "opportunity cost," meaning what you give up by choosing one option over another. For example, let's say you've got $100.00. If you put the money in an account that earns 5 percent interest, you'll have $105.00 at the end of the year. If you spend it on new clothes, you won't earn that extra $5.00, although you should still have the clothes. But if you wanted to sell them, they'd probably be worth less, especially if they're used or out of style.

✓ **Save and Invest for the Long Term:** Perhaps the best protection against risk is time, and that's what young people are fortunate to have the most of. On any day the stock market can go up or down. Sometimes it goes down for months or years. But over the years, investors who've adopted a "buy and hold" approach to investing tend to come out ahead of those who try to time the market.

✓ **Investigate Before You Invest:** Another way to reduce risk is to do your homework before you part with your hard-earned cash. Call your state securities regulator to check up on the background of any person or company that you're considering doing business with. You'll find that number in the government section of your phone book. Find out as much as you can about any company before you invest in it. Companies that issue stock have to give important information to investors in a booklet called a "prospectus" and, by law, that information is supposed to be truthful. Always read the prospectus. And beware of "get rich quick schemes." If someone offers you an especially high rate of return on an investment or pressures you to invest before you've had time to investigate, it's probably a scam.

✓ **Avoid the Costs of Delay:** Time can also be the most important factor that will determine how much your money will grow. If you saved five dollars a week at eight percent interest starting from the time you were 18 years old, you'd have $134,000 saved by the time you're 65. But if you wait until you're 40 years old to start saving, you'll have to save $32 a week to catch up. In fact, just one year's delay—waiting until you're 19 years old to start saving five dollars a week at eight percent interest—will cost you more than $10,000 by the time you're 65.

Digging Deeper

Federal Deposit Insurance Corporation (FDIC)

http://www.fdic.gov/.

The Federal Deposit Insurance Corporation (FDIC) is an independent agency created by Congress to maintain the stability of and public confidence in the nation's financial system by insuring deposits, examining and supervising financial institutions, and managing receiverships.

Financial Industry Regulatory Authority

http://www.finra.org/index.htm

The Financial Industry Regulatory Authority (FINRA) is the largest non-governmental regulator for all securities firms doing business in the United States. All told, FINRA oversees over 5,000 brokerage firms, about 172,000 branch offices, and more than 674,000 registered securities representatives. Created in July 2007 through the consolidation of the NationalAssociation of Securities Dealers (NASD) and the member regulation, enforcement, and arbitration functions of the New York Stock Exchange, FINRA is dedicated to investor protection and market integrity through effective and efficient regulation and complementary compliance and technology-based services.

Securities and Exchange Commission (SEC)

http://www.sec.gov

The mission of the U.S. Securities and Exchange Commission is to protect investors, maintain fair, orderly, and efficient markets, and facilitate capital formation. This is the home page of the SEC, with extensive resources on every aspect of the securities field.

How Does Compound Interest Work?

http://www.fdic.gov/consumers/consumer/news/cnsum06/amazing.html

People who put even a small amount of money into a savings account as often as they can and leave it untouched for years may be amazed at how big the account grows. The reason? A combination of saving as much as possible on a regular basis and the impact of interest payments (what the financial world calls "the miracle of compounding"). This webpage explains how you can slowly build a large savings account and experience the miracle of compounding.

Chapter 69

Putting Your Money to Work

New York Stock Exchange (NYSE)

Once you've established your investment plan you can determine which financial products are best suited for your goals. Besides stocks, a growing number of other types of securities trade on the New York Stock Exchange (NYSE).

Part I: Types of Stock

The two main categories of stocks are common stock and preferred stock. Preferred stockholders have priority over common stockholders in terms of dividend payout and in recouping their investment if the company fails or liquidates. However, preferred stockholders, unlike common stockholders, cannot vote for directors of the company.

Part II: Five Basic Categories of Stock

1. Income Stocks pay unusually large dividends that can be used as a means of generating income without selling the stock, but the price of the stock generally does not rise very quickly.

2. Blue-Chip Stocks are issued by very solid and reliable companies with long histories of consistent growth and stability. Blue-chip stocks usually pay small but regular dividends and maintain a fairly steady price throughout market

ups and downs.

3. Growth Stocks are issued by young, entrepreneurial companies that are experiencing a faster growth rate than their general industries. These stocks normally pay little or no dividend because the company needs all of its earnings to finance expansion. Since they are issued by companies with no proven track record, growth stocks are riskier than other types of stocks but also offer more appreciation potential.

4. Cyclical Stocks are issued by companies that are affected by general economic trends. The prices of these stocks tend to go down during recessionary periods and increase during economic booms. Examples of cyclical stock companies include automobile, heavy machinery, and home building.

5. Defensive Stocks are the opposite of cyclical stocks. Defensive stocks—issued by companies producing staples such as food, beverages, drugs and insurance—typically maintain their value during recessionary periods.

Part III: Mutual Funds

The most common way for individuals to invest in the stock market is through mutual funds. Mutual funds pool money from all their investors and buy different stocks with it. The risk and reward from all of the stocks is shared by all of the investors. This is a way for investors to diversify their risk and own many stocks with not a lot of money.

There are all kinds of mutual funds, including index funds that track market segments, and more specialized funds that invest in a certain industry or use a certain strategy. Many people invest through their employer with 401(k) retirement accounts, which generally allow employees to choose from a list of funds.

Part IV: Exchange Traded Funds

An exchange traded fund (ETF) is an index fund representing a basket of stock that trades on an exchange throughout the day and are bought and sold like common stocks with continuous pricing (compared with mutual funds, which are bought and sold at the end of the trading day at their end-of-day net asset value (NAV). Investors get the advantages of trading a diversified "basket" of stocks that reflects the performance of a market index, industry, sector, style, or region—all in one security. They also offer diversified exposure and lower expense ratios than traditional mutual funds.

Part V: Fixed-Income Securities

Bonds are considered fixed-income securities. The term bond, debenture and note are often used interchangeably. All three represent debt obligations of the issuing entity. The majority of these instruments are issued in multiples of $1,000 face amounts at a specified coupon, or interest, rate, with a set maturity date at which time the obligation must be repaid. Many debt issues may be redeemed, or called, by the issuer prior to the maturity date if specified in the issue's indenture.

Part VI: Structured Products

The NYSE also trades debt and equity structured corporate issues.

Part VII: Options

An option is a contract to buy or sell a specific financial product, which is called the option's underlying instrument or underlying interest. For equity options, the underlying instrument is a stock, ETF, or similar product. The contract itself is very precise. It establishes a specific price, called the strike price, at which the contract may be exercised. And it has an expiration date. When an option expires, it no longer has value and no longer exists. Options are most frequently used to remove market risk in owning or trading in an individual security or market segment.

Digging Deeper

Protect Your Money: Check Out Brokers and Investment Advisors

http://www.sec.gov/investor/brokers.htm

The SEC offers guidance and links to databases to help consumers check out brokers, brokerage firms, and investment advisors.

An Introduction to College Saving Plans (529 Plans)

http://www.sec.gov/investor/pubs/intro529.htm

A 529 plan is a tax-advantaged savings plan designed to encourage saving for future college costs. Legally known as "qualified tuition plans," 529 plans are sponsored by states, state agencies, or educational institutions and are authorized by Section 529 of the Internal Revenue Code. This website provides details on how these plans work and how they should be used for long term college saving.

Certificates of Deposit (CD): Tips for Savers

http://www.fdic.gov/deposit/deposits/certificate/index.html

The Federal Deposit Insurance Corporation (FDIC) provides details about certificates of deposit, since many investors use them as a savings vehicle. This website offers many tips for savers about where to obtain CDs, as well as differences in rates offered by different institutions.

Part XVI

Learning About Taxes

Chapter 70

All About Federal Income Taxes

Internal Revenue Service

Introduction

Throughout history, every organized society has had some form of government. In free societies, the goals of government have been to protect individual freedoms and to promote the well-being of society as a whole.

To meet their expenses, governments need income, called "revenue," which it raises through taxes. In our country, governments levy several different types of taxes on individuals and businesses.

- The federal government relies mainly on income taxes for its revenue.
- State governments depend on both income and sales taxes.
- Most county and city governments use property taxes to raise revenue.

Part I: Government Services

- **Free Enterprise System**

Our American economy is based on the free enterprise system. Consumers are free to decide how to spend or invest their time and money. The goal of producers is to make profits by satisfying consumer demand. Open competition among producers usually results in their providing the best quality of goods or services at the lowest possible prices.

☛ Services Best Performed by Government

The free enterprise system does not produce all the services needed by society. Some services are more efficiently provided when government agencies plan and administer them. Two good examples are national defense and state and local police protection. Everyone benefits from these services, and the most practical way to pay for them is through taxes, instead of a system of service fees.

Other examples are the management of our natural resources, such as our water supply or publicly owned land, and the construction of hospitals or highways. Taxes are collected to pay for planning these services and to finance construction or maintenance. Revenue is also collected through user fees, such as at the entrances to national parks or at toll booths on highways and bridges.

☛ Monopolies and Antitrust Laws

The free enterprise system is based on competition among businesses. With competition, only the most efficient businesses survive. To ensure that a degree of competition exists, the federal government enforces strict "antitrust" laws to prevent anyone from gaining monopoly control over a market.

☛ Government Regulation

The free enterprise system assumes that consumers are knowledgeable about the quality or safety of what they buy. However, in our modern society, it is often impossible for consumers to make informed choices. For public protection, government agencies at the federal, state, and local levels issue and enforce regulations. There are regulations to cover the quality and safety of such things as home construction, cars, and electrical appliances. There are also regulations for financial services provided by banks, insurance companies, and stock brokers. Another important form of consumer protection is the use of licenses to prevent unqualified people from working in certain fields, such as medicine or the building trades.

☛ Public Education

Our children receive their education mainly at public expense. City and county governments have the primary responsibility for elementary and secondary education. Most states support colleges and universities. The federal government supports education through grants to states for elementary, secondary, and vocational education. Federal grants used for conducting research are an important source of money for colleges and universities.

☛ Social Programs and the "Safety Net"

Since the 1930s, the federal government has been providing income or services, often called a "safety net," for those in need. Major programs include health services for the elderly and financial aid for the disabled and unemployed. Other major programs include financial aid to families with dependent children and social services for low income individuals and families.

Part II: Taxes in the United States

Governments pay for these services through revenue obtained by taxing three economic bases: income, consumption, and wealth. The federal government taxes income as its main source of revenue. State governments use taxes on income and consumption, while local governments rely almost entirely on taxing property and wealth.

Taxes on Income

- **Personal Income Tax:** The earnings of both individuals and corporations are subject to income taxes. Most of the federal government's revenue comes from income taxes. The personal income tax produces about five times as much revenue as the corporate income tax. This tax is most commonly collected through payroll taxes.

- **Capital Gains Tax:** Not all income is taxed in the same way. For example, taxpayers owning stock in a corporation and then selling it at a gain or loss must report it on a special schedule. This item and any other gains or losses get calculated separately before they are added to other income.

- **Taxes on Interest and Dividends:** By comparison, the interest taxpayers earn on money in a regular savings account gets included with wages, salaries, and other "ordinary" income.

- **Tax-Exempt and Tax-Deferred Investments:** There are also many types of tax-exempt and tax-deferred savings plans available that impact people's taxes.

Payroll Taxes

Payroll taxes are an important source of revenue for the federal government. Employers are responsible for paying these taxes, which include social security insurance and unemployment compensation. Employees also pay into the social security program through money withheld from their paychecks. Some state governments also use payroll taxes to pay for the state's unemployment compensation programs.

Over the years, the amount paid in social security taxes has greatly increased. This is because there are fewer workers paying into the system for each retired person now receiving benefits. Today, some workers pay more social security tax than income tax.

Taxes on Consumption

The most important taxes on consumption are sales and excise taxes. Sales taxes usually get paid on such things as cars, clothing, and movie tickets. Sales taxes are an important source of revenue for most states and some large cities and counties. The tax rate varies from state to state, and the list of taxable goods or services also varies from one state to another.

Excise taxes, sometimes called "luxury taxes," are used by both state and federal governments. Examples of items subject to federal excise taxes are heavy tires, fishing equipment, airplane tickets, gasoline, beer and liquor, firearms, and cigarettes.

The objective of excise taxation is to place the burden of paying the tax on the consumer. A good example of this use of excise taxes is the gasoline excise tax. Governments use the revenue from this tax to build and maintain highways, bridges, and mass transit systems. Only people who purchase gasoline—those who use the highways—pay the tax.

Some items get taxed to discourage their use. This applies to excise taxes on alcohol and tobacco. Excise taxes are also used during a war or national emergency. By raising the cost of scarce items, the government can reduce the demand for these items.

Taxes on Property and Wealth

The property tax is local government's main source of revenue. Most localities tax private homes, land, and business property based on the property's value. Usually, the taxes are paid monthly, along with the mortgage payment. The entity that holds the mortgage, such as a bank, keeps the money for taxes in an "escrow" account. Payments then are made for the property owner.

Some state and local governments also impose taxes on the value of certain types of personal property, called personal property taxes. Examples of frequently taxed personal property are cars, boats, recreational vehicles, and livestock.

Property taxes account for more than three-fourths of the revenue raised through taxes on wealth. Other taxes imposed on wealth include inheritance, estate, and gift taxes.

Part III: Principles of the Federal Income Tax

A basic principle underlying the income tax laws of the United States is that people should be taxed according to their "ability to pay." Taxpayers with the same total income may not have the same ability to pay. Those with high medical bills, mortgage interest payments, or other allowable expenses can subtract these amounts as "itemized deductions" to reduce their taxable incomes. Similarly, taxpayers may subtract a certain amount on their tax returns for each allowable "exemption." By lowering one's taxable income, these exemptions and deductions support the basic principle of taxing according to ability to pay.

Those with high taxable incomes pay a larger percentage of their income in taxes. This percentage is the "tax rate." Since those with higher taxable incomes pay a higher percentage, the federal income tax is a progressive tax.

Sales and excise taxes, by comparison, are considered regressive taxes. Since the goods get taxed at the same percentage, those with lower incomes pay a larger percentage of their income in sales and excise taxes. Federal income taxes are collected on a "pay-as-you-go" withholding system. Most employers must withhold taxes from their employees' paychecks and send the money for deposit into the General Fund of the U.S. Treasury.

Self-employed individuals and businesses must pay their taxes in regular installments known as estimated tax payments. Paying taxes through withholding or estimated taxes during the year helps reduce the government's expense for borrowing money. It also provides an easier method for taxpayers to pay their taxes. To keep collection costs down, the Internal Revenue Service expects all taxpayers to comply with the law voluntarily. Most taxpayers figure out how much tax they are supposed to pay and file their income tax return by the date it is due. Without this voluntary compliance, it would cost the Internal Revenue Service a great deal more to collect the same amount of revenue.

Part IV: Your Federal Dollar—Where It Goes

The federal government operates on a fiscal year that begins on October 1 and ends on September 30. Most of the federal government's revenue comes from personal income taxes. Other sources of revenue include social security and other insurance taxes and contributions, corporate income taxes, and excise taxes. Federal receipts are spent on many programs, including the following:

- 1. Social Security
- 2. Medicare
- 3. National defense
- 4. Interest on the public debt
- 5. Income security programs
- 6. Health care
- 7. Education and social services
- 8. Veterans benefits
- 9. Transportation, highways, mass transit, airports
- 10. Other government programs, domestic and international, including protection of natural resources, environmental protection, maintenance of recreation areas and public land, disaster relief, and community and regional development.

Digging Deeper

Internal Revenue Service (IRS)

http://www.irs.gov

The Internal Revenue Service website is an extensive source of information on federal taxes. A look at the Site Map shows dozens of links related to individual taxes, charitable gifts, self-employment, student taxation, armed forces taxation, tax refunds, and numerous types of information for current tax filers, such as tax rates for individual and married filers, deadlines, and estimated tax payment dates.

IRS: Frequently Asked Questions

http://www.irs.gov/faqs/index.html#Category

Dozens of typical questions from taxpayers and their answers can be found at this section of the IRS website. Issues can be searched by category or keyword and cover every possible subject.

USA.gov: Federal and State Taxes

http://www.usa.gov/Citizen/Topics/Money/Taxes.shtml

Although it contains much information directly from the IRS website, this section of USA.gov offers explanations and articles covering electronic filing (E-filing), tax preparation help, hybrid vehicle tax credits, tax violations, taxpayer rights, and tax education. There are also useful links to state information, such as state income tax rates, state revenue departments, and state tax forms.

Chapter 71

An Overview of State and Local Taxes

U.S. Department of the Treasury

Ever since the beginning of our history, the states have maintained the right to impose taxes. The federal government has always recognized this right. When our Constitution was adopted, the federal government was granted the authority to impose taxes. The states, however, retained the right to impose any type of tax except those taxes that are clearly forbidden by the United States Constitution and their own state constitutions.

Today, the states acquire the necessary revenue to maintain their governments through tax collection, fees, and licenses. The federal government also grants money to the 50 states. With the revenue that the states receive from the federal government, taxes, licenses, and fees, they provide public services to their citizens. Examples of these public services are public schools, police protection, health and welfare benefits, and the operation of the state government.

Among the common types of taxes that many states impose are personal income tax, corporate income tax, sales tax, and real property tax. Throughout the 1930s and 1940s, personal income tax and sales tax were introduced in many states because additional revenue was needed to finance public services.

Personal Income Tax

Today, most, but not all, of the states require their residents to pay a personal income tax. These states generally use one of two methods to determine income tax. These two methods are the graduated income tax and the flat rate income tax, and both methods first require the taxpayer to figure his or her taxable income.

State Sales Taxes

A sales tax is a tax levied on the sale of goods and services. Very often you pay sales tax when you purchase something. There are three different types of sales tax: the vendor tax, the consumer tax, and the combination vendor–consumer tax.

Consumer Tax

A consumer tax system taxes the retail sale. The vendor at a store collects the tax from the buyer and then sends the tax money to the state. For example, if you bought a record album, you would pay a tax in addition to the record price.

Sales Tax: A Regressive Tax

All states that apply a sales tax have an established rate. This established rate can pose problems. All people, no matter how much money they earn, pay the same percentage of tax. Such a tax is called a regressive tax because the people with smaller incomes pay a larger percentage of their money into the sales tax system than people with higher incomes. However, since all of us use state services, such as state highways, state public schools, and state medical institutions, all should pay a tax for using these services.

Exclusions and Exemptions

To help those groups that are adversely affected by a regressive sales tax, exclusions are often used by the states that levy a sales tax. Exclusions in sales tax often include food, clothing, medicine, newspapers, and utilities. For example, because food is a necessity, some states do not tax food.

Use Tax

In addition to the sales tax, many states also have a use tax. A use tax is very similar to a sales tax and is imposed for the storage, use, or purchase of personal property which is not covered by the sales tax. Usually, it is applied to lease or rental transactions, or to major items purchased outside the state, such as automobiles.

Property Tax

The revenue from property taxes usually goes toward financing public services, such as public schools, police protection, and sanitation. The amount of tax to be paid is figured on the total value of the property or on a certain percentage of the value. People usually pay property tax to the county, school district, local government, or water district. It is, however, the state that establishes the guidelines under which local government can impose property taxes.

Other State Taxes

In addition to personal income tax, sales tax, and property tax, there are other taxes that states may impose, including fuel tax, inheritance tax, and corporate income tax.

Digging Deeper

U.S. Census: State Tax Collections

http://www.census.gov/govs/www/statetax.html

Interesting data on the amounts different states collect for each type of tax they levy can be found at this U.S. Census website. Although certain states do not have an income tax, they still collect many other types of taxes which are listed here.

Federation of Tax Administrators

http://www.taxadmin.org/fta/link/forms.html

Tax information and forms can be obtained for any individual state by clicking on the convenient map at this website for the Federation of Tax Administrators.

Chapter 72

Taxes and the Self-Employed

Internal Revenue Service
U.S. Department of Treasury

We live in the era of entrepreneurship. Many people, young and old, are starting and operating their own businesses. This chapter examines how taxes are collected and paid by individuals who are self-employed.

Are You Self-Employed?

If you are in business for yourself, or carry on a trade or business as a sole proprietor or an independent contractor, you generally would consider yourself a self-employed individual. You are an independent contractor if the person for whom you perform services has only the right to control or direct the result of your work, not what will be done or how it will be done.

According to the U.S. Census Bureau, over three-quarters of all small businesses are self-employed individuals with no employees. Many government programs and services have been created to assist the self-employed grow and manage their businesses and comply with government regulations.

Employment Taxes

Both employers and self-employed individuals are responsible for paying federal, state, and local taxes. If you have employees, you must withhold certain taxes from your employees pay checks. Employment taxes include income taxes, Social Security and Medicare taxes, and the federal unemployment tax (FUTA). If you are self-employed, you are responsible for paying a self-employment tax that is similar to the Social Security and Medicare taxes withheld from the pay of most wage earners.

What Is Self-Employment Tax?

Self-employment tax (SE tax) is a Social Security and Medicare tax primarily for individuals who work for themselves. It is similar to the Social Security and Medicare taxes withheld from the pay of most wage earners. You must use either your social security number or an individual taxpayer identification number to file self-employment taxes.

Estimated Taxes

Federal income tax is a pay-as-you-go tax. You must pay the tax as you earn or receive income during the year. You generally have to make estimated tax payments if you expect to owe tax, including SE tax, of $1,000 or more when you file your return. There are two ways to pay as you go: withholding and estimated taxes. If you are a self-employed individual and do not have income tax withheld, you must make estimated tax payments.

Part-Time Business

You do not have to carry on regular full-time business activities to be self-employed. Having a part-time business in addition to your regular job or business also may be self-employment.

Sole Proprietors

You are a sole proprietor if you own an unincorporated business by yourself, in most cases. If this is your situation, the income and expenses of your business are reported on your federal and state tax returns. In addition, you are normally subject to self-employment tax, which helps you build up credits within the Social Security system toward your retirement benefits.

Operating Through a Limited Liability Company (LLC)

If you choose to operate your business as a single-person limited liability company (LLC), you can report your income and expenses on your personal tax returns, or you may elect to be taxed as a corporation.

Digging Deeper

Business.gov: Employment Taxes

http://www.business.gov/guides/taxes/employment.html

For those interested in starting a new business, the federal government provides a business website which focuses on employment issues, taxes, business law, human resources, advertising and marketing, and numerous other topics.

Business.gov: Starting and Managing a Business

http://www.business.gov/guides/start/

Numerous advisory publications and guides are offered by Business.gov, which helps the visitor navigate through the maze of issues related to new businesses. There is information on obtaining an employer identification number, choosing a business structure, obtaining permits and licenses, setting up business records, and much more.

Business.gov: Small Business Taxes

http://www.business.gov/guides/taxes/

Tax planning for new businesses depends upon the type of organizational structure selected. Although very popular, the limited liability company (LLC) is not the only entity discussed. There are links for sole proprietorships, partnerships, regular corporations, "s" corporations, which are taxed on a personal tax return, employers, and tax forms. There are also articles on numerous other tax and general business topics listed on the page, including environmental compliance, franchises, imports and exports, occupational safety and health, and non-profit entities.

Small Business Administration (SBA)

http://www.sba.gov/

Leading the way in helping small businesses, the SBA has a valuable website for help with grants and loans, business organization, regulations, training, compliance, marketing, and contracting with the federal government. The SBA has regional offices around the country where business counselors can be helpful in organizing and expanding a new business.

Chapter 73

Know Your Taxpayer Rights

Internal Revenue Service

The Internal Revenue Service (IRS) has published the following document to protect the rights of taxpayers in general, as well as in any dealings they have with the agency and its employees:

Part I: Taxpayer Rights at the Federal Level

Protection of Your Rights

IRS employees will explain and protect your rights as a taxpayer in your contact with the IRS.

Privacy and Confidentiality

The IRS will not disclose to anyone the information you give us, except as authorized by law. You have the right to know why we are asking you for information, how we will use it, and what happens if you do not provide requested information.

Professional and Courteous Service

If you believe that an IRS employee has not treated you in a professional, fair, and courteous manner, you should tell that employee's supervisor. If the supervisor's response is not satisfactory, you should write to the IRS director for your area or the center where you file your return.

Representation

You may either represent yourself or, with proper written authorization, have someone else represent you in your place. Your representative must be a person allowed to practice before the IRS, such as an attorney, certified public accountant, or enrolled agent. If you are in an interview and ask to consult such a person, then we must stop and reschedule the interview in most cases. You can have someone accompany you at an interview. You may make sound recordings of any meetings with our examination, appeal, or collection personnel, provided you tell us in writing 10 days before the meeting.

Payment of Only the Correct Amount of Tax

You are responsible for paying only the correct amount of tax due under the law—no more, no less. If you cannot pay all of your tax when it is due, you may be able to make monthly installment payments.

Help With Unresolved Tax Problems

The Taxpayer Advocate Service can help you if you have tried unsuccessfully to resolve a problem with the IRS. Your local Taxpayer Advocate can offer you special help if you have a significant hardship as a result of a tax problem. For more information, call toll free 1–877–777–4778 (1–800–829–4059 for TTY/TDD) or write to the Taxpayer Advocate at the IRS office that last contacted you.

Appeals and Judicial Review

If you disagree with us about the amount of your tax liability or certain collection actions, you have the right to ask the Appeals Office to review your case. You may also ask a court to review your case.

Relief From Certain Penalties and Interest

The IRS will waive penalties when allowed by law if you can show you acted reasonably and in good faith or relied on the incorrect advice of an IRS employee. We will waive interest that is the result of certain errors or delays caused by an IRS employee.

When dealing with tax collection authorities in different states, you can consult those agencies to learn about similar rights that you possess as a taxpayer.

Part II: Taxpayer Rights at the State Level

In addition to taxpayer rights related to the payment of federal income taxes, as set forth above, there are corresponding rights and protections within each state to ensure that taxpayers' civil rights are protected, as well as their rights to fair treatment. To learn about taxpayer rights in an individual state, visit the state revenue office and find a link to taxpayer rights.

Digging Deeper

IRS: More on Taxpayer Rights

http://www.irs.gov/advocate/article/0,,id=98206,00.html

The IRS offers extensive information on taxpayer rights, including a link to the formal Taxpayer Bill of Rights passed by Congress. Of paramount importance to the IRS is respect for the civil rights of citizens. The website also offers information on the agency's taxpayer assistance programs, taxpayer advocacy, rights of representation, and the appeals process.

Part XVII

Safety and Emergency Preparedness

Chapter 74

Ready America: Prepare, Plan and Stay Informed

U.S. Department of Homeland Security

Introduction

The U.S. Department of Homeland Security has a website dedicated to emergency preparedness. It is called *www.ready.gov*. The site offers details on each of the following subjects:

1. Preparing an Emergency Supply Kit
2. Making a Family Emergency Plan, and
3. Recommendations for Staying Informed

Part I: Putting Together an Emergency Kit

When preparing for a possible emergency situation, it's best to think first about the basics of survival: fresh water, food, clean air, and warmth.

- Water, one gallon of water per person per day for at least three days, for drinking and sanitation
- Food, at least a three-day supply of non-perishable food
- Battery-powered or hand-crank radio and a NOAA weather radio with tone alert and extra batteries for both

- Flashlight and extra batteries
- First aid kit
- Whistle to signal for help
- Dust mask, to help filter contaminated air and plastic sheeting and duct tape to shelter-in-place
- Moist towelettes, garbage bags, and plastic ties for personal sanitation
- Wrench or pliers to turn off utilities
- Can opener for food (if kit contains canned food)
- Local maps

Part II: Making a Family Emergency Plan

Your family may not be together when disaster strikes, so it is important to plan in advance how you will contact one another, how you will get back together, and what you will do in different situations. Here are some recommendations:

1. Family Emergency Plan

   It may be easier to make a long-distance phone call than to call across town, so an out-of-town contact may be in a better position to communicate among separated family members.

   Be sure every member of your family knows the phone number and has coins or a prepaid phone card to call the emergency contact. You may have trouble getting through, or the telephone system may be down altogether, but be patient.

2. Emergency Information

   Find out what kinds of disasters, both natural and man-made, are most likely to occur in your area and how you will be notified. Methods of getting your attention vary from community to community. One common method is to broadcast via emergency radio and TV broadcasts. You might hear a special siren, or get a telephone call, or emergency workers may go door-to-door.

3. Emergency Plans at Work or School

   You may also want to inquire about emergency plans at places where your family spends time: work, daycare, and school. If no plans exist, consider volunteering to help create one. Talk to your neighbors about how you can work together in the event of an emergency. You will be better prepared to safely reunite your family and loved ones during an emergency if you think ahead and communicate with others in advance.

Digging Deeper

Ready America

http://www.ready.gov

The U.S. Department of Homeland Security has developed this website to help Americans prepare for national emergencies. It includes sections for individuals and families, workplaces, and children. There is an important link to information by state and tabs for older persons, disabled Americans, and pet owners.

Federal Department of Homeland Security

http://www.dhs.gov/index.shtm

Important tabs at the homepage of the Department of Homeland Security cover Information Sharing and Analysis, including the national security alert system, Prevention and Protection, Preparedness and Response, Research, Travel Security, and Immigration.

Federal Emergency Management Administration (FEMA)

http://www.fema.gov/

The agency that comes to the aid of people caught in floods and other disasters is FEMA, the Federal Emergency Management Administration. FEMA's homepage provides information on disasters, applying for assistance, recovery, and rebuilding. There is also an active headline news section and a listing and description of types of disasters.

State Emergency Management Agencies

http://www.fema.gov/about/contact/statedr.shtm

Aside from the federal agency (FEMA), each state has its own emergency counterpart, which can be accessed through this website, including the programs and initiatives developed by each state.

Chapter 75

Guidelines for Consumer and Workplace Safety

Starting Out!® Research Group

The federal government and most states provide extensive resources on every type of safety, including food safety, highway safety, product safety, and occupational safety.

The annotated web links below will lead you to the most reliable safety information in each category.

I. Automobile, ATV and Highway Safety

- ATVSafety.gov
  http://www.ATVSafety.gov
  Safety tips, national data, state data, state legislation, injuries, and training are all topics at this website, which is devoted to the safe use of all-terrain vehicles.

- National Highway Traffic Safety Administration (NHTSA)
  http://www.nhtsa.dot.gov/
  The NHTSA is devoted to saving lives, preventing injuries, and reducing vehicle-related crashes. There are numerous topics posted on the left margin related to traffic safety guidelines, articles, national campaigns, and news.

- Safercar.gov
  http://www.safercar.gov/

Vehicle safety information from the federal government is offered at this website. There are links to safety ratings, recalls, safe driving guidelines, plus extensive topical resources on individual vehicles, equipment, and safety promotion programs.

II. Cyber Safety

- Computer Emergency Readiness Team (US-CERT)
  http://www.us-cert.gov/
  The United States Computer Emergency Readiness Team (US-CERT) is a partnership between the Department of Homeland Security and the public and private sectors. Established in 2003 to protect the nation's internet infrastructure, US-CERT coordinates defense against and responses to cyber attacks across the nation. The website posts alerts and tips, information resources, and news about efforts to improve internet safety and functionality.

III. Drug Safety

- Drug Safety Initiative at the Food and Drug Administration
  http://www.fda.gov/cder/drugSafety.htm
  The Food and Drug Administration has ongoing initiatives to improve drug safety. This website offers links to resources on safe drug use, drug safety podcasts, drug alerts and recalls, and an extensive list of drug-specific information arranged alphabetically.

IV. Fire Safety

- Firesafety.gov
  http://www.firesafety.gov/
  Helpful recommendations, as well as mandatory fire safety regulations, are offered at this government webpage, including information on smoke alarms, escape plans, fire safety practices, sprinkler, and other

topics. There are also news postings, product recalls, and statistical data sources.

V. Food Safety

- Foodsafety.gov
  http://www.foodsafety.gov/
  This Gateway to Food Safety provides consumer advice, product recalls, national food safety programs, and links to federal and state agencies involved with food safety. There are sections on foodborne pathogens, food safety training videos, and other program areas.

VI. Personal Safety

- CDC: Violence Prevention
  http://www.cdc.gov/ncipc/dvp/dvp.htm
  Resources on violence prevention are posted at this webpage maintained by the Centers for Disease Control and Prevention, including social and public health issues, electronic and Internet aggression, child maltreatment, partner violence, sexual violence, suicide, youth violence, international violence, and statistical data.

- National Coalition Against Domestic Violence
  http://www.ncadv.org/
  This non-profit organization is devoted to efforts to address and reduce domestic violence through programs, education, public policy, and victim assistance.

VII. Product Safety

- U.S. Consumer Product Safety Commission
  http://www.cpsc.gov/
  Extensive resources on product safety are offered through this website

of the Consumer Product Safety Commission, including recalls, reports of unsafe products, product safety standards, news, and regulations for business.

- Recalls.gov
  http://www.recalls.gov/
  To coordinate product recall alerts for the American public regarding unsafe, hazardous, or defective products, six federal agencies with vastly different responsibilities have joined together to create www.recalls.gov—a "one stop shop" for U.S. Government recalls. The agencies include the U.S. Consumer Product Safety Commission, the National Highway Traffic Safety Administration, the U.S. Coast Guard, the Food and Drug Administration, the U.S. Department of Agriculture, and the Environmental Protection Agency.

- Household Product Safety Database
  http://householdproducts.nlm.nih.gov/
  The National Library of Medicine, part of the National Institutes of Health, has compiled a database of household products relative to safety issues. Products are organized in broad categories, but there is also an ingredients database for those seeking more detailed information. There are also Material Safety Data Sheets that can be accessed by product name.

VIII. Public Safety

- USA.gov: Public Safety and the Law
  http://www.usa.gov/Government/State_Local/Safety.shtml
  Public safety and legal resources relative to public safety are located at this website of USA.gov, including crime news and statistics, information from the FBI and other enforcement agencies, and information from state correctional departments, drug enforcement agencies, and other federal organizations engaged in this field.

IX. Worker and Workplace Safety

- Occupational Safety and Health Administration (OSHA)
  http://www.osha.gov/
  All aspects of occupational safety and health are administered by OSHA, with extensive public information available at this homepage. There is a huge alphabetical, topical database, as well as fact sheets, regulatory and compliance resources, state agency links, and enforcement information.

- National Institute for Occupational Safety and Health
  http://www.cdc.gov/niosh/
  Within the Centers for Disease Control and Prevention, the National Institute for Occupational Safety and Health provides publications, news, individual program information, grant and training resources, and major links to affected industries and occupations, hazards and exposures, diseases and injuries, chemicals, safety and prevention, emergency preparedness, and data and statistics.

Digging Deeper

Personal and Public Safety Resources

http://www.usa.gov/Citizen/Topics/PublicSafety/Safety.shtml

Dozens of links to personal and public safety resources are provided at USA.gov, covering such topics as disaster preparedness, elder abuse, all forms of violence, human trafficking, safe schools and neighborhoods, and sexual offender databases.

National Safety Council: Fact Sheet Library

http://www.nsc.org/library/facts.htm

The National Safety Council website divides its public information into broad categories, providing recommendations and guidelines for safety on hundreds of topics. Categories include agricultural safety, safe living, environmental safety, road safety, and school bus safety.

National Transportation Safety Board (NTSB)

http://www.ntsb.gov/

The NTSB investigates major accidents relating to air travel, rail, highways, pipelines and hazardous product transportation. It is also engaged in transportation disaster assistance. Each of these topics has a dedicated section on the website.

Medlineplus: Safety Resources

http://www.nlm.nih.gov/medlineplus/safety.html

Consumer articles and resources on a wide variety of health and safety resources are offered at this page of Medlineplus, the database operated by the National Library of Medicine. There are overviews, news, a discussion of specific conditions, and related issues organized in outline form, with article links.

Mine Safety and Health Administration

http://www.msha.gov/

Dealing with mine safety and health, this federal agency's website offers an extensive list of topical links on the left margin of the site, as well as press releases and a data retrieval system. There is a list of special initiatives of the agency, along with technical assistance and statistics.

Chapter 76

Towards a Safe and Healthy Environment

U.S. Environmental Protection Agency

Part I—Air

- EPA: Air Resources
  http://www.epa.gov/ebtpages/air.html
  The Environmental Protection Agency (EPA) offers extensive resources on air quality and air pollution, the changing atmosphere, and ozone depletion, as well as information on abatement, remediation, and treatment of different forms of air pollution.

- AIRNow.gov
  http://www.airnow.gov
  For information on air quality in real time, AIRNow.gov offers up-to-the-minute data when a user clicks on a map of the United States. The Air Quality Index is discussed at this site, which provides information on the areas that are experiencing the highest levels of air pollution.

Part II—Water

- EPA: Water Resources
  http://www.epa.gov/ebtpages/water.html

Issues of water safety and types of pollution, as well as drinking water, ground water, storm water, surface water, waste water, and water treatment are all major topics at this section of the EPA's website.

Part III—Ecosystems

- EPA: Ecosystems
  http://www.epa.gov/ebtpages/ecosystems.html
  Risks to major ecosystems from all forms of pollution as well as the effects of climate change are examined at this website, which also has information about soils, landscaping, endangered species, watersheds, forests, and wetlands.

Part IV—Climate Change

- EPA: Climate Change
  http://www.epa.gov/climatechange/
  The broad subject of climate change is examined at this site, including past and more recent climate changes, greenhouse gases and their effects, the nation's climate policy, and practices that can be pursued by individuals and businesses to reduce adverse climate effects.

Part V—Wastes

- EPA: Wastes
  http://www.epa.gov/ebtpages/wastes.html
  The Wastes section of the EPA site addresses animal waste, solid waste, liquid waste, hazardous waste, and radioactive waste, as well as waste generation, disposal, transportation, and treatment.

Digging Deeper

Environmental Protection Agency

http://epa.gov/

The mission of the Environmental Protection Agency is to protect human health and the environment. The website offers extensive resources on every aspect of the environment, as well as all forms of environmental risks. Dozens of major topics have links at the top of the site, from acid rain to wastes, and additional links along the left margin cover laws and regulations, FAQs, educational resources, and statistics. The center of the site is devoted to current news articles.

Department of Energy, Office of Health, Safety, and Security

http://www.hss.energy.gov/index.html

The Department of Energy's Office of Health, Safety, and Security deals with scientific issues, energy sources and efficiency, the environment, national security matters, and personal health issues regarding safety and security. Chemical safety, nuclear safety, and facility safety are among the topics examined.

CDC National Center for Environmental Health

http://www.cdc.gov/nceh/

The National Center for Environmental Health is located within the Centers for Disease Control and Prevention. Its mission is to plan, direct, and coordinate a national program to maintain and improve the health of the American people. It is engaged in promoting a healthy environment by preventing premature death and avoidable illness and disability caused by non-infectious, non-occupational environmental and related factors. The site offers numerous links to data sources, emergency response, health hazards, regulations, educational information, and news.

Part XVIII

Conservation and the Green Economy

Chapter 77

Jobs for a Greener Economy

Starting Out! Research Group

Numerous new jobs are being created in the 21st century as we begin to clean up our planet, tackle environmental problems, harness new sources of energy, improve agricultural practices, re-design products, and increase recycling.

Ex-offenders who are re-integrating into society after incarceration have the opportunity to find new types of jobs in the "green economy" that not only will bring them needed income, but will also serve an important public purpose.

Below is a summary of some of the jobs that have attracted increasing employment in recent years:

Public Works and Clean-Up

Communities are spending money cleaning up parks and public places, greenways along highways, and inner city areas that can become gardens instead of fields of litter. Graffiti is being removed from subway cars, buildings, and overpasses, and public gardens are being brought back to life. Ask the personnel or public works department in your town or city for a full- or part-time job doing municipal clean-up projects.

Waste companies work in almost every community, and workers are employed by the town or city or by a contractor serving the municipality. Trash removal jobs can be well-paying since they do not appeal to many people and require heavy labor.

Recycling: Part or Full-Time

A significant number of people make a living in the recycling field, either on their own by collecting cans and bottles, or by working for recycling companies that serve towns and cities.

Organic Occupations

Although organic products are generally more expensive than non-organic products, consumers have been buying them in greater numbers in recent years. The promise of organics' higher price tags has not been lost on farmers. According to the U.S. Department of Agriculture, land used for organic crops increased from 48,000 acres in 1997 to 122,000 acres in 2005. That increase has created new jobs on working farms and in farmers' markets across the country.

Some people are even creating new small farms on an acre and a half to two acres, according to Bill Duesing, executive director of the Connecticut Northeast Organic Farming Association (NOFA). And there is more job potential around farmer's markets. According to U.S. Department of Agriculture (USDA) figures, farmer's markets increased seven percent between 2005 and 2006, to 4,385.

But that is not all. There are also jobs in farmland protection, food preparation, and product distribution, as demonstrated by Albert's Organics, the nation's leading organic foods distributor which supplies 5,000 supermarkets, natural food stores, and restaurants with some 250 seasonal fruits and vegetables.

Construction and Renovation

High energy prices have caused every building owner to examine the cost of heating and air conditioning. The government has established attractive tax incentives so homeowners install attic insulation, double- or triple-ply windows, and more efficient boilers and appliances.

This new wave of energy-consciousness has produced large numbers of skilled and unskilled jobs, many offered by small contractors in communities across the country. Spraying attic or wall insulation is a job that any able-bodied worker can do. With carpentry skills, there is also the removal of old windows and re-installation of energy-efficient windows and doors. And with mechanical abilities, there are jobs involving the installation of new boilers, clock thermostats, attic fans, and other special equipment.

Firewood, Biomass, and New Composite Fuel Pellets

The price of firewood continues to rise, and woodcutting companies are always looking for new workers. Special mills transform wood into composite pellets that are sold for a whole new line of space heaters. Interest in these fuels has produced new jobs in mills, warehousing, trucking, and distribution, especially in rural areas.

Fuels are now produced from natural growing products, such as grains, corn, wood, and soybeans. Diesel fuel can be made from soybeans and corn. Biofuel from non-food sources, called biomass, however, is more desirable since it does not limit the food supply. Numerous jobs that never existed in the past are "growing" out of this new industry.

Other Energy Jobs

In parts of the country where the oil and gas industry is active, such as in southern and western states, there are numerous heavy labor jobs around oil and gas wells. Operators have been returning to old wells as the price of energy has been on the increase, giving rise to additional jobs in the oil and gas industry in many areas.

Environmental Products and Services

There are many new businesses that offer a wide range of environmental products and services that utilize people with mechanical and installation skills, such as installing solar panels, wind turbines, solar hot water heaters, fuel-efficient boilers, and similar equipment. Check the Yellow Pages for environmental equipment companies and inquire about different kinds of jobs.

Job Fairs Offer Green Jobs

Across the country there are now job fairs that offer green jobs, such as those described in this article. Job fairs are announced in newspapers or can be found on the internet. You will get many different employment ideas at a job fair, not just involving green jobs.

Chapter 78

Conserving the Environment

U.S State Department
U.S. Department of the Interior
U.S. Department of Agriculture

Part I: A Global Perspective

An expanding global population, rapid conversion of critical habitat to other uses, the spread of invasive species to non-native habitats, air and water pollution, and waste management are a few of the problems that pose a serious threat to the world's natural resources and to all of us who depend on them for food, fuel, shelter, and medicine. Every year, there is a net loss of 22 million acres of forest area worldwide. Toxic chemicals, some capable of traveling thousands of miles from their source and lasting decades in the environment, are released into the earth's atmosphere. Other worldwide concerns include ozone depletion, species extinction, contamination of food and water, and global climate change.

Part II: Opportunities to Advance Conservation

Each of the federal and international agencies described in this article has a website that includes opportunities for both employment and volunteer involvement in tackling conservation problems in the United States and abroad.

Part III: What Federal Agencies Are Most Involved With Conservation?

Addressing these problems and achieving sustainable management of natural resources here at home as well as worldwide requires the cooperation and commitment of the public, businesses, and industries. Here are some of the federal agencies engaged in conservation:

- U.S. Department of the Interior

  The mission of the Department of the Interior is to protect and provide access to our nation's natural and cultural heritage and honor our trust responsibilities to Native American tribes and our commitments to island communities.

  - The Office of Environmental Policy and Compliance (OEPC): OEPC develops U.S. policy on environmental issues in the area of air pollution, toxic chemicals and pesticides, hazardous wastes, and other pollutants.
  - Bureau of Land Management: The Bureau of Land Management (BLM) manages 264 million acres of surface acres of public lands located primarily in the 12 western states, including Alaska.
  - National Park Service: The American system of national parks was the first of its kind in the world, and provides a model for other nations wishing to establish and manage their own protected areas. Beyond national parks, the National Park Service helps communities across America preserve and enhance important local heritage and close-to-home recreational opportunities.
  - U.S. Fish and Wildlife Service: The U.S. Fish and Wildlife Service (FWS) is the only agency of the U.S. Government whose primary responsibility is fish, wildlife, and plant conservation.
  - Bureau of Reclamation: The mission of the Bureau of Reclamation is

to manage, develop, and protect water and related resources in an environmentally and economically sound manner in the interest of the American public.

- Office of Surface Mining: The Office of Surface Mining (OSM) mission is to carry out the requirements of the Surface Mining Control and Reclamation Act in cooperation with states and tribes.
- Bureau of Indian Affairs: The Bureau of Indian Affairs (BIA) is responsible for the administration and management of 55.7 million acres of land held in trust by the United States for American Indians, Indian tribes, and Alaska Natives.
- U.S. Geological Survey: The U.S. Geological Survey (USGS) serves the nation as an independent fact-finding agency that collects, monitors, analyzes, and provides scientific understanding about natural resource conditions, issues, and problems.

➤ U.S. Department of Agriculture

Conservation of environmental resources that are an integral part of farming is a major goal of the USDA. Agriculture uses land, fertilizers, pesticides, water, and other inputs to produce food and fiber. How these inputs are used has implications for the health of the environment, including air quality, water quality, soil quality, wildlife, and human health.

- Natural Resources Conservation Service: Provides leadership in a partnership effort to help America's private land owners and managers conserve their soil, water, and other natural resources.
- U.S. Forest Service: The Forest Service manages public lands in national forests and grasslands, which encompass 193 million acres.

- Environmental Protection Agency

The mission of the Environmental Protection Agency is to protect human health and the environment. There are numerous conservation programs around the country administered by the EPA, as listed under "Digging Deeper."

- U.S. State Department

  » Bureau of Oceans and International Environmental and Scientific Affairs works with other federal agencies to forge international cooperation and obtain commitments through a variety of diplomatic approaches globally, regionally, and bilaterally.

  » The Office of Ecology and Natural Resource Conservation (ENRC) coordinates the development of U.S. foreign policy approaches to conserving and sustainably managing the world's ecologically and economically important ecosystems, including forests, wetlands, drylands, and coral reefs, and the species that depend on them.

Digging Deeper

National Park Service (NPS): History of Conservation

http://www.nps.gov/history/history/hisnps/NPSThinking/nps-oah.htm

The article posted at this webpage of the National Park Service addresses issues of conservation and preservation in the U.S. from an historical perspective, including the conservation movement, wilderness exploration, anti-pollution campaigns, and the recent evolution of the environmental movement. You can also find a state-by-state directory at the NPS homepage.

U.S. Department of the Interior

http://www.doi.gov/

There are links at this homepage for the Department of Interior's principal initiatives, along with issues of interest, quick facts, bureaus and offices, web cams, and numerous educational resources.

USDA Forest Service

http://www.fs.fed.us/

Organizational structure, recreational activities, forest management, fire protection, projects and policies, educational information, photos and videos, careers, and other related topics are available for review at the homepage of the U.S. Forest Service, within the Department of Agriculture.

EPA: Geographic Conservation Programs

http://www.epa.gov/epahome/places.htm

Major individual conservation programs around the country are featured at this webpage from the Environmental Protection Agency. Each program link sends the visitor to a more in-depth page of information.

Natural Resources Conservation Service

http://www.ct.nrcs.usda.gov/

News, programs, technical resources, partnerships, legislation, educational information, news, and other links are provided at the home page of the Natural Resources Conservation Service, an agency of the U.S. Department of Agriculture

U.S. Fish and Wildlife Service

http://www.fws.gov/

Extensive information on birds, fish, habitats, hunting, recreation, permits, educational resources, and other topics each have links on the homepage of the U.S. Fish and Wildlife Service. Fisheries and Habitat Conservation is of the many topics explored.

Federal Conservation Incentive Programs

http://www.defenders.org/programs_and_policy/biodiversity_partners/

Federal tax incentive programs to support conservation efforts for farming, fish and wildlife, and forest preservation are described at this webpage.

State Environmental and Conservation Agencies

http://www.epa.gov/epahome/state.htm

State agencies dealing with the environment and conservation can be accessed through this webpage of the Environmental Protection Agency.

Chapter 79

The Benefits of Recycling

U.S. Environmental Protection Agency

Introduction

Recycling is one of the greatest environmental success stories of the late 20th century. Recycling, which includes composting, diverted over 72 million tons of material away from landfills and incinerators in 2003, up from 34 million tons in 1990—doubling the recycled tonnage in just 10 years.

Recycling turns materials that would otherwise become waste into valuable resources. As a matter of fact, collecting recyclable materials is just the first step in a series of actions that generate a host of financial, environmental, and societal returns.

Why Recycling Is Beneficial

Recycling:

1. Protects and expands U.S. manufacturing jobs and increases U.S. competitiveness in the global marketplace.
2. Reduces the need for landfills and incineration.

3. Saves energy and prevents pollution caused by the extraction and processing of virgin materials and the manufacture of products using virgin materials.

4. Decreases emissions of greenhouse gases that contribute to global climate change.

5. Conserves natural resources such as timber, water, and minerals.

6. Helps sustain the environment for future generations.

What Materials Are Not Safe to Throw in the Trash

Chances are, there are certain items or products in your house that you should not throw out in the trash. Many common household items, such as paint, cleaners, oils, batteries, and pesticides, contain hazardous components. Leftover portions of these products are called household hazardous waste (HHW). These products, if mishandled, can be dangerous to human health and the environment.

Certain types of HHW can cause physical injury to sanitation workers, contaminate septic tanks or wastewater treatment systems if poured down drains or toilets, and present hazards to children and pets if left around the house. Some communities have special programs that allow residents to dispose of HHW separately. Others allow disposal of properly prepared HHW in trash, particularly those areas that do not yet have special HHW collection programs in place. Call your local department of sanitation or department of public works for instructions on proper disposal. Follow their instructions and also read product labels for disposal directions to reduce the risk of products exploding, igniting, leaking, mixing with other chemicals, or posing other hazards on the way to a disposal facility. Even empty containers that used to contain HHW can pose hazards because of the residual chemicals inside.

How to Start a Recycling and Composting Program in Your Community

Starting a local recycling program might not be as tough as you think. Your first step should be to get in touch with the proper authorities in your area. Most communities have recycling coordinators—government officials who have information on local recycling resources. Look in your phone book under "recycling coordinators" or contact your local department of public works or department of sanitation.

You also can visit the "Waste: What you can do." page located at this website: *(http://www.epa.gov/epawaste/wycd/index.htm)* as well as the EPA's Waste-Wise website located at: *(http://www.epa.gov/wastewise/wrr/r-pubs.htm)* to find information and resources to help you start, maintain, or expand a recycling program in your community.

Digging Deeper

U.S. Environmental Protection Agency (EPA)

http://www.epa.gov/

This is the home page of the Environmental Protection Agency, offering information on all aspects of the agency's mission, including recycling and waste management.

EPA: Recycling

http://www.epa.gov/msw/recycle.htm

The EPA Recycling page provides facts and figures and addresses the recycling process, business and industry recycling, publications, educational materials, news, and organizations promoting different types of recycling.

Frequently Asked Questions About Recycling and Waste Management

http://www.epa.gov/msw/faq.htm

Numerous common questions about recycling and waste management are posted at this EPA webpage, including very specific answers. Such issues as the economics of recycling and landfill space are among the topics covered.

National Recycling Coalition

http://www.nrc-recycle.org/

The National Recycling Partnership (NRP) is a coalition committed to improving recycling programs in the United States and reinvigorating recycling among consumers. Under the direction of the National Recycling Coalition (NRC), grocery, food, and beverage producers and retailers are engaged in two major initiatives to maximize the potential of recycling programs nationwide.

Chapter 80

Learning About Renewable Energy

National Renewable Energy Laboratory, U.S. Department of Energy

Part I: Renewable Energy for Homeowners

There are a number of renewable energy technologies that you can use in your home. Some are best incorporated into new homes when they are built. Others can easily be added to existing homes.

Technologies that are commercially available today include:

1. **Biofuels**

   Unlike other renewable energy sources, biomass can be converted directly into liquid fuels, called "biofuels," to help meet transportation fuel needs. The two most common types of biofuels are ethanol and biodiesel.

2. **Geothermal direct use**

   When a person takes a hot bath, the heat from the water will usually warm up the entire bathroom. Geothermal reservoirs of hot water, which are found a couple of miles or more beneath the earth's surface, can also be used to provide heat directly. This is called the direct use of geothermal energy.

In the United States, most geothermal reservoirs are located in the western states, Alaska, and Hawaii.

3. **Geothermal heat pumps**

   The ground, several feet below the surface, maintains a nearly constant temperature between 50° and 60°F (10°–16°C). Like a cave, this ground temperature is warmer than the air above it in the winter and cooler than the air in the summer. Geothermal heat pumps take advantage of this resource to heat and cool buildings.

4. **Passive solar heating and daylighting**

   Step outside on a hot and sunny summer day, and you'll feel the power of solar heat and light. Today, many buildings are designed to take advantage of this natural resource through the use of passive solar heating and daylighting.

5. **Photovoltaic (solar cell) systems**

   Solar cells, also called photovoltaics (PV) by solar cell scientists, convert sunlight directly into electricity. Solar cells are often used to power calculators and watches.

6. **Solar hot water systems**

   The sun can be used to heat water used in buildings and swimming pools.

7. **Wind energy**

   We have been harnessing the wind's energy for hundreds of years. From old Holland to farms in the United States, windmills have been used for pumping water or grinding grain. Today, the windmill's modern equivalent—a wind turbine—can use the wind's energy to generate electricity.

8. **Wood heating (biomass energy heating)**

   We have used biomass energy or "bioenergy"—the energy from plants and plant-derived materials—since people began burning wood to cook food and keep warm. Wood is still the largest biomass energy resource today, but other sources of biomass can also be used.

Part II: Renewable Energy for Transportation

Improving the fuel economy of vehicles and using alternative fuels help decrease our reliance on imported petroleum and produce fewer tailpipe emissions. To reduce our nation's petroleum fuel consumption, the National Renewable Energy Laboratory (NREL) conducts research to develop and advance the following transportation technologies:

1. **Advanced vehicle systems**

   Advanced vehicles—such as plug-in hybrids and fuel cell vehicles—can be quite different from conventional vehicles. Therefore, they require different vehicle systems. These systems and their components not only help make these vehicles more fuel efficient but also can help reduce tailpipe emissions.

2. **Alternative fuels**

   When you drive an alternative fuel or flexible fuel vehicle, you don't have to rely entirely on petroleum as a fuel. You can use an alternative fuel designed for the vehicle. Using alternative fuel will help reduce our dependency on imported petroleum and produce fewer harmful tailpipe emissions.

3. **Fuel cell vehicles**

   For decades, NASA has used fuel cells to provide auxiliary power in its spacecraft. Today, we can use fuel cells to provide auxiliary power for such things as lights in vehicles as well as the power that moves the wheels—propulsion. Fuel cell vehicles aren't yet commercially available because of their cost, but in the future they could provide us with a pollution-free transportation fuel option—hydrogen.

4. **Hybrid electric vehicles**

   Today hybrid electric vehicles (HEVs) are a familiar sight on the road. They're everywhere, from small cars and SUVs to large trucks. On the outside, some are indistinguishable from conventional vehicles.

   But unlike a conventional vehicle, a hybrid electric vehicle typically combines an internal combustion engine with an electric battery and electric motor. This combination offers greater fuel economy and fewer emissions compared to a conventional vehicle.

5. **Plug-in hybrid electric vehicles**

   Plug-in hybrids—the next generation of hybrid electric vehicles—are emerging. Compared to standard hybrids, plug-in hybrid electric vehicles offer even greater fuel economy and diversity and fewer emissions.

   Plug-in hybrids have a larger battery pack than a standard hybrid electric vehicle. This allows plug-in hybrids to operate predominantly on electricity for short trips. For longer trips, a plug-in hybrid draws liquid fuel from its onboard tank, which provides comparable driving range to a conventional vehicle. The vehicle's onboard computer chooses when to use which fuel most efficiently.

Digging Deeper

Energy Efficiency and Renewable Energy: Understanding the Technologies

http://www.eere.energy.gov/

Energy efficiency and renewable energy are explored in great detail for the benefit of the public at this webpage of the Department of Energy. Each principal method of alternative energy generation is discussed. There are also links to other related resources, news, and popular topics, such as tankless hot water heaters and buying green power.

Consumer's Guide to Energy Efficiency and Renewable Energy

http://www.eere.energy.gov/consumer/

This Consumer's Guide from the Department of Energy examines practical steps that homeowners can take to improve the efficiency of their homes, locate energy-efficient products, and benefit from tax incentives for energy efficiency.

Renewable Energy and Energy Efficiency

http://www.nrel.gov/learning/index.html?print

Renewable energy and energy efficiency technologies are key to creating a clean energy future for not only the nation, but the world. This website describes NREL's research in renewable energy technologies and provides information on energy efficiency and various applications of renewable energy.

FuelEconomy.gov

http://www.fueleconomy.gov/

FuelEconomy.gov addresses fuel prices, fuel economy ratings, hybrid cars, mileage tips, alternative fuel vehicles, and related topics to assist consumers in finding ways to reduce their cost of vehicle transportation.

NOTES

NOTES